# Enchantments & Escrows

Book One: Spellbinder Series

J. Wint

# THE LAND OF
# AMBRIEL

HUMAN
AUTHORED™
AG The Authors Guild
1470190

Edited by Caroline Barnhill www.1stagemedia.com
Artwork by J. Wint - photoshop

**SPELLBINDER SERIES:**

BOOK ONE: *ENCHANTMENTS & ESCROWS*

BOOK TWO: *(forthcoming)*

BOOK THREE: *(forthcoming)*

**A CHARADE OF IMMORTALITY:**

BOOK ONE: *A STORM of IMMORTALITY*

BOOK TWO: *A SHROUD of IMMORTALITY (forthcoming)*

BOOK THREE: *A RAGE of IMMORTALITY (forthcoming)*

**THE SKYLIGHT SERIES:**

BOOK ONE: *THE PRISM EFFECT*

BOOK TWO: *THE SKYLIGHT FALLOUT*

BOOK THREE: *THE HELIOGRAPHI MEMOIRS*

BOOK FOUR: *THE SERPENT EFFECT*

BOOK FIVE: *(forthcoming)*

www.theskylightseries.com

## CONTENTS

## PART ONE: A WALK WITH THE DEAD



## PART TWO: SPELLBINDER'S GAME

**PART THREE: THE DEVIL'S PADDOCK**

# PART ONE

## A WALK WITH THE DEAD

# CHAPTER 1
## *A WALK WITH THE DEAD*

IT HAD BEEN proclaimed in Ambriel for centuries that spirits couldn't feel grief. But Gwenevere Arris knew that theory was false. The haunted house across the street was all the proof she needed.

Gwen's next appointment was approaching, yet she lingered, enjoying the lazy afternoon in the northeastern province of Kalispell. Typical late autumns in this region were gray and overcast. But it had been unseasonably warm of late, and she intended to soak up every last ray of sunlight before she entered the haunted property.

The older cottages in this part of Kalispell were cute, quaint and somewhat affordable. Although prices had shot through the roof, even in a small town like Kalispell, this was as close to a starter home as a newlywed couple could afford. What the new buyers didn't know was that nearly every cottage in this district was haunted.

Just down the street was the Cornell Mansion Museum. Speculation that the museum was haunted had been rumored around Kalispell for nearly a century. That mysterious vibe had trickled into the very fabric of every house near the historic museum. Gwen had sold a handful of the cottages in the area, all of them haunted. Though Gwen was aware of the spirits, she didn't completely understand why they clung to certain areas of town. Unfinished business, or perhaps an unfair shake in death? Regardless of the reason, she had sensed spirits since the day her friend Kriss had been murdered. It had also been the same day she'd stolen her friend's ruby amulet.

Gwen stood and strolled past the Cornell Museum. The lush, manicured gardens and stately trees surrounding the grounds belied the historical mansion's more sinister nature. Bright pops of marigolds and mums pocked the lower wainscot of the large keep. A craggy stone fence surrounded the property: aged, dull and bereft of joy. The impressive shape of the steeply pitched roofline and brick chimneys struck an impressive profile on the majestic Ambriel sky. But to her eyes, she saw a decaying, gray cedar shake mansion, screaming to be saved.

Across the street stood 316 Olive Branch Avenue. The single-story cottage was simple, no frills. Its dark-green siding gave the cottage a charming street presence, though. There were three picturesque gables over arched windows, a small entry porch and plenty of repairs just waiting for the right family—all for just a shade under half a million steam tokens. Not bad, except for the grief-stricken apparition haunting the home.

Gwen had stopped by the foreclosed home half a dozen times over the last few weeks. She'd known the cottage was haunted from the beginning. One only needed to look at its constant listings on the assessor's sheet. Sold, followed by listed. Like clockwork, every six months, and no one ever asked why. Of course, the homeowners were afraid to say anything, concerned it might sour the salability of the property. Then it was the next unfortunate owner's nightmare.

Gwen stepped onto the porch, placed her key in the lock and opened the door. She had about an hour and wanted to make sure she could complete the job before the buyers arrived. Gwen walked through the rooms with her wand held high, the crooked rosewood haft warm against her sweaty palm. She kept her other hand wrapped around the amulet at her neck, rubbing the glowing ruby for clarity. She methodically went through each room and stood in the very center. A few minutes were all she needed to confirm what she already knew.

She felt nothing.

There was no hint of sway or whispers. Her mind was clear and unobstructed.

Now for the real test. The basement.

That had been the primary disturbance all along, and it had taken her several trips in the beginning to piece it all together. A young girl named Vivian had died from a tumble down the basement stairs some thirty years ago. The family's heartache still lingered within the walls of the small cottage. In weeks past, Gwen could hear those cries of pain and agony. Her trips into the basement had given her a mournful, unsettled feeling. Like all her past cleansings, this cottage was no different. She first had to discover the cause, then rectify the unfinished business for the trapped spirit. In turn, young Vivian would be free to rejoin her deceased parents. It was always a challenge, unraveling the mystery. But the reward was freeing young Vivian, and that made the effort worth it.

Thanks to her years in the ministry, her degree from Encantar University, and her heritage as a green witch, discovering Vivian's cause of death hadn't been too difficult. Gwen had simply 'phased' into the ethereal realm and observed the young girl, who'd been caught in a ghost loop for the past thirty years.

Sadly, and with heartbreaking realization, Gwen had discovered the loose step on the staircase. Surely, it was something the family had known about but hadn't repaired. Then, it was too late.

Gwen glided down the unfinished wooden stairs. The aged railing was warped, cold and creaky. She paused at the sixth step and cast a luminance spell, her rosewood wand creating a soft green glow within the basement's stillness. She set her wand down and pulled out a hammer and six nails from her satchel. As she knelt, she felt the basement go dim—that moment when energy was near. She was exposed here, even in the middle of the day. The witching hour was upon her, and she wasn't in her phased state, nor was she in a safe zone. But this was how it had to be. The step needed to be repaired while Vivian's presence was near. Her spirit needed to see this, needed to know it was safe to leave the basement and rejoin her family…a family that waited for her return.

Gwen hurried, her hands cold and shaking. With her back turned to the basement, she felt unnerved as she hammered home the sixth nail. Then, she quickly stood and took up her wand, dropped the hammer and began pulling trinkets from her satchel. They were tiny toys, stuffed animals, shiny bells and other childlike objects. She set one on each step until she reached the bottom. Then she grasped her amulet and felt it warm her frozen hand. Almost immediately, energy flooded through her body, along with a sense of relief.

Gwen stepped into the center of the frigid basement, sat down and crossed her legs. With her wand in one hand and the amulet in her other, Gwen closed her eyes and finally passed into the ethereal realm.

It took only a few seconds before she had completely phased into a shadow. Now, she was in a whole new world of danger. There were rules she couldn't break while phased, and she had to take caution to obey them. When Gwen was in her shadow state, she was vulnerable. Malicious spirits could attack, she could get drawn into a ghost loop, or she could become a lost soul like the ones she was trying to help.

But all she really needed to do now was coax Vivian's spirit up the stairs, one step at a time. Gwen stood and paused on the bottom step.

She waited patiently until she felt a tug on her green robe.

Vivian was there…

…and Gwen had her trust.

Together, they moved to the next step. Gwen waited until she felt the tug at her robe again. They repeated the process, each step coming in quicker succession. Gwen knew then that Vivian was ready to go home, even before they reached the top step.

Gwen breathed a sigh of relief, one hand over her forehead and the other on the amulet as she sat in a chair in the living room and waited.

The Gunter family arrived ten minutes early. The newlywed gnome couple brought the stroller with young Harriet. The nine-month-old was a darling: light blonde hair, curly at the tips, and inquisitive green eyes to match her skin. She smiled up at Gwen and tried to take her hand when Liz and Jeff stepped into the living room.

"One last look around?" Gwen said and smiled at them.

"We're so excited, Gwenevere." Liz gave her a hug. The lady was young with a lean and toned runner's physique. There was a confidence in her eyes that reminded Gwen of her old friend, Kriss.

Jeff stood behind them, beaming. "Thank you, Gwen. You've been so kind."

*They have no idea,* Gwen thought. *But at least they'll sleep in peace.* And that knowledge made her smile. The extra effort to cleanse 316 Olive Branch Avenue was worth it, no tip necessary.

"All in a day's work, Jeff," she said and smiled back.

Gwen followed the couple around the house (it was their fifth visit) as they checked the floors, opened and closed the doors. Jeff inspected the kitchen again, pointing out a few cracks in the paint for the tenth time. But the Gunters were sold.

"Everything's in place," Liz said. "Financing came through earlier today." She gave Jeff a smile, barely able to contain her joy. "Let's do this, honey!"

Jeff reached over and hugged her, holding little Harriet between them, and she giggled. That made Gwen's heart melt just a little more.

Though she felt a pang of jealousy, she couldn't help but laugh with them.

Twenty minutes later, they were all sitting in the mortgage company, *Kalispell Title & Trust*, signing away. The Gunters transferred nearly half a million steam tokens from their account, which was Ambriel's preferred form of payment. Everything was traded, bartered and sold in steam, even property. The happy family accepted the keys to their new cottage and left.

Of course, Gwen didn't have to stay for the closing, but she always found satisfaction in it, and this sale was even more enjoyable. She was helping the Gunters more than they realized, and she'd never tell them about it either. She couldn't care less about the attention. Creating a safe home for little Harriet Gunter was something Gwen had never experienced in her own youth. That, and freeing Vivian, was the only reward she needed.

# CHAPTER 2

## *A STRANGE OFFER*

WITH SEVERAL MORE goodbyes, and a few tearful hugs of joy, the Gunters left as happy homeowners while Gwen made her way back to the office. Though it was late, she wanted to file some paperwork and close down for the evening.

When she arrived, the downtown district was filled with festive lights. The Autumn Séance Festival was near, and Kalispell was in full celebration mode. Kids ran through the cobbled streets with streamers and kites. Adults gathered around the parks and chatted, mugs of cocoa in their hands. It was, in truth, one of her favorite times of the year. There was an energetic vibe in the small province, enhanced by the trees' brilliant orange, red, and gold tones, which wasn't normal for this late in the year. Usually, most of the leaves had fallen, but the unseasonably warm temperatures had stretched the months beyond their rhythmic schedule.

Her home base wasn't much more than a couple of offices, a restroom and a small kitchenette. The wood cabin had a steep slate roof and a quaint stone chimney poking up, which was slightly slanted. The coach's wheels pushed through the gravel lot, and the horses swished their tails as she entered her small office. On her desk was a handwritten note, which had been flattened out with a few paperweights pinning the corners down.

No one ever left messages for her, especially in Kalispell, and she wondered if this was some joke. Gwen looked around for her partner, expecting him to barge into her office. If there were clients in need, they would always visit her. But the place was empty, and she assumed her partner, Daniel Harris, was probably sitting at the local pub.

A few rays of fading sunlight filtered through the small window as Gwen sat down and picked up the letter. At the top, written in official letterhead with an aloe plant sigil, was the name of a prominent realtor, Lorenzo Kershaw. His company, Aloe Realtors, was headquartered in the southeastern region of Ambriel. The mega realtor was a world-renowned real estate agency that sold high-end properties, both residential and commercial.

Gwen leaned back and read the letter.

*Greetings, Miss Arris*

*My name is Lorenzo Kershaw with Aloe Realtors. I'd like to chat with you about a job opportunity that I believe you might find intriguing. I recruit the finest talent in the business, and your skills have come to my attention. If you are interested, please send a raven so that we can discuss this opportunity further.*

*Sincerely, Lorenzo Kershaw*

Gwen reread the message, flipped it over a few times, then set it down and furrowed her brow. She'd heard of Kershaw—any realtor worth their salt had, of course. The man was practically a legend in the industry. But why the hell would someone of his caliber be so interested in a green witch who'd sold nothing of importance? The type of customer she represented was likely a joke compared to his clientele. Plus, small three-room cottages in the sleepy town of Kalispell didn't seem to fit his market. In fact, she doubted Kershaw had even heard of Kalispell prior to him sending the letter. However, she was curious about what he had to say.

Later that night, Gwen took a coach home but opted for the long way so she could think. The winding roads lined with tall evergreens, along with the sound of the horses clomping, always set her at ease. In the back of her mind was the letter from Lorenzo Kershaw. She was so intrigued that by the end of the ride, she'd decided it couldn't hurt to at least hear what he had to say.

Thirty minutes later, she stepped into her two-bedroom bungalow and tossed her satchel onto the entry table. Under her robe, she unstrapped her rosewood wand and laid it on the table, glad to be rid of the gnarled branch. She started a pot of tea in the kitchen when her cat, Jewel, appeared at her feet. The tabby intertwined at her ankles, ready for her dinner.

Gwen sat in her favorite chair, a fire crackling in the corner hearth. Surrounding her were all sorts of plants, which created a wall of green in her living room. The emerald tones comforted her as she flipped through her scrapbook, which she'd recently pulled from the attic. She'd been thinking about her good friend, Kriss Blackwell, since the tenth anniversary of her death was near. In the middle of the scrapbook, like some oversized bookmarker, was a picture of her and Kriss hugging each other. She recalled the day of Kriss's funeral and visiting her home afterwards. Miss Blackwell had tearfully invited her in and allowed her to sit in Kriss's bedroom—closure perhaps. Gwen could still remember the musty smell, the hopeless, forlorn feeling of the empty space…the pinpoints of light where the stray bolts had come through the thatched wall and pierced Kriss in the chest. She'd often wondered about that day and why she had stolen her ruby amulet. Kriss had been a fantastic marksman and had won dozens of tournaments and amulets. But this particular amulet seemed to call to Gwen that day. Of course, she'd felt guilty about taking it and fleeing the Blackwells' cottage. She hadn't spoken to Kriss's family since then. If there was ever an experience she didn't want to go through again, that was it.

Gwen finally lifted the amulet and held it to the firelight. The large ruby twinkled at her like it was trying to say something. She took a long, steady breath and placed the amulet around her neck. She sat back and sipped her tea, reminiscing about the next ten years after Kriss's death, which had been a life-changing event for Gwen.

Not long after the incident, the authorities had caught and imprisoned the shooter, a male genie from a neighboring town. Of course, that had set off a firestorm of riots and clashes. Given the disdain between witches and genies, it had taken years for the squabbles to recede. Gwen had often wondered how Kriss would've reacted, had she known the strife her death had caused. Kriss's kind and caring nature had been considered abnormal for most red witches, who tended to be more aggressive and somewhat belligerent compared to green and yellow witches. Over the years, Gwen had struggled to accept the fact that Kriss's bright future had been stolen by a genie. Although it had never been proven that the shooting was premeditated, Gwen still harbored ill feelings toward the genie. That often made her feel ashamed.

During the following years, she had found solace through support groups filled with grieving parents, siblings or friends. But the one group she'd stuck with was unique from the others.

It had been for those who could walk with the dead.

And that had all started on the day she'd stolen Kriss's amulet.

Gwen traced the large ruby with her finger.

Over time, she'd grown comfortable with her new ability. That strange voice often filled her dreams, a presence that always seemed close, as if looking over her shoulder…constantly haunting her.

A sudden tapping at her door caused her to jump. Jewel shifted in her lap and flattened her ears back.

Gwen set her teacup down and opened the door. Standing on the doormat was a large raven, a message tied around its talon. Gwen bent low and took the rolled-up piece of parchment, then shooed the raven off. It cawed at her before taking flight into the night sky.

Scrawled on the outside of the note was an address, which Gwen knew to be from a southeastern region of Ambriel. There was no name written on it.

She sat down and thought about throwing the note into the fireplace. Something about it felt ominous. She wasn't sure if she wanted to read what was written within…

…because she knew it would change her life.

*Is that what I really want right now?*

Then again, it might be *exactly* what she needed.

Gwen rolled the note between her finger and thumb for a few seconds longer. Then she untied and read it.

*Greetings, Miss Arris*

*I apologize for contacting you again so soon. I'm afraid my company's situation is dire.*

*You possess a special skill, one that I've been searching for. I know that you have served in the ministry in the investigation department. You are a clue solver, something natural for green witches like yourself. I am also aware of your history regarding the supernatural. You happen to be a talented realtor as well. It's quite the combination of skills, which makes you a perfect candidate for the department I am developing. I would like to offer you a position as the head of this new department. Currently, I represent a very high-profile client who is in need. This would be your first assignment. I propose that you come to our headquarters, Aloe Realtors, in Valeside Beach. I would like to speak in person to go over the details of my offer, one that I think you will find very attractive. All expenses will be paid, including a stipend for your time. If you decline the offer, you may keep the stipend and return to your life in Kalispell.*

*Included in this letter is a round-trip ticket for this weekend. I hope you will consider my offer. Adventure awaits.*

*Sincerely, Lorenzo Kershaw*

Gwen found the train ticket and held it up to the candlelight—one round-trip pass to Valeside Beach. She knew of the region, though she'd never been there, or to any beach for that matter. Gwen had only known the cooler climates of northern Ambriel.

She perused the note again. Kershaw seemed intent on speaking with her. This was the second message in the same day. She wondered what would happen if she ignored him. Would there be ravens on her doorstep and notes at her office until she did respond? But in truth, she'd already made up her mind. She was intrigued. But before she did return his message, Gwen wanted to run it by her partner first. He always seemed to see things clearly. And she knew just where to find Harris.

# CHAPTER 3
## *A MOUNTAIN OF TROUBLE*

"YOU DID WHAT?" Gwen blurted, trying to hold her voice down. Her partner, Daniel Harris, sat across from her in their favorite booth. The pub, *The Thirsty Thistle*, was busy at this time of evening, and most of the locals knew Gwen and Harris by name. The air was a bit smoky with pipe weed, and colorful lights illuminated the bar.

Harris pushed his ruddy hair to one side. His cheeks were their typical rosy-red color, which matched his bulbous nose. He wiped a bit of froth from his thick mustache and leaned in, lowering his voice. "Sorry, Gwen. What can I tell ya? I got carried away, or maybe it was the ale…I just knew I could win." Harris hammered his fist into his palm.

"But you didn't," Gwen said and leaned into the table, her elbows thumping onto the wooden top. "You just gambled the deed to our company away! What were you thinking?"

"I wasn't…apparently." Harris didn't look Gwen in the eyes and leaned back. "I'm sorry. Won't happen again."

"Well, I don't guess it will, since we don't have a company now." Gwen sat back and shook her head. She'd placed a lot of trust in her partner over the years. She'd known Harris to be risky; it was one reason they even had a company. Regardless, her partner had, for the first time, placed them in a dubious spot, though. He'd always held his risk-taking in check after they'd established their company. His gambling nature had gone dormant. Owning a successful business had required him to be more thoughtful with his decisions. But deep down, Gwen had always feared Harris might slip back into his old habits. She just wouldn't have guessed he'd gamble their company away.

"There's more," Harris said, the bashful look on his face returning. "I…might have taken out a loan to try and get our deed back. Then I lost that as well." Harris flinched, waiting for Gwen's verbal backlash.

"How many steam tokens?" Gwen said, trying to maintain the waver in her voice. She failed.

"It's a lot…over a million."

"You're serious?" Gwen continued, gripping the table. "This isn't some deranged prank of yours?"

Harris could only nod, his lips pursed tight. "I'm sorry, Gwen. I don't know what to do."

Gwen watched Harris, her arms crossed. She wanted to reach across the booth and throttle him. "Who did you take the loan from?"

"Bam Jino."

Gwen felt her head loll forward. "Oh no," she whispered and ran her fingers through her dark green hair.

There was an awkward silence; the noise of the bar in the background, with glass clanking and muffled conversations filled the space between them. Harris waited silently for Gwen to speak. But Gwen's mind was racing, and the recent opportunity with Kershaw kept coming to the forefront. The timing seemed almost too good to be true. Was it a blessing? Either way, it would seem to be their best hope to get the tokens they needed.

"Bam Jino runs a mob," Gwen said. "That's the last person you should have gone to."

"Honestly, he was the only one with the amount I needed to get our deed back."

"He's a mountain troll, Harris."

"Yeah, I'm aware."

"His cronies are going to be all over you…all over us. Why didn't you come to me in the first place?"

"I know. I'm sorry, partner."

As if on cue, the door to the pub thudded open, and the patrons grew silent. Gwen shifted to see a large troll hunch through the door, followed by several other trolls.

"Great!" Harris hissed and tried to slouch in the booth. He held a hand over his brow, trying to hide his face.

The large troll waded through the crowded bar and stopped in front of their table. Gwen looked up at the brute. Bam Jino was gray-skinned, with thick wrinkles along his arms and neck. He wore a plaid kilt with dozens of leather belts strapped across his large chest. Bam Jino's calling card was his purple beret, which had two dragon's teeth pushed through the brim. He was homely, as were most mountain trolls, and patchy silver hair lined his muscled jawline. He was so tall that he nearly disappeared into the rafters of the pub. Gwen had a sense that everyone in the bar had stopped what they were doing to watch and listen.

"Oi, it's Harris and his kitten," Bam Jino chuckled. The three trolls next to him guffawed.

Gwen felt her skin heat up. She felt for her wand but remained calm. She knew the troll wasn't there for a scuffle if he wanted his payment back. This was how things worked in Kalispell. Bam Jino wasn't as interested in the steam tokens as he was in controlling others. Though it was a sizable amount they owed, the troll had plenty of tokens. No, this was all for show and intimidation. She relaxed her grip on her rosewood wand.

"What are the terms of repayment?" Gwen said coolly.

Bam Jino crossed his arms. "Well. I can see who has the brains in your company, Gwenevere Arris. Never thought I'd get to you through your partner. You sure you won't just join my team? I'd wipe away the entire debt, just like that. I could use a green witch like you—"

"Just get to the terms, Bam Jino," Gwen continued.

"Oh, let's see." The troll shoved Harris to the side and somehow managed to fit into the booth across from Gwen. Bam Jino held her gaze, his large black eyes staring into her hazel eyes, like he was trying to determine how much he could manipulate her. "I'll give you till Saint Halving Day, green witch. If you want to save your partner, and your business, you have till then to pay me back, with interest." The mountain troll pulled a piece of parchment from his kilt and waved it in her face. It was the deed to their company.

"Where'd you get that?" Harris blurted.

Gwen glanced at Harris, who was squished between the wall and the massive troll. His skin was pale, like he'd be nauseous at any moment. "Doesn't matter," Gwen said. "You'll have your tokens by Saint Halving Day. And when you get it, you leave Harris and me alone. No more loans."

"Well, you'll have to work that out with your partner. I'd suggest you get that gambling habit under control, though." Bam Jino elbowed Harris and nearly sent him through the wall. "Till then, I own your agency, and any steam tokens that come of it. Till then, I own the two of you."

# CHAPTER 4
## *VALESIDE BEACH*

GWEN AND HARRIS watched as Bam Jino and his crew left the pub. The din and clamor returned as the patrons bent back to their conversations and drinks as if nothing had happened.

"What're you thinking?" Harris asked.

Gwen could hear the nerves in his tone. Harris was rattled, and quite honestly, so was she. But her anger was overriding her nerves at the moment. She wanted to yell at Harris for getting them into this predicament. But as angry as she was, she couldn't stay upset at him. She looked at her partner of nearly a decade and could only shake her head.

"You know, the worst part about this is your disappointment," Harris said. "I thought I had it under control. I guess those old addictions don't just go away. I can't tell you how sorry I am, Gwen."

Gwen reached across the table and took his hand. "It's okay. I think I might have a plan."

The look on Harris's face was a mix of elation and curiosity. "What is it?"

"I just got a raven, tonight in fact. A realtor in Valeside Beach wants to talk to me about a business deal. His name is Lorenzo Kershaw."

"Lorenzo Kershaw?" Harris squinted his eyes. "Oh, I dunno. I've heard rumors about him."

Gwen threw up her hands. "What else is there? Selling homes in Kalispell isn't going to net us the tokens we need to pay our debt and get our business back."

Harris held her gaze, then scratched at his red hair. He gulped down the rest of his ale, then gave the waitress a nod and held up his mug. "Kershaw's slick. I just hate to see ya get taken advantage of."

"I don't know that we have a choice. Either I go to Valeside, or we fold our business, and Bam Jino takes the rest out of our hides."

"Yeah, I know." Harris folded his hands under his arms, a nervous habit he'd always had. "It's just… Valeside Beach, and, well, what if this new opportunity means that you don't come back to Kalispell? It sounds selfish of me, but I just don't want to lose you. This community needs you, Gwen. No one else can do what you do."

Gwen waved it away. "I don't know about that."

"Don't deny it. Think about all the families you've helped because of your ability, like the Gunters…like Vivian. Plus, I don't want to train another partner. We're perfect together."

Gwen smirked, somewhat in shock. "You've got a bounty on your head from a mountain troll, we're about to lose our business, and all you can think about is me coming back to Kalispell?"

Harris tilted his head. "Well…yeah, I guess. I mean, I don't want to lose you."

Gwen reached across the booth and patted his arm. "Don't worry about me. You just focus on staying alive and selling homes. I'm going to hear what Kershaw has to offer and hope it's enough to bail us out. I'll be back before you know it."

"Did Kershaw say why he wanted you?"

"Apparently, he's done some research and found out about my special ability."

Harris eyed her, then lifted his chin at her as the waitress dropped another mug of ale and left. "Gwen. I've known you too long. Tell me what this is about."

Gwen chewed at her cheek, then brushed her dark green hair back. "I've told you about my past."

"The interviews? Yeah, so? What's that gotta do with a realtor like Kershaw?"

"Says he wants me to head up some new division of his company." Gwen chuckled.

"Head up, as in lead?" Harris craned his head back. Gwen recognized the look and waited for the explosive laughter. "So, you'd be leading a group of other paranormal realtors?"

"Keep it down, Harris." Gwen glanced around.

Harris slowly frowned, his smile fading. "Look, Gwen. It just sounds a bit sketchy, don't it? I mean, you get a mega realtor calling you in Kalispell, offering you a major job to head up a division at Aloe Realtors, probably a huge salary bump…" Harris sat back, shaking his head.

Gwen took a sip of her green tea and gently set it down. She shuffled her feet a bit, suddenly feeling uncomfortable. "Sure, the timing is a bit odd, considering what just happened with Bam Jino. Regardless, this could be our ticket out of this mess."

"Yeah, well, I guess the weather's pretty nice down there this time of year."

Gwen reached across the table and gave the stocky man a hug. "You've been a good partner, Harris. Despite the mess you've gotten us into, you're like a brother to me, and I'm thankful for that. I'm going to find us a way out of this, okay?"

"I know you will, Gwen. You've got a knack for figurin' things out. Bam Jino's right about one thing, you *are* the brains. You discovered how to cleanse all those unsellable cottages. No one else in Ambriel could have done it. Otherwise, we don't have a business. I'm really not surprised that someone finally contacted you. Just…watch after yourself, alright?"

Gwen stopped by the post office the next day and sent a raven to let Kershaw know she was on her way. That weekend, she was on the train out of Kalispell, with just one brief layover in Roiling Springs.

Once she reached the Valeside terminal, the hubbub picked up, which was annoying, since she hadn't really traveled in years. She was used to the slower pace of Kalispell, where she knew most of the people.

Eventually, she found a coffee shoppe, and a chai latte settled her nerves. Then she followed the directions in the letter and saw a lady holding a sign that read, Gwenevere Arris.

The lady was petite—probably a full foot shorter than Gwen—with a blue-skinned complexion to match her long, powder-blue hair. She was toned, a runner or fitness coach, Gwen guessed, and her facial features were almost pixie-like, though she had a vertical scar across her left eye and cheek. The blouse she wore exposed her midsection and was a bit too tight, although it did show the lady's curves nicely. She was bejeweled with golden trinkets: bracelets, rings, necklaces. Genies had an affinity for golden jewelry, and this lady matched that stereotype perfectly. However, there was a glowing golden chain around her thin waist that didn't look normal. It was delicate, had a strange pattern, and looked to have an enchantment upon it.

The genie stared at Gwen with golden eyes as she approached.

"Great," Gwen muttered under her breath. She was familiar with genies, thanks to the long history between their two races. Wars had been fought over genies' wish-magic and their ability to generate steam. Genies and witches were natural enemies, some had declared, not to mention the death of her friend Kriss at a genie's hand. Though the last war had been nearly a decade ago, there was still plenty of animosity between their races.

Gwen looked down at her and noticed some steam beginning to rise from her skin, which was a common trait amongst genies. Cold mist or heated steam, depending on their mood. *Good. The easier to read her,* Gwen thought to herself.

At first, Gwen didn't think the genie would even speak to her. But she finally lowered the sign with a look of distaste, crossed her arms and looked up at Gwen. "Tall, with striking features. A pencil-thin nose, high brows and cheekbones, strong jawline, long, dark-green flowing hair with matching hazel eyes…" the lady paused and looked closer at the back of the sign again, as if reading something. "And one wide-brimmed witch's hat. The exact description, straight from Mister Kershaw himself. You're Miss Arris, I take it?"

It wasn't difficult to miss her sarcasm. Gwen could see she wasn't happy about the assignment either.

"None other," Gwen said and unshouldered her satchel. She held it out to the genie, who promptly ignored her.

"I'm not a bellhop, Miss Arris. I'm only here to escort you to Kershaw. Carry your own items."

"Do all of Kershaw's employees treat his guests this way?"

"No, just me," the genie said.

Gwen took her satchel back, giving the girl a cheeky smile. "Fine. Might as well get to know each other then. You can call me Gwen."

"Patricia Oshner," the lady said and gave a dramatic, if not overly sarcastic, curtsy. "I go by Posh. Not to rush you, but we should get moving if we want to beat the traffic."

"I'm in no hurry," Gwen said.

"Well, I am. Mister Kershaw doesn't wait for anyone."

Posh turned and started walking down the concourse without another word. Gwen stepped up her pace to walk beside her.

At the curb was a fancy coach with a man holding the door open for them.

"Here we are. Thank you," Posh said, giving the chauffeur a pat on the cheek. The man smiled at her, his eyes lingering on her bare midriff. Then he took Gwen's satchel and started to put it in the trunk.

"I'll hang on to it, thank you." Gwen took a seat across from Posh.

Soon, they were merging into the traffic Posh had mentioned. Gwen settled back, finally catching her breath and taking a sip from her now lukewarm latte. "Was this Kershaw's idea? Placing you in charge of ferrying me around town?"

Posh held her gaze, letting one arm drape across the bench seat. "Yes. And I can see you're not thrilled about it. Neither am I. But people don't say no to Mister Kershaw around here."

"I see. And have you been working for him for very long?"

"Long enough to have his *trust.*"

Posh placed just enough emphasis on the word to make Gwen understand that there was very little between them at the moment, which was fine by her. But deep down, she was beginning to wonder how this would all work out. If Posh was Kershaw's personal assistant, this was going to be a long weekend. And furthermore, assuming she even took Kershaw's offer, there was no way in hell she was going to work alongside someone like Posh. That just wouldn't do.

"Lots of talk from upper management about you," Posh said. "I wonder what's so special? Last time I checked, green witches could barely cast any meaningful enchantments."

"Is that so?" Gwen said. "I'm happy that you think so highly of us. Can't say that I've ever met a genie who could stay out of trouble. I'm shocked that Kershaw would even employ one. I thought he'd be a bit more discerning."

Posh's blue skin blanched, and a jet of steam filtered up from her arms. Gwen felt for her wand but remained calm.

Posh gave her a strained chuckle, then waved it away. "Well, I guess I'll let you be the judge of that. Be cautious what you say around Kershaw. He may come across as non-discerning, but don't underestimate him."

"So, now you're giving me tips for my own protection? Am I to take your word for it?"

Posh shrugged. "Take it or leave it. But the man is determined. Whatever he brought you here for, he'll get it. Believe me."

"Is that how he was able to land you?"

That made Posh sit forward.

Gwen was good at reading others. It was something that came with being a realtor for a decade. Posh's little hesitation told Gwen there was something more between her and Kershaw.

"I'm not really allowed to discuss that," Posh said. "It's not relevant anyway. What's relevant is our clientele. We have a confidentiality clause, and we don't share information. Whatever this is about, it must stay between you and Kershaw. If word gets out, our reputation will be damaged. You'll probably have to sign a non-disclosure agreement before he'll discuss anything with you."

"Any idea who this client is?"

Posh shook her head. "And if I did know, I wouldn't say. We represent a lot of celebrities, like movie stars, actors, musicians, athletes, investors…you name it. You'll have to wait for the rest of it."

Posh, somewhat reluctantly, offered her a drink, which Gwen declined. She continued to sip halfheartedly on her now cold latte while avoiding Posh, though it felt as if the genie was trying to be polite. But Gwen wondered if that was from fear of Kershaw more than anything else.

Thanks to the traffic, it took about an hour before they pulled up to a tall skyscraper. The coach maneuvered into a drop-off lane and parked. The chauffeur opened the door and helped Posh out. Gwen ignored the man and shouldered her satchel. They stood in front of the glass façade building with a large porte-cochere. Massive planters with tropical aloe plants lined the entry vestibule. Tall palm trees dotted the manicured front lawn as the gentle coastal breeze tugged at Gwen's dark-green robe.

She craned her neck up, holding onto her hat so it didn't tumble off. The high-rise building was perhaps thirty, or more, stories tall. In the diminishing sunlight, the glass was a deep green color that reminded her of the nearby ocean. A vibrant green light wrapped the top parapet with a backlit sign that read, *Aloe Realtors Inc.* A spiked plant in simplistic fashion followed—minimal and to the point. The main south-facing façade was curved and reflected the waning sun.

The coach left as Gwen and Posh stood under the porte-cochere. Gwen basked in the warmth of the sultry air. There was a slight bit of humidity, but it was still comfortable. Much better than Kalispell for late autumn.

"Right this way," Posh said and stepped into the glass vestibule.

They were greeted by a doorman who wore an expensive-looking suit. The entry lobby was decadent with a slightly modern touch: snowshed marble flooring with gold leaf adorning nearly every inch of the wood trim. It felt like floating in a white cloud. She could see her reflection on almost every surface.

Their concierge led them to an elevator bank with four cabs on either side. Background music gave off a soft island jazz vibe, making Gwen feel like she was on vacation. She had to keep pulling herself back—this was business, not playtime. Still, she was enjoying the scenery.

The sleek, magical elevator zipped them up to the 35th floor, leaving her stomach behind. She could hear the steam propulsion system rumble beneath her feet as they ascended higher. Soon, they stepped off the lift and passed through another lobby before finally being seated in a contemporary-style boardroom. The table was mahogany, the chairs wrapped in a supple, saddle-brown leather. The artwork adorning the walls appeared to be originals by a local artist, based on the coastal theme. She didn't care to guess the worth of the pieces, but assumed it was well beyond what she had in savings. But it was the view that stole her breath. Beyond was the nightlife of Valeside Beach, which was just getting into full swing. Colorful fairy lights graced the other tall buildings surrounding the shoreline, which looked pastel in the evening sun. In the distance was the Green Sea, dark and foreboding. It reflected the final light of the setting sun like a mix of tangerine and turquoise, awash in some boiling cauldron.

The city of Valeside, like most other towns in Ambriel, was steam powered and fortified by magic. It allowed for the lifts, lighting, electricity and plumbing. Even most of the vehicles, like trains and airships, utilized the same combination of steam and magic. This arcane fortification, coupled with the technological contraptions that produced the steam, allowed the residents to live in relative comfort. As a result, the lower downtown area was cloaked in steam and lit in multiple colors.

Gwen sat uncomfortably in the leather chair, trying to straighten out her green hair and robes. She disliked boardrooms. They were too uptight and stuffy for her liking, not to mention she'd spent the last eight years working out of a cubicle on a fold-up table and chair. She much preferred those.

The doors opened, and a man walked in with several others following behind. Lorenzo Kershaw looked exactly as he did in all the articles she'd read. Tall, toned, and impeccably dressed. He wore a blue pinstriped suit and tie. His dark hair was feathered perfectly to one side, and his tanned skin told Gwen he'd been a native of this region for a long time. He flashed a smile, then walked over and shook her hand with both of his. Gwen stood to greet him, halfway thinking the man was going to give her a hug. It was more than awkward.

"Gwen, so good to meet you. Anything we can get you? Water, snacks?"

The entire entourage of people in the room stood silently, waiting for Kershaw to give them the 'as you were' command.

Gwen blinked a few times. "Uh, no. I'm fine. A bit tired, to be honest."

"You can sleep soon, I promise. Let me apologize for the late meeting, but I had to see you tonight."

Gwen waited as Kershaw took a seat at the head of the long conference table. Everyone else finally relaxed.

"Mister Kershaw—"

"Please, Gwen. Kershaw will do."

Gwen nodded and cleared her throat again. "Kershaw. Is all of this really necessary?"

The man looked around at all the people dressed in business attire, then chuckled. "Of course not. Forgive me. I'm so used to having my assistants near me." He nodded to the others in the room, who turned and left. Posh started to walk out, but Kershaw motioned to her. "Posh. I would ask that you stay, please." It came off a bit too direct. Gwen watched Posh's expression and could tell that she was annoyed at having to stay.

Posh bowed subtly and took a seat near Kershaw and steepled her hands under her chin.

"Shall we talk now?" Kershaw said. He leaned forward and placed his hands on the table, drumming his fingers. But to Gwen, he seemed a bit nervous, and perhaps he was simply trying to cover it up.

"You seem a bit uptight," she said.

Kershaw pursed his lips. "Is it that obvious? I forgot that you've been in the business a while. As a realtor, I, too, learned to read others' emotions. But you're right, Gwen. This is important to me and our company. I've mentioned that you possess a unique blend of skills. There aren't many with your abilities."

"So you've said. But what exactly are these skills? Selling three-bedroom cottages in a small northern province doesn't seem to align with your company's business model. My clients are young couples just starting out, not celebrities with bank accounts loaded with steam tokens."

"I'm not concerned about who your clients are, or how many tokens they have or how big the property is, Gwenevere. What I am interested in is your problem-solving skills. You're a green witch, adept in this. You have a paranormal background and can walk in both planes. You're also a realtor. I know you've helped many couples, just like the Gunters, by cleansing haunted homes, while also freeing trapped souls. And yet, you take no thanks for your work. All that ability, with a heart of gold on top of it all." Kershaw held out his hands. "Why *wouldn't* we want you here at Aloe Realtors? You may be the best-kept secret this side of Ambriel."

Gwen listened to Kershaw while watching his movements, facial expressions, and tone. Obviously, he was trying to flatter her. Big deal, she didn't care about that. She was trying to detect if he was being genuine. Either Kershaw was the best liar in Ambriel, or he *was* being one hundred percent honest with her, though. "What are you offering, and what exactly would my job be?"

"Your first assignment will be a castle known as Hidden Palm Grove. It's prime beachside property. It's large. It's haunted. None of our realtors will go near it. The client wishes to remain anonymous, and we have been directed to keep the property's status a secret until it has been cleansed."

Gwen considered. It was close to what she had guessed. A large estate owned by a wealthy client, likely on prime real estate…but haunted. "I'll need access to resources around town, a place to stay, transportation, records—"

Kershaw held up his hands. "We'll handle that. Posh knows her way around Valeside. She'll be your personal assistant while you're here."

Posh sat forward to say something, but one look from Kershaw made her settle back, arms crossed. A bit of steam flitted from her skin.

Kershaw continued. "As far as living arrangements, we have a cozy beachside property that you can stay at. Assuming you can crack the case and cleanse the castle, then you can keep the beach property for your efforts."

"How bad is the castle?"

"First, I want you to hear my full offer."

"I'm not accepting *any* offer until I inspect the castle."

"You'll have a chance to see it in person soon enough. Not only does our offer include the beachside property, but also a large stipend. If you choose not to accept our offer, then you're free to go back to Kalispell. You may keep the stipend for your trouble."

Kershaw stood and paced the boardroom, holding his hands behind his back. "If you enjoy working for Aloe Realtors, you'll be heading up the paranormal department. I want you to lead a group of realtors. There's an entire market of haunted, unsellable homes out there, sitting on prime real estate. And not just here in Valeside. All across Ambriel, there are countless properties on the market right now. It's an untapped resource that we intend to capitalize on."

"Sounds interesting," Gwen said. "I'm listening."

"Good. Let's talk about the salary." Kershaw pulled an envelope from his breast pocket and slid it across the table.

Gwen took it and held it up. It was addressed to her with the word *confidential* written across the front. Inside was the salary, with what she assumed was one too many zeros. Kershaw's proposed salary was more than enough to cover what she needed for Harris, with plenty of tokens left over, assuming she could cleanse the castle. There was also a contract inside. Gwen took it out and paged through it, trying to hide her enthusiasm.

"That's the contract, along with the non-disclosure agreement. Whether or not you accept the offer, I would ask that you sign the NDA. Realtor to realtor, please do me that favor."

"Sure," Gwen said. "When do you need an answer, though?"

"Two days."

Gwen nodded. "That seems fair. Kershaw, you know I can't guarantee that I'll be able to cleanse Hidden Palm Grove."

"I understand. I'm only asking you to consider my offer. I think you'll find the challenge exhilarating, more so than any other property you've sold. I believe you have a perfect record of cleansing homes. Isn't that correct?"

Kershaw almost seemed to read her mind. She'd never failed before; her record was perfect in that department. But honestly, she wasn't thrilled about working with a big company like Aloe Realtors or having a genie as her assistant. And she certainly didn't like the idea of treating haunted properties as 'capital'. That felt somewhat sacrilegious.

But it was also an intriguing offer, and the challenge of cleansing a larger property like Hidden Palm Grove enticed her. Gwen was already wondering if the spirits there were any different than the smaller properties.

"Okay, Kershaw. I'll give you two days."

# CHAPTER 5
## *JAVA HOUSE*

THE COACH WAS waiting outside for them. Posh walked impatiently in front of Gwen, not speaking to her. The chauffeur held the door, this time avoiding Gwen's gaze. Once they were seated, Posh settled in with a dramatic sigh.

"Kershaw has directed me to show you around town," Posh said. "I imagine you're tired and would rather call it a night—"

"Actually, I'd prefer to see Valeside."

The look on Posh's face was a mixed expression of disappointment and slight annoyance. But she also detected a bit of curiosity.

Posh picked at her nails. "Well…I guess we could start by visiting one of my favorite coffee shoppes."

"Oh, coffee?" Gwen said. She tried to hide her excitement and settled back. "I mean, that would be nice. I love coffee shoppes."

Posh gave the leather seat a few taps. "Good. There are quite a few, but the best one in town is *Sephora Bean.* The beachfront view is amazing and there's easy access. Best lattes in town, I might add. It's rumored that they brew their coffee beans in gold pixie dust. Anyway, if you're with me, we'll be making a lot of stops there."

Gwen had to practically sit on her hands to keep from clapping.

Though it was getting late, and she was tired, Gwen hadn't had a night out in a while. And maybe she could glean some more information about Kershaw as well.

Their coach dropped them at the seaside coffee shoppe called *Sephora Bean*, which also had a pub on the upper level. There was some soft music playing from inside and, surprisingly, the coffee shoppe wasn't very crowded. It was an open-air lounge with some mood lighting and a low-slung roofline.

The interior was wide and airy with an unobstructed view of the ocean beyond. The soft crooning of crashing waves melded with the music in a way that made Gwen feel like she was on vacation. It was like being on another planet compared to the cold slopes of Kalispell.

Posh spoke softly to the host, who led them to the back and onto a patio, the sound of conversation and steam frothers filled the space. The patio had a few well-manicured gardens and high palm trees that swayed gently in the sea breeze. The wicker furniture was low and inviting and faced the ocean. A linear firepit emitted a subtle flame that sent off a bit of heat. Gwen practically melted into the lounge sofa and inhaled the scent of saltwater.

"Very nice," Gwen murmured in a dreamlike tone, letting her eyelids droop.

"Like I said, it's one of my favorite coffee shoppes. Hard to get a seat unless you know the right people."

"Like Kershaw?" Gwen asked.

"Working at Aloe Realtors can be challenging, but it has its perks."

"You don't strike me as a coffee fanatic," Gwen said.

"It's the hair, right?" Posh said. Gwen sensed that her walls had dropped for just a split second. Now they were back up.

Gwen shrugged. "I've never met a coffee-loving genie before, that's all."

"Can't say that I've met a coffee-loving green witch either."

Their waiter stepped up to take their order. Posh ordered a mint latte. Surprisingly, it was the exact same fashion that Gwen usually had hers brewed, and she simply held up two fingers.

As the waiter hurried off, Gwen gave Posh a serious look. "I didn't mean to offend you, Posh."

"Yeah, you did," Posh said, but her expression softened. "Look. I really don't care if you dislike me. I know that our two races don't get along. But this is business. I have a job to do, and I'd prefer to keep Mister Kershaw on my good side. It'd be nice if we could get along while you're here."

"And what if I choose to take Kershaw's offer? Is that going to be a problem?"

"I doubt I'd be working underneath you."

"What if Kershaw makes you my personal assistant?"

"I'd probably use my wish-magic and send him away."

Gwen held her gaze, trying to determine if the genie was serious. But Posh finally cracked a smile.

"I'm joking, of course. Wish-magic is forbidden. I would do as he asks. So, let's play nice with each other."

"Looks like you've already used one of your wishes," Gwen motioned to the vertical scar along Posh's left eye. "What's to keep you from using the other two?"

Posh didn't seem to care, and she remained silent. Gwen could tell that particular topic wasn't open for discussion, and to be honest, Gwen didn't know the extent of wish-magic anyway, nor did she care to know.

The waiter returned and dropped their lattes on the table. Posh picked hers up, cupped it in her hands and inhaled the steam. "I don't think I'll ever get tired of that smell."

Gwen did the same and let out a moan. "Oh, that is good."

"I told you so," Posh muttered in a dreamy tone.

They both sat in their lounge chairs, feet up and silent. Gwen sipped her mint latte and kicked her leather boots off, letting the gentle breeze tickle her toes. She'd lost track of time until Posh cleared her throat.

"Enjoying the experience, I see."

Gwen opened her eyes. "Kind of hard not to, especially when you've spent most of your life in Kalispell."

"Right. Kalispell," Posh said. "You went to Horsehair Academy, where you met your friend, Kriss. Took archery together, where she won regionals and earned a scholarship to Recurve University. But she was tragically killed in her own bedroom before making it to college. That's when you got into the paranormal support group, is that correct?"

Gwen stared at Posh, her mug hovering near her lips. "How did you know about the support group? Only a handful of people—"

"Kershaw has nearly unlimited access to everyone, Gwen. If there's a secret out there, he knows about it. Considering he's making such a high-level job offer, he's double-checking everything about you."

"And you've seen the files on me, too?"

Posh nodded. "I'm his assistant, so I review almost everything for him. Not to pry, of course."

Gwen set her mug down and faced Posh. "So, do you think I'm crazy?"

"Why? Because you can walk in two realms? Why would I think you're crazy?"

"Because almost everyone who knows about my ability does. It's one reason I try to keep it quiet."

Posh looked out at the ocean, which was dark and brooding now. The sinking sun shone neon across little fingernail-shaped waves, which appeared and vanished just as quickly. Gwen waited for Posh to respond.

"I'm a genie, which means I've been around for a long time. I've never met someone who could walk in two realms. That said, I know there are many strange things in Ambriel. So, what if you can walk with the dead? Why would that change my opinion? My job for Kershaw is to analyze everything. You learn to view people more diplomatically that way. Short answer, no. You're not crazy, and if you were, I really don't care. But I'm not the one you have to impress."

"Who says I'm trying to impress anyone?" Gwen said.

Posh held her mug up. "Exactly. If I could take on that attitude, I would."

"Then why don't you?"

"Because I work for Kershaw. I can't afford to."

"So, what is it between you two?"

"That's really none of your business," Posh said, her voice back to monotone. "I suggest you focus on your upcoming decision with Kershaw and his job offer."

Gwen held up her hands. "Fair enough."

"Out of curiosity, what was it like?" Posh asked. "I read about some of the support group experiences, but it doesn't go into detail on phasing into the ethereal realm."

Gwen looked away, not ready to discuss it, especially with a genie she barely knew.

Posh seemed to catch her hesitation. "I don't mean to pry, of course."

"Yeah, you did," Gwen said.

Posh grimaced, then finished the last of her latte. "Let's go for a walk."

Posh led the way from the patio and onto the beach.

Gwen followed behind her a few steps. She draped her boots over her shoulder and let her toes sink into the warm sand. It was a sensation she'd never felt before. It was soothing in a way she couldn't put into words. She felt grounded, alive.

When she caught up to Posh, she slowed her pace. "So…this Java House is where I'm staying?"

"That's where we're heading."

Gwen narrowed her eyes. "Wait. Java House is close by?"

"Yes. One of the best perks about Valeside Beach is that almost everything you need is along the coast and within walking distance."

They followed the white sand beach, soaking up the final rays of sunlight. Gwen ventured closer to the water's edge, letting the seafoam lap onto her green robe.

"Over there, see it?" Posh nodded, then pointed at a large castle perched on a craggy rock outcropping. In the waning sunlight, two large palm trees resembled a pair of massive horns. The shape of the outcropping looked like a skull, and the whole thing sat on three large pillars of stone. Surrounding the base was a thicket of pink and green thorny rose nettle.

Gwen stopped, and Posh had to backtrack.

"That's Hidden Palm Grove?"

Posh nodded. "One of the oldest castles along Ambriel's coastline. Nearly one hundred and fifty thousand square feet of prime real estate. You'll get your chance to visit it tomorrow."

"It's…incredible."

"Oh, there are plenty of potential buyers. As of now, it hasn't hit the market, and it won't until we figure out how to cleanse it. There's a lot at stake with this property. It's been dubbed *The Devil's Paddock* by the locals. I think you can see why."

It took only ten minutes to reach Java House. Posh had been right. The view was spectacular.

Facing the ocean was a wall of windows. Leading to the house was a raised boardwalk, sun-bleached and twisting its way through the thick beach reed grass and thorny rose nettle. The elevated bridge had a slight incline that dead-ended into one of the cutest decks Gwen had ever seen. It stretched the length of the modern beach house with a few tables and pastel-colored umbrellas. A porch swing hung near the patio door, and an outdoor fireplace made of stone stood to one side.

Posh led the way across the boardwalk, eventually stopping in front of the wall of windows. Like the other nearby beach homes, this one had a pitched roofline that opened toward the ocean. White stucco, in a simplistic Art Deco style, gave the home a clean, yet sophisticated presence.

"Like a dream, yeah? Splendid view of the Green Sea." Posh unlocked the aluminum door slider, and the telescoping system opened the full width of the living space inside. Interior lights dimmed to a low level. The other systems also came online: large ceiling fans whirred to life, sending a soothing breeze through the space. Soft music played in the background, and a fire popped magically into the corner hearth.

"Let me give you the tour," Posh said. "Over here, we have a state-of-the-art interactive system, temperature settings, alarm system, cameras, and motion detection. On to the kitchen, right this way."

They moved to the open kitchen, and Gwen felt the urge to sprawl out across the massive marble island.

"Seating for eight with waterfall edges, and a two-tone marble color to match. Top of the line appliances," Posh motioned to the refrigerator and gas range, "and my personal favorite, the breakfast nook." She waved at the corner where a booth and table were tucked discreetly near a casement window. Beneath the banquet booth was a bookshelf stocked with all the latest bestsellers.

"Bedrooms, you ask?" Posh continued and led the way down a wide corridor, which was clad with marble tile and had high ceilings. "Four bedrooms, each with its own bathroom. A private study and library for research. All of the rooms have a view of the ocean. And here…we have the master suite."

Gwen followed Posh into the suite, trying to keep herself calm. She'd never seen anything like it. The beach house was a far cry from her humble two-bedroom bungalow in Kalispell.

The suite was massive, with floor-to-ceiling windows and gossamer sheer drapes. The bed was built into the wall with a white oak headboard and a skylight above it. A walk-in closet took up half the space, which was tucked behind the bed's wall. Gwen could only shake her head at the size of the shower and tub.

"Well…I'm impressed," Gwen laughed. "But I'm afraid it's just too tiny."

"Count yourself lucky. Not many people get to stay at Java House. Kershaw uses it as a recruiting tool. From what I gather, you're one of the most important potential employees to come along in a while. Better enjoy it."

They walked out and sat on the sofa, looking at the Green Sea beyond.

Gwen tucked her legs under herself and draped an arm across the back of the sofa. "So, where do you live?"

Posh stood and shook her head. "That's on a need-to-know basis. I suppose I'm at your beck and call, but don't bother if you hear anything go bump in the night."

"I'll keep that in mind."

"We meet Kershaw at Hidden Palm Grove at nine in the morning. I'll be here at eight thirty to escort you over."

# CHAPTER 6

## *HIDDEN PALM GROVE*

GWEN WAS AWAKE at six in the morning. Force of habit. She put on her shorts and a t-shirt but left her running shoes behind, and hit the beach for a quick morning jog.

Running in the sand was difficult compared to running in the snow. Her feet could never seem to find purchase, while in the snow, there was eventually firm ground beneath. She tried running in the darker sand, which was wet from the waves washing up the beach and found the footing much better.

Fifteen minutes later, Gwen recognized the beachside coffee shoppe called Sephora Bean. She stepped up to the waiter, hoping to get a seat and one of the splendid mint lattes.

"Sorry, ma'am," the waiter said. "Unless you're on the guest list, I can't allow you inside."

Gwen recognized the waiter from the night before: a tall pixie with pink skin. "I was here last night with a lady. I'm a guest of Mister Kershaw."

The waiter's skin blanched, and then his eyes went wide. "Oh…Gwenevere Arris. Forgive me. Right this way."

The waiter led her to the patio, where she took a seat at the same table as the night before. Soon, she had a mint latte in her hand and her feet propped up on the wicker ottoman. Gwen found a paper and read the morning news. As she skimmed the pages, she noticed most of the articles in the local paper revolved around real estate, which made sense, considering the resort-like atmosphere. The asking prices were eye-popping though, compared to Kalispell. Of course, at the center of it all was Aloe Realtors and Kershaw. Almost every beachfront property was their listing. It wasn't difficult to see who the king of the hill was in Valeside.

Gwen finished her latte and made the jog back to meet Posh. She showered and dressed in an oxford shirt and dark green business slacks, which was slightly more appropriate than her long robes and hat.

At eight thirty sharp, Posh knocked on her door. She wore a pinstriped powder-blue blazer and pants, her blue hair pulled back into a half ponytail. Her midriff was still visible—Gwen wondered if she owned a normal shirt—and of course, she looked like a walking jewelry store with all the golden trinkets adorning her body.

Posh marched right through the house and to the back patio, where she slid the door open. "Shall we?" Posh said, sounding cheerier than yesterday.

"Thought we were taking the coach?" Gwen asked.

"Why take the coach when we can enjoy the weather? It's a quick stroll, come on." Posh guided Gwen by the shoulder outside and toward the beach, shutting the door behind them.

Gwen walked along the boardwalk, noting how Posh's tone and attitude seemed to be more accepting today. Only yesterday, they'd practically ignored each other at Aloe Realtors. Gwen wondered if Posh was just playing nice, or perhaps she was finally accepting the fact that they might be stuck together, at least for the foreseeable future.

"Have you been to Hidden Palm Grove?" Gwen asked.

They walked beside each other once they made it to the beach.

Posh removed her sandals and held them over her shoulder. "Heavens, no. That place gives me the heebie-jeebies."

"What do you mean?"

Posh gave her a side glance, like she was trying to decide how much to share. "Not that I want to frighten you, but that castle has a strange, almost macabre vibe, in my opinion. I've heard about shifting halls, dimensions that magically change. The caretaker and lawn keeper both claim there are strange things that happen at nightfall. Neither Thomas nor Natalie will go inside the castle after dark."

"Have they talked about these things in detail?"

"I've never asked. Kershaw's probably heard all the tales, though. I don't bother to ask because I really don't care." Posh picked up a smooth rock and skipped it across the rolling waves. "How do you manage it, anyway?"

"Excuse me?" Gwen asked.

"How do you remain so calm? We followed up with your partner, Daniel Harris. He told us that you're the only person he's ever met who felt at home around the paranormal."

Gwen gritted her teeth. She was going to have a long chat with Harris next time she saw him. He should know better than to share her personal information. "I'm surprised you got anything out of him," Gwen said, trying to hide her frustration.

"Don't blame your partner. Kershaw has a way of getting what he wants."

"Apparently," Gwen continued. "Harris is usually tight-lipped." Gwen sighed as she stuck her hands in her back pockets, still trying to decide if she even wanted to talk about the paranormal and how she grew into her ability. She wasn't sure if she trusted this genie just yet. What if she was simply trying to spy on her for Kershaw?

"I can see you don't want to talk about it right now," Posh finally said. "It's fine, I understand. We barely know each other, and it seems to be a sensitive topic anyway."

"It's a long story," Gwen said. "Maybe later, assuming I take the job."

"Fair enough," Posh said.

Soon, they could see the rock outcropping. Even in the morning light, it still looked like some demonic idol, towering over the white sand beaches. In the daylight, Gwen could see more detail now. The three pillars of stone that jutted into the sand were larger than she'd originally thought. It was ominous, like a massive pitchfork thrust into the sand. The pink and green rose nettle surrounded the rock, partially obscuring the lower portion. Posh led them to the base of it and around the back. Gwen was shocked to see a natural spiral staircase carved into the rock.

"A little backdoor I found while venturing around." Posh led the way up the hidden staircase, which wound around and in between the three stone pillars. Eventually, they crested the top of the cliff, which spilled out onto a lush, manicured lawn.

Gwen steadied herself from the sea breeze and took in the view.

The main road leading into the estate was paved with brick and twisted its way around hundreds of tall palm trees. In fact, the entry road was nearly hidden amongst the dense trees. Behind Gwen was a panoramic view of the Green Sea. They stood at least one hundred feet above the beach, with some dense shrubs the only thing between them and a sheer drop off. To her left was the castle. To say it was large would have been an understatement. At first, Gwen had difficulty counting how many levels and turrets there were. It was unlike any castle or manor she'd seen, though. This one had a unique design that defied most norms. It was a mixed style of medieval and Renaissance, with a twist of modern architecture. The stately details of limestone around the windows, doors, and cloisters hinted at a much older building. Yet the doors and windows had a sleek and sophisticated feel. The roofline was steep, clad in a dark green slate, and numerous chimneys poked up through the roof. The keep was framed by the morning light, casting a halo around it.

"Here we are, Hidden Palm Grove," Posh said. "Hope you're ready for this."

Gwen and Posh stepped onto one of the many crushed granite pathways that led to the castle. As they drew closer, Gwen began to notice the keep's state of disrepair, though. A tangle of reed grass and thorny rose nettle had encroached into the flowerbeds, and a few of the palm trees barely clung to the cliff, due to erosion along the back of the property. One detail Gwen had missed was the tallest turret. It extended up high above the rest of the castle and had a cone-shaped roof, reminding her of a lighthouse.

"It was originally built as a lighthouse in case you're wondering," Posh said. "Then the castle continued to expand over the centuries as it changed hands. Now, it's one hundred and fifty thousand square feet of prime real estate."

"Intriguing doesn't begin to explain it," Gwen said, wondering how the hell she was going to sell a property of this size. She couldn't get her head around it, unlike all the other three-room cottages she was accustomed to in Kalispell. But Gwen could easily see how this location would be the key factor. If ever a piece of real estate was carved into a prime location like Valeside Beach, then it was Hidden Palm Grove. This castle would likely go in a bidding war once it hit the market.

"Notice the lighthouse," Posh said with a nod at the tall turret. "It's been said to light up sometimes, like it's searching for something…or someone. The beacon has been without steam power for over fifty years."

Posh led the way over to a cloister along the front of the castle. Walking across the wood planks, Gwen noticed several that needed replacing. They finally stopped at the entry's large double doors, which arched up in an intricate pattern of stone and ironwork. It was a true marvel of past craftsmanship with elaborate scrollwork and trim at the top transom of the doorway. The ironwork pattern crisscrossed the colorful stained glass, reflecting interesting patterns across the porch.

Posh fumbled with a set of keys to unlock the doors. But before she could find the right one, the doors swung open.

Kershaw stood in the foyer, waiting with his hands behind his back. "Right this way, ladies," he said and stepped to the side.

Gwen walked tentatively into the main foyer and let out a gasp.

It felt like she was standing inside a cloud.

The floor was clad in an oversized snowshed marble tile with gold veining. The plaster on the walls and ceiling was pristine and unblemished. It all reflected a soft pink color from the morning sunlight, which poured in through the high, clerestory windows overhead. The ceiling soared above them, perhaps twenty-five feet, and intricate motifs were cast into the panels and painted in shades of white. A massive chandelier hung in the center, its crystals refracting prismatic colors onto the far wall, though it had a few cobwebs clinging to it. Beyond was a wide circular staircase that spiraled up to an expansive balcony. The staircase's balustrade was wrought from iron that ended in a white marble newel post.

"Well?" Kershaw said.

"It's breathtaking," Gwen said, stunned. "I mean…wow."

"Isn't it?" Kershaw whispered and closed his eyes like he was trying to breathe in the scent of the space. "One hundred and fifty thousand square feet of opportunity…for the right person. And it'll be your job to make that person's dreams come true, Gwenevere."

That thought brought Gwen back to reality. She turned to face Kershaw. "Okay, you have my attention. I'm listening."

Kershaw clapped his hands together. "Before we discuss the specifics, let me give you the full tour. I don't want to leave anything uncovered. After all, I'm a realtor, indulge me, won't you?"

Kershaw walked off, followed by Posh. Gwen stepped in behind them, still taking in all the details of the castle.

"We'll start in the back and move our way forward," Kershaw said.

Before long, the three of them were standing in the back of the castle, which was the kitchen and pantry area. It was easily the largest kitchen Gwen had ever seen. It was, in fact, larger than most of the cottages she'd sold in Kalispell. There were four islands, all the size of a large dining table, and several doors along one side, which she assumed were for dry storage and freezers. On the opposite side was a wall of windows with an unobstructed view to the Green Sea. But Gwen knew this kitchen was meant to serve large events and weddings. Though it was impressive, she felt overwhelmed in the vastness—it didn't have the charm of a more intimate kitchen like Java House. It might turn some potential buyers away. Then again, anyone with the amount of steam tokens to purchase this castle would likely have the same size ego.

"I can sense what you're thinking, Gwen," Kershaw said. "This kitchen might not work for every buyer, which is why there are two kitchens." Kershaw led them through a doorway and into another, more manageable kitchen.

It was about a third the size of the larger kitchen, and Gwen breathed a sigh of relief. "This is more like it," she said.

Along one side was a cute little breakfast nook, where she could see herself having coffee and reading a book as she stared out at the crashing waves.

"Come along. We still have a lot to see," he said. "Over there is the butler's pantry."

Gwen walked in to see storage and prep tables. The closets were stocked with canned goods, bread and utensils, which Gwen assumed had been left behind. Everything looked pristine and undisturbed, if not a bit dusty. Even the appliances had been abandoned, it seemed. "This will all need to be cleaned and staged before it hits the market."

"Yes, of course," Kershaw said.

Gwen pointed at the countertop and a set of emerald bejeweled knives still sitting there. "Looks like the owner left everything in a hurry. That's an expensive set of knives."

Kershaw smiled, then turned without saying anything and led them through the next doorway.

If the main foyer was impressive, then the living room was beyond comparison.

The orientation of the chamber faced outward toward the ocean with a view framed by the veranda porch, providing a postcard moment. Above, the ceiling seemed to disappear in a way that made her feel like she was standing outside. A long line of windows hovered high on the wall, highlighting the morning clouds like pink cotton balls. White leather lounge seating was sprinkled strategically around the sunken space, while colorful rugs hopscotched just under each grouping of furniture. A large modern-looking fireplace adorned the west wall, clad in glass and snowshed marble. High-end track lighting accented expensive art hanging on the tall walls. Though the subject matter wasn't one Gwen found tasteful, she could see that it was original artwork and probably very expensive.

"Rodrick Tanzier," Kershaw said, catching Gwen's gaze. "He's one of the up-and-coming local artists in Valeside."

"What's the subject matter?" Gwen asked. "There's such a jumble of shapes and geometries that I can't seem to focus on anything." But even as Gwen looked on, the shapes continued to morph in a way that kept her mesmerized, as if she were in a magical trance.

"That's a really good question," Kershaw said. "The castle's owner has an affinity for paintings, and apparently this artist spoke to her. As I've heard it explained, they are based on *The Friar's Inferno*, and the Three Rings of Hell, at least that's the word on the street. This art was commissioned by the owner specifically for Hidden Palm Grove."

Of course, Gwen had heard of the ancient tale called The Friar's Inferno, though she knew very little about the specifics. Regardless, the paintings gave her an unsettled feeling.

Kershaw led them out of the living area, down several wide corridors and into the upper portions of the castle. Near the back and facing the ocean, they finally came to the master suite. Kershaw flung the doors open, as if to say, *ta-da!* Gwen was immediately taken by the panoramic view. Of course, she knew the selling point for the property wasn't just the location to the beach and the surrounding town. It was also the view, and the original designer had laid it out in a way to maximize every angle from inside the castle.

She stepped into the suite and then walked onto the elevated private balcony. She felt her heart leap to her throat as the full view sank in. She could smell the salt water. She could feel the soft morning breeze ruffling her hair like it was trying to seduce her. A few beach joggers passed by below like tiny polka dots on a white canvas. The imprints of their feet were barely visible until the ocean erased them seconds later, like nature's broom, sweeping away any presence of human life. Gwen wanted to stand there forever and soak it all in. Just listening to the gulls and the crashing waves gave her a heady rush of yearning. She wanted to retire to this place, become one with this castle… *let it take over me.* She wanted to give in to that desire in a way she'd never known before. Kalispell had its own charm. But Hidden Palm Grove was special…

…and dangerous.

Gwen tried to hide her wide grin from Kershaw and Posh as she basked in the moment.

Kershaw and Posh stood silently and waited for her as she leaned against the stone railing and didn't say anything.

"I can see that you're taken with it," Kershaw finally crooned, breaking the silence. "I felt the same way. There's something special about this place."

"Yes, I'd say so," Gwen said. "Which makes me wonder why the owner is so anxious to sell it."

"Gwenevere. We don't ask those sorts of questions. Our job is to sell property, not to understand the rationale of our clients. Their business is their own. You've been a realtor long enough to know that much."

"Still, it makes you wonder, doesn't it?"

Kershaw gave her a quick smile. "Perhaps. But I see it as another potential sale for my client."

Gwen took a deep breath, as if getting one last inhale of the salt-laden air, then turned. "Okay, Kershaw. I'm in."

# CHAPTER 7

## *LOOSE ENDS*

KERSHAW AGREED TO give Gwen a few days to travel back to Kalispell and wrap things up. Gwen had made up her mind. She no longer wanted to be in Kalispell, not that she disliked the town. After all, she'd grown up there, met her friend Kriss there, and had run a successful business there. But something called to her from Valeside. Like a mystical siren's song, it seemed to be reeling her in. Though she couldn't put it into words, she only knew that this was the right time to relocate. Now, she had to break the news to Harris, and he probably wouldn't be happy about it.

Of course, Aloe Realtors would cover the cost of moving her belongings to Valeside Beach, which in truth wasn't much: a few personal items, knick-knacks, and pictures. Her cat, Jewel, she could give to Harris, who in fact had a soft spot for the tabby. All of her furniture she planned to donate to the local homeless shelter, since the furniture at Java House came with the property.

Kershaw had also presented Gwen with a contract and a nondisclosure agreement, as well as a signing bonus. She signed the contract and the NDA. The work contract gave her the resources she would need to sell Hidden Palm Grove. She had an office at Aloe Realtors but knew she wouldn't use it. With Java House, the study was supplied with everything she'd need to work remotely. The contract also stipulated that Posh was to work alongside her. Gwen wasn't thrilled about that part. Even when she'd had Harris as her partner, Gwen mostly preferred to work alone. But Kershaw seemed to be sticking to his guns on this—*Posh will be by your side, like it or not.* Still, Gwen thought it strange that he was so insistent on this. Surely, he knew she was capable without any help.

The signing bonus went directly into her new bank account and would cover any costs incurred to relocate. Though it wasn't nearly enough to pay Bam Jino's debt, she set up an account in the Kalispell bank and would send tokens each week by raven to help Harris.

With her new job came a clothing allowance as well. Kershaw had told her to dress professionally and that Posh could help with it. But Gwen preferred her green robes and wide-brimmed hat. She imagined eventually she'd gravitate back to that dress code, regardless of what Kershaw preferred.

That Tuesday, Gwen arrived back in Kalispell by steam train. She took a coach to the local bank and had a check made out to roughly a fourth of what her hefty signing bonus had been. Despite how much she needed the steam tokens, she addressed the check to Miss Blackwell.

That night, Gwen met Harris at the local pub.

She plopped down at their usual table and waited. Harris was perpetually ten minutes late, and not to disappoint, he strolled in at eleven minutes past the hour.

"Well?" Harris said and sat down. His thinning red hair was a bit windblown from the late autumn wind. His cheeks and the bulb of his nose were a bright red, reflecting the cooler temperatures already dipping past freezing in Kalispell. His right eye was black and swollen shut.

Gwen immediately reached over to touch his face. "What happened?"

Harris shooed her hand away. "Ah, yeah. That'd be Bam Jino's guys. A little reminder. Forget it. Tell me about Valeside."

Gwen sat back, a concerned look on her face. "Before I break the news, I have a bone to pick with you."

"Oh, right. About that lad named Kershaw."

"You know better than giving out my information. I've been trying to tamp down the rumors about me for years."

"Gwen, it's public knowledge. He was bound to find out sooner or later. So what?"

Gwen took a deep breath, then shook her head. "Well, you'll be happy to know that I'll have the tokens, assuming I can sell a haunted castle called Hidden Palm Grove before Saint Halving Day."

Harris leaned forward and gripped her hand. "Thank you. After that, we can get back to business as usual."

Gwen pushed her glass of tea away from her. "Well, about that."

"What do you mean?" Harris blurted.

Gwen shrugged. "I'm thinking about moving to Valeside, maybe stay on with Kershaw."

"What!" Harris barked. He started to stand, then settled back. "You said you'd be back to Kalispell. I need you here as soon as possible."

"Harris, listen. I feel like I need to make this move. I can't explain it; I just need to do it."

The waiter dropped a mug of ale in front of Harris. He promptly picked it up and drained it, then wiped his ruddy mustache with the back of his arm. "You sure about this?"

"Yes, and I want you to sell my bungalow."

Harris's eyes went wide, and he almost stood up again. "Gwen. You sure you don't want to think this over?"

"No. I've made my decision, and selling my cottage gives me some closure. I think it'll also help me focus on getting this castle sold. Assuming I do, you can keep our business."

"What if you don't sell the castle and you have to return? Why not hang onto your bungalow just in case?"

But Gwen shook her head. "I'm not coming back to Kalispell, Harris."

Harris held her gaze, and Gwen could see the shock and sadness in his expression.

"Okay, fine. *Fine!* Sounds like a good opportunity for you anyway. Besides, who am I to argue? You're the one bailin' me out. How can I be upset? I reckon there's plenty of potential realtors that would be happy to step in for you. But I'm gonna have to change the business model without you around."

Harris held up his mug for another round, then pulled the business section of the local newspaper from his breast pocket. "I'm prepared. I kinda knew this was coming. Let's see…there's Isabel, she's a snow fairy, can't trust them…some gnome named Brannel—I can't stand gnomes…um, Erica. Ooh, she's cute. What do you think?"

Gwen could only shake her head. "Maybe you should wait before you hire anyone. I have to close the deal in Valeside first."

"Right." Harris slid the newspaper back into his pocket. "Wow…Valeside Beach. I'll have to break out my swim trunks when I come to visit."

Gwen frowned at the thought of Harris in a bathing suit but then chuckled and shook her head. She'd expect nothing less from him, though.

Harris smiled, then reached across the table and grasped Gwen's hand in his fat-fingered grip. "Listen, Gwen. I know what you mean to this community, even if no one else does. We're gonna miss you."

"Stop it—"

"No, listen. It scares the hell out of me, that part of you. How you can phase into the darkness is beyond me. Just promise you'll be careful, okay? This isn't all fun and games."

"Of course. I'm always cautious."

"Look. Maybe I'm out of line, but you know you can't bring her back. Kriss is gone—"

"I know that, Harris," Gwen said, a bit too harshly. A few nearby patrons looked their way.

Harris finally let go of her hand.

Gwen immediately regretted her tone. She knew her partner of nearly a decade was only concerned about her well-being. "Harris, I appreciate all you've done for me over the years. You're like family. But this ability—as frightening as it may be to you—is who I am. Maybe Valeside is calling to me for that reason?"

"I know you like a challenge, Gwen. I know you're driven to fix homes and families because it's something you didn't have growing up. Hell, it shows by how many people you've helped over the years. Just don't get into a place you can't get out of. Sometimes, you need to be reminded to look after yourself. I can't do that for you in Kalispell."

"Maybe I'll meet someone who can."

"Are you trying to atone for what happened to Kriss?"

"I don't know," Gwen said. "Maybe it's guilt about making a profit from flipping all these homes? Have I used my ability to take advantage of others?"

"No, of course you haven't. Sure, we made some capital, but not enough to retire on. And probably not nearly as much as you should have been paid, considering what you've done for these families."

"And yet, the amount of steam tokens Kershaw is paying me is more than all the realtors combined in Kalispell."

Harris shrugged. "Thank goodness, because we're gonna need it."

The next morning, Gwen finished packing her items and then showered. She made a few calls around town with her crystal globe, letting her close contacts know she was relocating and giving her full support to Harris. She left the door unlocked for the movers, signed all the documents and let Harris handle the sale of her two-room bungalow.

Fifteen minutes later, she was in a private coach and pulling away. She gave her small cottage a last glance, wondering again if she was doing the right thing. A small voice was telling her to get out of the coach and forget the trip to Valeside Beach. But Gwen had never shied away from a challenge. The excitement at what lay ahead could not be quelled.

Gwen had a few last-minute things to wrap up before she left Kalispell. Her first stop was to the Chesterfield Cemetery on the edge of town. When she arrived, Gwen asked the coach to wait nearby.

It was a cloudy day, and there was no hint of the sun. A heavy mist fell across the manicured lawns of the cemetery. A few groundskeepers roamed the fields, scraping away snow.

Gwen walked along the landscaped trails, wondering why she'd decided to stop by. Being back at Chesterfield Cemetery brought a flood of emotions, which was something she probably didn't need just before starting a new job. Perhaps it was the desire to tie up loose ends or, better yet, maybe it was the closure she needed before moving on to the next chapter in her life.

She noticed how everything had grown in the ten years since she had last been there. Gwen recalled the day Kriss had been laid to rest. At that time in her life, Gwen had been trying to decide what college to go to and where her future might lead her. She'd been in a rush to flee her foster home and leave Kalispell.

And then Kriss had been murdered by a genie.

That event had plunged her into a time of confusion and grief. Needless to say, college had been put on pause during that time. Once she had gotten the courage to emerge from that dark period, she went on to university to become an investigator and eventually spent several years in the Ministry of Green Witches. Seeking clues on the battlefield, while witnessing the horrors her race had wrought upon genies had

shaken her beliefs. Moving on from that trauma to becoming a realtor had gone a long way in healing those scars. Now, she felt like she'd come full circle, being back here at Kriss's gravesite.

Gwen continued along the gravel trails, winding between the tall, leafless trees, until she stood in front of the placard that belonged to Kriss Blackwell. It was a simple granite slab with a picture of her friend. She'd been a bubbly, red witch with chestnut eyes and a mischievous grin. Below the etched photo were two dates, the latter was one Gwen would never forget. It had been the worst day of her life.

Gwen sat at the foot of the grave and pulled her knees up to her chest and buried her face. She thought back to that day when she'd gotten word about the accident. She'd spent the morning sitting in her favorite chair, going through her scrapbook. Kriss had lived in an upscale neighborhood, which had never seen such an event. Random shootings were a thing of myth, something that happened across town in the Horsehair District or Arcane Heights—never on the northside. Of course, shock had settled in, and word had spread like wildfire around Kriss's neighborhood of King's Wood.

Gwen had always met Kriss on Saturday morning in the open field beyond King's Wood to practice their archery. When Kriss hadn't shown up on that Saturday, Gwen knew something was wrong.

Kriss had been a terrific archer, well beyond Gwen's skill level. But red witches were natural archers, unlike greens, who excelled in sleuthing and arcane botany. Still, Kriss had worked with Gwen, hoping they could both go to Recurve University together, where she'd been given a full-ride scholarship. Gwen often wondered if she'd met Kriss at her cottage that day instead of the field, would she have avoided the stray bolt that entered her bedroom and taken her life?

Gwen wiped her eyes and stood, looking around and listening to the birds, the stillness…

…the voices from the graves.

Gwen found the ruby-red amulet beneath her robe and clutched it tightly.

Coming to visit her friend's gravesite should have been quiet and peaceful. But the constant voices from around the cemetery were the main reason she'd never returned. She wanted to remember Kriss as she had been in life: kind, energetic, confident. She wanted to remember the love she'd felt for her best friend. She wanted to relive those memories of being invited into Kriss's home to stay the night or have family dinner. Those little reprieves from her own broken home had provided an escape from the yelling and abuse and violence of her foster parents.

But seconds later, Gwen stood and sprinted out of Chesterfield Cemetery, unable to quell the voices from the spirits there.

# CHAPTER 8

## *A FAMILY HEIRLOOM*

GWEN HOPPED INTO the coach and asked the driver to take her to King's Wood via the 'scenic' route. The coach moved slowly, past old neighborhoods and landmarks that Gwen hadn't seen in a decade.

Eventually, the coach turned into Kriss's old neighborhood. To say King's Wood had gone downhill would be polite. The once stately cottages were mostly overgrown with weeds, and the residents hadn't bothered to paint the flaking facades or fix the dilapidated fences. Many of the cottages had broken-out windows or the thatched roofs had fallen in.

When the coach pulled up to Kriss's old residence, Gwen sat there for several minutes, trying to decide if she was doing the right thing. The Blackwells' cottage was in remarkably good condition, compared to the others. The lawn was cut, the paint was fresh, and the roof's thatching looked fairly new. She finally pulled herself from the seat and marched up to the front porch. After a brief pause, Gwen knocked on the door.

The heavy wooden door cracked slightly, then it opened all the way. A witch with dark red skin and gray-flecked auburn hair stared at Gwen, a confused look on her face.

"Miss Blackwell?" Gwen said. "It's me, Gwenevere Arris, Kriss's old friend."

Recognition finally lit across the lady's face, and she stepped out and gave Gwen a hug. "Gwen? Oh, thank goodness. It's so good to see you! Come in, please."

Miss Blackwell ushered Gwen inside and quickly shut the door, latching multiple locks. "Come. Have a seat," she said and guided Gwen to an old terrycloth sofa.

Gwen settled in apprehensively. Everything was the same as it had been a decade ago. Even the aroma was familiar: a scent of orchids and oranges. The pictures on the wall hadn't moved, and the flooring was the same. Gwen had a sense that Miss Blackwell was still trying to live in the past, maybe afraid to let go.

Miss Blackwell clasped her hands between her knees and seemed to study Gwen. She gave her a brief, almost sad smile. "It's alright, Gwenevere. I can talk about it now."

But Gwen questioned that. Based on what she was seeing, Miss Blackwell didn't look like she was okay. Then again, it wasn't really Gwen's place to ask such a question. "I…just happen to be on this side of town and…I'm actually starting a new job, and, well, I guess I wanted to come see you—" Gwen paused, feeling like her tongue was tied in knots.

"It's okay, Gwenevere," Miss Blackwell said again. "I've accepted what happened to my daughter."

But Gwen was still frozen, uncertain how to begin. She needed to do this. She had to confess what she had done, and she wasn't leaving until she did.

Miss Blackwell finally stood and pulled out an old scrapbook. She leafed through several articles about Kriss. Gwen saw them all: Kriss winning state in archery, her acceptance letter to Recurve University, and about a dozen other contests she had won. Miss Blackwell finally stopped on an article and held it out to Gwen. "You might say I've been keeping up on your career."

Gwen took the article and read it. In the photo, she was accepting her diploma. In the next article, she was enlisting with the Ministry of Green Witches. The next article showed her and Harris standing in front of their office with Arris & Harris Realtors etched onto the window.

"I guess you know about the support groups too?"

"Yes." Miss Blackwell held up a hand, as if to say, *so what?*

"I'm not the same person I was ten years ago. Does it bother you that I was a part of those groups?"

"Why should it? What happened was traumatic for everyone who knew my daughter. We all cope in our own way." Miss Blackwell nodded to the furniture, pictures, and flooring around the living room. "I suppose I'm still reluctant to let go of the past. Maybe that's the reason I latched onto your career."

Gwen felt her eyes begin to sting and wiped a hand across her cheek. "Miss Blackwell. I need to confess something to you. I've been afraid to do it, maybe that's why I never visited you. And now that I'm leaving, I don't know if I'll ever come back to Kalispell."

"Whatever it is, it'll be okay. You don't have to tell me. I forgive you and so would Kriss—"

"I need this, please," Gwen interrupted her. She waited for Miss Blackwell to give her permission, though.

Miss Blackwell held Gwen's gaze. She could see that the lady didn't want to hear it. Perhaps it would bring back painful memories, and Gwen could see the resistance on her face. But Miss Blackwell finally nodded.

Gwen slowly pulled out Kriss's amulet.

Miss Blackwell's hand went to her mouth, and she began to cry.

Gwen wanted to hug the elderly lady. But she sat quietly and waited for Miss Blackwell to yell or scream or curse at her.

But the screaming never came.

"That amulet is one I gave her just a week before her death," Miss Blackwell said. "It's a family heirloom, passed down from red witches in our lineage for a millennia."

"I am so sorry," Gwen said.

"So, the day you came over after my daughter's funeral. I said you could keep one of her archery medals. You took the amulet instead."

"At first, I wasn't sure. When I picked it up…I heard her voice. It spoke to me and…I ran. I'm sorry I stole it." Gwen took the amulet off and held it out to Miss Blackwell. "I needed to tell you the truth, and I am here to return this."

Miss Blackwell looked at the amulet, the ruby a perfect match against her skin. "This is a powerful relic. My mother gave it to me, and my grandmother to her." The lady stared at the amulet as Gwen held it out. But she didn't touch it. "I have no daughter…other than you, Gwenevere."

"Me?" Gwen said.

"I can gift it to you. And, if you are hearing Kriss's voice through it, then it was meant for you." Miss Blackwell reached out with both hands and clasped them around Gwen's outstretched hand. She gently forced the amulet back. "I forgive you, Gwenevere Arris. You have my blessing. I never want to see this amulet again."

Gwen bowed her head and broke down. She felt Miss Blackwell wrap her arms around her and hold her.

They sat on the floor for a long while and cried together.

When Gwen felt ready, she pulled back. "Why don't you come with me? I have enough room to put you up at my place in Valeside. It's much warmer than Kalispell. My partner, Harris, could sell your place; you wouldn't have to worry about anything."

But Miss Blackwell shook her head. "No. This is where I belong."

"I just worry about you. The area's declined."

"Don't you worry. I still know quite a few enchantments." Miss Blackwell tapped her satchel and her wand.

That made Gwen smile. It's exactly how Kriss would have reacted.

"Promise me one thing." Gwen pulled out an envelope. Inside was the check made out to Miss Blackwell. "Open this after I leave town, but not until then."

Miss Blackwell took the envelope. "I can do that, as long as you promise to keep Kriss's spirit alive with the amulet."

Gwen could only nod and smile as she hugged the elderly lady one last time.

# CHAPTER 9

## *DOWN TO BUSINESS*

THE TRAIN TERMINAL wasn't busy when Gwen arrived—tourist season in Kalispell didn't hit until early December. Amidst the sounds of steam and horns, she boarded her train, which had another brief layover in Roiling Springs again. She was back in Valeside Beach the following afternoon.

When she arrived, Posh was there, waiting. She wore some loose-fitting pants and a tight tank top in powder blue, of course.

"I hope everything went splendidly for you in Kalispell?"

Gwen caught the slight hint of cynicism. "Yes. Just needed to wrap a few things up—you know, sell my house and pretty much my old life." Posh either didn't catch the return sarcasm or didn't care.

"You're my primary client now. I've been directed to assist you in all matters. That does *not* mean that I serve you." Posh gave Gwen a long look, her arms crossed and her golden eyes glinting a bit brighter.

"Well, I'd never," Gwen said, still holding on to her sarcasm. Posh didn't smile.

"Good. Let's make our way back to Java House."

The coach dropped them at the curb, which was a short walk along a brick-paved path. Posh paused in front of the beach cottage's front door. "The code has been preprogrammed for you," Posh said and handed Gwen a sleek-looking key. She slid the other one into the pad. "You'll need the key and the code to enter. It's 3-6-9, by the way." She punched in the code, and the glass door swung open.

Posh led the way inside, where Gwen could see groceries sitting on the large island. "The pantry's been stocked, the refrigerator as well. Oh, before I forget…" Posh rifled through her satchel and pulled out a roll of drawings. "The blueprints for Hidden Palm Grove, as Kershaw promised. By the way, it's the entire set: site plan, floor plans, sections, elevations, even down to the door hardware, in case you're interested."

"Great," Gwen said with a yawn. "So, I guess I'll just call you in the morning and we'll get started?"

Posh nodded but lingered at the front entry door. "Mind if I ask how you plan to approach this? I mean, I've never seen a case this extreme. Where do you even start, ghosts and all?"

"Same as I normally do. I'll want to interview a few people, might spend some time at the local library. We need to do some historical research on the area. Maybe even talk to the builder and the architect as well. You never know where you'll find clues."

"So, once you unravel the issues, you cleanse it, and the ghosts just go away? House fixed, problem solved?"

"Something like that. Many homes have residual leftover, or an *energy*, which can be negative or positive. The spirits, or ghosts, hang around because they have unfinished business and won't vacate until that's done. I have to figure out why, then help them resolve it."

"Why the architect and the contractor? Seems like they'd be very little help."

Gwen shrugged. "Like I said, you never know where you might find clues." She took the architectural set of drawings and unrolled them on the large kitchen island.

Posh, suddenly interested, turned on the lights and stood next to Gwen.

"It's here, in the title block," Gwen said. "NoirMASS architecture studio. The wet seal says Arman Bernhardt."

"He's a very well-known local architect," Posh commented. "Does a lot of high-end residential work."

"Can you see about an appointment with him?"

"I'll see what I can do."

"And what about the builder…" Gwen muttered, then found the information at the top of the title block. "Harcourt & Laymon Construction. Any contacts there?"

"Honey, we have contacts everywhere," Posh said. "I'll make it happen."

"Great," Gwen said and stretched. She was ready for a power nap after being on the train all day. But Posh continued to linger. "Something else to add?"

"I need to confess something." Posh seemed hesitant, which Gwen was quickly learning wasn't typical. "Kershaw caught me off guard when he placed me on this assignment. He knew there'd be a conflict of interest between us, for obvious reasons. But he also knows what he's doing. He must think it's a good idea that we work together."

"Kind of surprised me too," Gwen said. "He was very insistent. You know him better than me, though."

"I…really need to keep him happy. I just thought you and I could extend an olive branch to each other—a truce, at least until this case is over and the castle sold."

"Agreed, assuming I can make that happen."

"And…I will do what I can to help." Posh hesitated again, then reluctantly stuck out her hand.

Gwen considered for only a few seconds. She realized that she was going to need all the help she could get, and if that meant teaming up with a genie, then so be it. She stepped over and shook Posh's hand. "Just until this is over, right?"

"Yes. The quicker the better," Posh said. "Besides, it goes without saying that I'm not the best around paranormal environments."

"Well, you'd better buckle up. Something tells me this is going to be one hell of a ride."

As tired as Gwen was, she got very little sleep that night. After Posh left, Gwen couldn't help but scour the old architectural drawings. Though she wasn't an architect, she found the documents fascinating. Over the course of her career, she'd reviewed quite a few blueprints. It was sometimes required that realtors understand them in order to relay information to their clients.

Although Hidden Palm Grove's remodel was dated just a few years back, the new drawings were superimposed over the original sketches, which were at least a few centuries old. Not much had changed from the original shape and footprint of the castle. The majority of the remodel consisted of finish upgrades, new technology, window replacements and new doors. By and large, the main walls had been left undisturbed with only a new coat of paint.

However, the shape of the castle was unlike anything Gwen had seen before. In fact, she hadn't noticed its true geometry during her visit. But looking at it in plan revealed several things.

The castle was essentially a three-sided triangle with three angled faces in between, which looked like a trident, or perhaps a pitchfork was a better description. Two of those sides faced the Green Sea, with the third side facing the entry drive. It was an aggressive, bold design. There were three massive chambers surrounding the central staircase on the ground floor: the living area, the kitchen quarters, and the dining area. When Gwen stepped back to get a better look, the floor plan resembled a human skull.

Posh let herself in at six a.m. and made a racket in the kitchen, brewing herself a latte. Gwen groaned and rolled out of bed and into the shower. She dressed in her green robes (she refused to wear the tight-fitting blazer and slacks Kershaw had asked her to) and walked into the kitchen with a yawn.

Posh had prepared breakfast: hashbrowns, scrambled eggs, and toast.

"I'm starving," Gwen said and sat down behind the island.

"Don't get used to this," Posh said, pouring Gwen some coffee. "Cooking breakfast isn't in my job description."

Gwen gave her a thumbs up as she dished up a plate.

Posh leaned forward, her hands splayed on the island. "Gwen. Don't take this the wrong way, but you need a serious wardrobe upgrade. When we're done today, I'm taking you shopping—"

Gwen held up her hand as she forked some hash browns into her mouth. "I'm not interested, Posh," she mouthed.

"You're not in Kalispell. We have an image to uphold."

"Do we have to?"

"Yes. It's on Aloe Realtor's account anyway. Besides, it'll be fun."

Gwen gave Posh a defeated look. "Fine. And what about chatting with the architect and builder? Any luck with that?"

"Fortunately, yes. Kershaw's name has some heft. We're on for 10:30 this morning at the architect's office."

The coach picked them up about an hour later. Posh gave the address to NoirMASS architecture studio, which sat in the heart of downtown Valeside. The high-rise building was sleek and modern, as Gwen would expect. The architect's office occupied the top floor.

They were greeted by a spectacular view of downtown Valeside when they stepped off the steam elevator. The greenish haze of the ocean seemed to saturate the horizon and reflect off the other tall skyscrapers. The office's interior design was sleek and minimal: matte finished anodized aluminum trim with a large format tile adorning the walls and floor. A soft blue light rimmed the ceiling and washed the walls in a soothing way. Around the lobby were some colorful clay pots with tropical plants to soften the space.

The receptionist checked Gwen and Posh in, where they sat in the lobby and waited.

Soon, a man stepped through the door. His skin was tan, and he was dressed in a button-down oxford shirt, patterned in a blue herringbone design with the sleeves rolled up like he'd already put in a full day's work. His pinstriped slacks matched his shirt, and his stature was lean, athletic and striking. His hair had hints of gray to match the light scruff peppering his jawline, and a pair of wire-rimmed glasses sat atop his head.

"Miss Gwenevere Arris. Patricia Oshner, correct?" the man said and stopped in front of them.

"Just Gwen and Posh will do, thanks," Gwen said.

"Very well. I'm Arman Bernhardt. I hear that you've come into possession of one of my projects."

"Well, we've been commissioned to sell one of them at least," Posh said.

"May I ask which one?"

Gwen gave Posh a quick glance, and she nodded her approval.

"Hidden Palm Grove," Gwen said. "We're hoping you might answer a few questions about the castle."

Arman rubbed the stubble on his chin, a bit anxiously, Gwen thought. "Why don't you come inside?" he said and held the door for them.

Arman led them through the office. It was mainly open cubicles with gnomes working behind drafting desks, and a few popped their heads up to see who was visiting. Arman stopped at a conference room and ushered them inside.

"This is our seaside conference room. There's a bit more privacy here. Let me grab the drawings. I'll be right back."

Gwen and Posh sat at the long conference table, which felt cold and uninviting with its thin, knife-like edges. The view through the floor-to-ceiling windows gave a commanding view to the beach, though Gwen wasn't interested in the view. There was more on her mind, and she studied Posh over the soft elevator music in the background.

Posh noticed and cleared her throat. "You caught his hesitation, didn't you?" she asked.

"Yeah, as soon as I mentioned Hidden Palm Grove. There's a story here, if we can get it out of him—"

Arman returned with a roll of drawings and quickly shut the door. He lowered the shades and turned up the light level. Then he rolled out the floor plans on the table. "I worked on the remodel for Hidden Palm Grove several years back. I've been trying to forget about that project ever since."

Gwen glanced at Posh. "What do you mean by that?"

Arman held her gaze, then shook his head. "It's nothing, don't mind me. So, Kershaw has accepted the owner's request to sell it. I'm curious if the owner was unhappy with my design."

"No, it's nothing like that, Arman." Gwen paused to gather her thoughts. "Kershaw has requested that I keep the real reason about the castle quiet. I hope you can appreciate that. Architects have the same confidentiality with their clients, correct?"

"Yes, primarily during the design phase."

"And now that your work is complete, can you discuss the castle?"

"That depends on what you need to know," Arman said.

"There must be a story behind its unique design."

"If you're referring to the original designer's inspiration, then yes. That, I can share." Arman brought his hand to his lower lip as if considering where to begin. "The castle was originally designed as a lighthouse to protect ships from the nearby rocks. That was several centuries ago. Eventually, the owner hired a well-known architect named Louis Holcomb. No doubt, you noticed the three prominent stone pillars that make up the foundations. Those massive pilasters penetrate the rock outcropping it sits on. That inspired Louis, and his design replicated the three pillars. Since then, it's been referred to as The Devil's Paddock. He loved to work in multiples of three, which underpinned his religious beliefs and inspiration from divinity. I find his work to be genius, to be honest. When my firm was approached to do the remodel, I jumped at the opportunity."

"You say your work was simply a remodel. Anything you noticed during construction?" Gwen asked.

Arman thought, then shook his head. "We stayed mostly on the surface, only a few walls came down. The entire castle is on the historic register, so we had to follow certain rules. The owner decided to go with a modern look, so we updated the finishes mostly. The directive was to 'make the interior float.' I believe I accomplished that."

"It's an odd shape, wouldn't you say?" Posh says.

"The three main chambers on the ground floor are equilateral triangles. Almost every dimension in the home is in multiples of three, at least when I did my survey, everything kept coming back to that. The strangest thing was when I went back, the dimensions were slightly different. It was like the walls kept moving. I thought I was going crazy. To this day, I still don't know if the plans are accurate."

"That is interesting," Gwen said. "Some say the floor plan resembles a skull," Gwen said.

Arman nodded. "You noticed that too. I have designed homes on a module before, the golden section, for example, but never to this extent. It's uncanny, accurate and unnervingly precise."

Gwen leaned against the conference table. "I assume you worked closely with the general contractor on this?"

"Very much so. It was a design-build approach to help keep the budget in line, though I don't think that was ever a concern with this project. Force of habit for me, at least."

"What do you mean?" Gwen asked.

"Money was never an object—I got the sense that was only a pretense. The owner just preferred to work with a particular contractor, whose fee was exorbitant. Harcourt & Laymon isn't the largest outfit, and certainly not one I would have recommended for something like this. They're a small boutique contractor, and they've never worked on a private residence of this size. But the owner insisted, for some reason."

"Do you still have the name of the job foreman?"

"Yes, I have his name, not sure if the company is still around, though."

Arman found a business card. When he handed it to her, he also slipped his own business card to her in a way that Posh didn't notice.

"Thank you," Gwen said, not calling attention to it. "I don't mean to take much of your time. We'll let you get back to work."

"It's no problem," Arman said, then he reached out and touched Gwen on the arm. "I understand you've signed an NDA, but are you certain you can't share the real reason you're here?"

"I'm afraid not," Gwen said, though she felt a bit guilty after everything Arman had shared.

"A word of advice," Arman said and lowered his voice. "If you're looking for answers, be cautious. The castle has a mind of its own. Do not get lost inside."

# CHAPTER 10
## *A HIGH-RISE MEETING*

GWEN AND POSH left the architect's office wondering if they'd actually gained any information. To Gwen, it felt like they had taken two steps backward. They decided to grab a bite at the diner across the street and gather their thoughts.

"What are you thinking?" Posh asked, forking some salad into her mouth.

"That mister 'starchitect' wasn't telling us everything," Gwen said.

"Yeah, I caught that too. Maybe he's still bound by the agreement he mentioned?"

"Some of it, sure. But there's more. Still, he coughed up quite a bit of information. Wonder what he meant by don't get lost inside?"

Posh raised her eyebrows. "I have no clue, but at least he gave us the contractor's name."

"And I'd like to pay him a visit as soon as possible."

Posh was already asking the waitress for an information directory, and she returned shortly with one. "Says Harcourt & Layton went out of business several years ago."

"Is that right?" Gwen slouched back and took a bite of her salad. "What about the foreman? Benjamin Holden?"

Posh thumbed through the pages. "Looks like he holds a position at Vorpal Construction. This is a much bigger construction company."

"Let's see if we can track him down," Gwen said.

They finished lunch and made a visit to the company's main office. Benjamin Holden was a field superintendent on one of the high-rise condos along Valeside Beach. Fifteen minutes later, Gwen and Posh were at the construction site, walking toward the job shack. It was a double-wide trailer with half a dozen subcontractors inside. They stood over a set of plans, arguing about a wall section detail. They turned when Gwen and Posh walked in.

"Can I help you?" a large ogre asked. It was a smattering of warlocks, ogres and gnomes. Like the others, he wore a hard hat, safety vest, jeans that hung low at the waist and heavy boots.

"We're looking for Benjamin Holden," Gwen said. "I hear he's the superintendent on this project."

The broad ogre looked Gwen over, then Posh. His gaze lingered on Posh, and Gwen could almost read his thoughts. "And who are you specifically? Are you two with the planning department or something?"

Gwen glanced sidelong at Posh, then gave the bearded ogre a nod. "We're field inspectors."

"Oh, right." The ogre snapped to attention. "Benjamin's on the twenty-third floor. You'll need to put on your PPE before you head up there."

"PPE?" Posh asked.

He gave them a funny look, then chuckled. "Yeah, good one. Personal protective equipment…who needs it, right?"

"Sorry," Gwen said. "My partner's new to this. We left ours at the office. Mind if we borrow some?"

The ogre raised a brow, then stepped into an office and returned with two hard hats, safety glasses and bright yellow vests. "No boots either?"

Gwen raised her hands in an apologetic manner. "We had a business meeting just before. Sorry."

He dug through the closet, then dropped a few pairs on the floor in front of them, causing dried mud to crumble off the boots' soles. "These might be a bit large, but they'll do."

Gwen and Posh took the lift to the twenty-third floor. The tall high-rise was mostly a concrete skeleton of columns, beams and slabs, with the formwork still in place on several floors. The top floor was wide open and made Gwen feel a bit uneasy. She gripped Posh by the arm while Posh did the same to her. Workers hurried by, seemingly unfazed by the height. Only a thin cable railing separated them from a freefall of a few hundred feet. Beyond was the expansive Green Sea with puffs of steam floating by like clouds.

Standing a bit too close to the edge was a thin man with a dark beard. He wore a black hard hat and brown overalls, which had his initials on them. He was busy yelling at a worker over improper dress code. After he dismissed the man, he turned and gave Gwen and Posh a stern look.

"Well? What do you want?" Then he paused and reset. "Oh…you two are with the planning department? Hey, look. I told that worker to keep his hard hat on. That's not my fault, okay? If you want to file a complaint, it's already been taken care of—"

Gwen held up a hand. "It's Benjamin, right?"

He paused again and looked at them closely. "Do we know each other?"

"No, not exactly. I just have a few questions that I'm hoping you can answer."

"What's this about?"

"My name is Gwenevere, this is Patricia. We work for Lorenzo Kershaw of Aloe Realtors."

The thin man furrowed his brow, as if thinking gave him a migraine. Then his eyes grew wide and his skin blanched pale in the warm Valeside sun. "You two are here about that castle, is that it? I washed my hands of that place years ago. I want nothing to do with it, okay?"

"You're not in any trouble, and there's nothing wrong," Gwen said.

Benjamin seemed to calm down a bit. "Oh…well, what is it?"

"We've been commissioned to sell the property—"

Benjamin started laughing. "Good luck with that."

Gwen gave Posh a quick look and shrugged.

"You don't know, do you?" he said. "Kershaw didn't tell you?"

Gwen waited for him to continue, her arms crossed. She knew then that Kershaw hadn't been as forthcoming about Hidden Palm Grove. Then again, she'd known that all along.

"Yeah, didn't think he would've said anything," Ben continued. "We lost three workers on that project."

"What?" Posh blurted.

"Three. All in bizarre accidents. The first was a simple cut, blood poisoning. Nothing that would raise suspicions. But then, a few weeks later, a second worker fell from the cliff and broke his neck. Again, no foul play, just an accident. In the twenty-six years I've been doing this, not once have I lost a worker. Suddenly, they're dropping like flies at this property."

Gwen rotated her head slightly to look at Posh. She stared back at Gwen, eyes wide.

"No," Posh said. "Kershaw never mentioned that."

"Right," Benjamin said. "It's all hush-hush, just like the owner wants it. And thanks to the NDA I signed, I'm not supposed to talk about it either. Still, word got out about it, though it was squashed as an urban legend."

"What about the third worker?" Gwen asked.

"That was the icing on the cake. On the final day, just before handing the keys over, a worker slit his own throat near the interior staircase. Course, we had to clean up the mess. After that, it was almost impossible to hire workers. Our small company quickly went out of business. It was like Harcourt & Laymon had been cursed."

"That's horrible," Posh said and looked away.

Benjamin kicked at the concrete slab, then looked out over the horizon. Gwen wondered if he was trying to find the castle along the coastline.

"You two really sure you want to sell Hidden Palm Grove? Personally, if I were you, I'd never step foot on that property again."

It was getting late in the evening when they left the construction site. Gwen could tell that Posh had had enough for one day, and frankly, so had she. Gwen flopped onto the couch when they arrived back at Java House.

"So, about tomorrow?" Posh asked. She leaned against the kitchen island, stretching one of her legs from a cramp.

"Let me think about our next step."

"Look. If I'm going to help, you need to keep me in the loop."

"What are you saying?" Gwen asked.

"I'll be here at the same time every morning, unless I say otherwise."

"Are you helping me, or are you in charge now?"

"Kershaw's in charge, whether we like it or not. He'll expect constant updates from me."

Gwen waved it away and wrapped her arms around a pillow. "Fine. One thing before you go. Are you certain you knew nothing about the accidents at Hidden Palm Grove?"

Posh pursed her lips to one side and avoided Gwen's gaze. At first, Gwen didn't think she would answer the question. "I do what Kershaw asks, how's that?"

"So, he made you keep that part quiet?"

Posh shrugged.

"Look. I know you're just doing your job. And I understand why Kershaw didn't want me to know, because it may have changed my mind about taking this job. But if you're going to be part of the team, I need you to be honest with me. I can keep a secret. Kershaw doesn't have to know what goes on between us."

Posh didn't flinch when she spoke. "Gwen. Kershaw knows everything."

After the horse-drawn coach had whisked Posh away, Gwen brewed a cup of tea and tried to relax on the deck. She couldn't stop thinking about Kershaw and Posh and felt a bit perturbed. Withholding information was sometimes required as a realtor, she knew that. But this felt different. Though she didn't blame Posh, who had been pressured by Kershaw, she wondered if Posh would ever go against Kershaw's orders. Would she be able to trust the genie without worrying that she was sharing everything with Kershaw? Gwen hoped soon that she and Posh might be able to. It was obvious that Posh was starting to soften toward her. And, in fact, Gwen was starting to change her tune toward Posh as well. But until there was a little more trust between them, Gwen would have to play it carefully. There were things she wasn't ready to reveal to Kershaw, like what was really happening at Hidden Palm Grove. She was beginning to think it was more than just a haunted castle.

Gwen kicked back on the deck sofa and watched some evening beachgoers stroll by. She listened to the crooning waves and thought about the three unexplained deaths Benjamin Holden had mentioned. Though she didn't know much about construction-related injuries, she felt Benjamin had been telling the truth. What if she was dealing with a negative energy in the castle?

Hoping to brighten her spirits, Gwen decided to make a call to Harris. He had a way of calming her, and she needed some cheering up. She grabbed her crystal globe and set it on the patio table. A few seconds later, Harris answered. Gwen could see immediately that her old partner had received another beating, no doubt at the hands of Bam Jino's mob.

"Harris!" she blurted.

"Hi, Gwen," he answered, then rubbed at his forehead. "Oh, the bruises. Yeah, I took a tumble."

Gwen glared at him. "Tell me what happened."

"What do you want me to say?" Harris blurted. "Look, you can't worry about me. You don't need these distractions. Bam's not going to do any permanent damage, he's just tryin' to mess with you. So don't concern yourself, alright?"

"But…Harris—"

He held up a hand and stopped her. "Gwen, please. Stop calling me. It's what he wants. You're making weekly payments, that's enough. I'll be fine, okay?" Harris gave her a brief smile, then hung up.

Unable to calm her racing thoughts, Gwen decided to go for an evening beach stroll. Seeing Harris roughed up had unsettled her more than she cared to admit, not to mention his short attitude with her. But Gwen knew Harris was simply trying to make her job easier by pushing her away.

She grabbed her sandals and a light sweater and crossed the boardwalk, gliding a meter above the sand and beach grass. She stepped onto the warm sand, letting it seep through her toes. Her tension eased, and her heart rate slowed. The salty air seemed to push through her and tug her hair like a sail. The moon waxed over the Green Sea with white hints on the cresting waves, and the palm trees rustled in the breeze.

Gwen walked aimlessly along the beach as couples passed by. With her mind at ease, she lost track of where she was until she noticed the business card that was still in her pocket.

She stopped walking, her sandals dangling in her other hand.

Why had Arman even bothered to give his business card?

He must have known she already had his information from the set of blueprints.

She pulled his card out and looked at it in the moonlight.
On the back, he had written a warning. *Beware of the lower levels.*

# CHAPTER 11

## *THE BONDS OF NEW HOPE*

THE NEXT MORNING, Posh was at Gwen's front door, as promised, and let herself in. She started a pot of coffee and breakfast. But Gwen continued to lie in bed, not ready to get up. Posh eventually walked into Gwen's room and flung the curtains open.

"Wakey, wakey, hon," she chimed as sunlight flooded in. Then she sat on the edge of Gwen's bed, which caused her to roll toward Posh.

Gwen finally pried one eye open. "It's still pretty early, Posh. Can't we sleep in a bit longer?"

"Afraid not. We have a big day."

Gwen rolled onto her elbow and shaded her eyes with one hand. "Big day?"

"Come on. You need to get moving. We got things to do." Posh waited in Gwen's bedroom to make sure she got out of bed. Gwen rolled her eyes, then got out and slipped a t-shirt and shorts on with Posh still watching.

Posh gave her a playful wink. "Shower first, then breakfast."

Gwen washed away the previous day in the spacious shower. Despite Posh's eagerness to get moving, Gwen lingered, letting the steam and hot water seep into her shoulders. Some thirty minutes later, Gwen sat down at the kitchen island. Posh was nowhere to be seen.

Gwen poured some coffee and shoveled down the now-cold hashbrowns and scrambled eggs. Just as she was finishing up, Posh walked in from the study. She had the morning paper and slid it in front of Gwen.

"What's this?" Gwen asked, pulling it closer.

"Rothmar & Vine."

Gwen raised her brow and shrugged. "I'm from Kalispell, remember?"

"It's a clothing store. A nice one."

"And you're showing me this because…"

"They're having a sale, for one. And two, it's the best perk about working for Kershaw and Aloe Realtors. You have a clothing allowance now. Might as well use it."

"Oh no," Gwen said, shaking her head.

"Oh yes."

"Why? I mean, this isn't a fashion show."

Posh turned Gwen's chair around and practically knelt in front of her with hands clasped. "Please, Gwen. Let me do this for you. I can get your wardrobe updated in one day's time."

"I happen to like my wardrobe."

"I need this," Posh pleaded.

"Oh. So, this is more for you than me?"

"Well, no...I mean, yes, kind of."

Gwen looked at Posh, somewhat dumbfounded. The genie had literally transformed into a teenage girl right in front of her. "Alright. But only if you promise there'll be no more secrets between us."

Posh stood and shook both of Gwen's hands excitedly. "Deal."

Gwen and Posh took the coach to Rothmar & Vine and made it there in record time. Posh was barely able to contain herself. The entire afternoon, she giggled and clapped as she pulled Gwen around the department store. Posh made her try on sundresses, joggers, shorts and practically every other type of clothing the store had to offer. Some of the clothing Gwen had never seen before. Posh insisted on sitting in the dressing rooms with her to judge the fit. For good measure, Posh also tried on everything.

They spent the better part of the day shopping, only taking a short break to eat. Then they were off again to another department store. The two of them window shopped, like a couple of old friends. Gwen found herself enjoying the experience—seeing Posh in a state of giddiness was worth the hours on her feet. To Gwen, it seemed like their relationship had finally turned a corner, and all it had taken was one day of shopping together.

Around dinner time, Gwen was spent. Still, she had to practically drag Posh out of the shoppe with a promise they'd return at some future date. In Gwen's opinion, they'd bought enough clothes to last her a lifetime, all on Kershaw's account.

This time, the coach took them to Posh's home first. It was an inner urban area, north of the central business district of Valeside. The beach was nowhere to be seen, and the streets were a bit dark. The long row of apartments had a low-slung roof and uninviting windows. The roof thatching and paint had seen better days.

"Thought you might want to come up," Posh said.

Though Gwen was ready for bed, she was also curious to see Posh's apartment and agreed to stay for a little while.

Her apartment was a basic one-room efficiency, nothing fancy, and Gwen found herself slightly surprised. She'd assumed that it would be some high-end condo along the beach, considering she was Kershaw's go-to assistant. Apparently, working for a prime realtor didn't have the same perks for Posh.

The apartment was on the second floor. Inside, the living space was small and dark, with a bedroom off to the side. There was a small kitchenette, a bathroom, and something that barely qualified as a balcony. The furniture looked used, cheap and didn't match.

Posh sat at the small round table. "I know what you're thinking."

Gwen sat across from her. "Oh?"

"You're impressed at how lovely my pad is," Posh said and flung her hands out, like she was presenting a prized possession.

Gwen grinned but folded her hands into her lap. "Seriously, Posh. What is going on? You work at one of the premier real estate companies in one of the hottest cities in Ambriel. This apartment doesn't align with any of that."

"Truth be known, Kershaw doesn't pay his assistants very well, ta-da."

"Then why are you with him? Sorry, I don't mean to pry, I just find it curious is all."

Posh shrugged. "Loyalty, I guess. I've been with him for a while, even if the pay isn't great."

"It could be better, though," Gwen said. There was still a hint of hesitation in Posh's response.

"Money isn't everything. I like my job."

That made Gwen think about the offer she'd just accepted from the same company and all the steam tokens that came with it. She felt a sudden pang of guilt and looked away.

"Tell me something," Posh said. "Why are you doing this? From everything I read, you seemed happy in Kalispell, successful business and all. Are you doing this just for the money?"

Gwen shrugged. "I don't know. Maybe I just wanted a new challenge."

"You don't sound convinced of that," Posh said. "Tell me. I can keep a secret."

"Can you? I thought you were sworn to share everything with your boss?"

"I can classify this as personal and not business," Posh said somewhat tentatively, as if trying to justify the conversation.

"I thought you and Kershaw had already done the background checks on me? He knows everything, right?" Gwen chided good-naturedly.

"We did some checks, yes. That's standard for all our potential employees. But there are always things hidden from us."

"Why are you so interested all of a sudden? Just a few days ago, you barely wanted to speak to me."

Posh shrugged again. "It's like you said, looks like we'll be spending some time together. Might as well get to know each other."

Gwen thought about how she'd tried to keep her support group interviews quiet for so long. She had no doubt Kershaw knew about them, but she wasn't sure how much Posh knew. "It's complicated, and it's a long story."

"I've got plenty of time. Maybe a summary if nothing else." Posh stared at her, chin propped in one hand.

"Do you have any tea?" Gwen said.

Posh grinned, then walked into her small kitchen. A few minutes later, she had brewed a pot of lavender tea and served it in a cup. "Here you go. Now…about you."

Gwen swirled her tea and inhaled the aroma, then settled back. "You and Kershaw know about the support groups, correct?"

"Of course. We pulled your files. But we don't know what happened inside the groups."

"Then you'd know that my friend Kriss was murdered by a genie."

"Yes," Posh said. "That was very unfortunate, but I hope you're not blaming me for that."

Gwen watched Posh carefully, though she detected no sarcasm in her tone this time. Posh seemed to be genuinely remorseful, and Gwen felt no angst toward her anyway. Posh was right, it wasn't like she had anything to do with Kriss. "Well, I stole this amulet from her room." Gwen pulled the ruby amulet from beneath her shirt and held it out.

Posh's eyes lit up at the glint of gold. "That looks like more than just a piece of jewelry."

"It is, and I had no idea when I took it. This amulet unlocked something within me that I didn't know I had, or maybe it was something dormant. The support groups were mostly folks grieving for lost loved ones: fathers, daughters, siblings. Kriss was like a sister to me."

"Why all the secrecy? Were they bad people?"

"No. I wouldn't say they were bad. The support group that I was part of included people who had a connection with the supernatural, like me. We practiced phasing into the ethereal realm to see if we could contact them. Some of the interviews got leaked, and it just came off the wrong way. A lot of people didn't understand what we were doing. People are afraid of what they don't know, and there was a lot of pushback. So, we decided to disband the group. I couldn't get away from the mark it left on me and eventually decided to go off to college. Encantar University allowed me to get away from all the negative publicity."

"Sorry to hear that," Posh said, and Gwen felt that she really meant it.

"Actually, I think it was for the best. I needed to get away, and five years at Encantar helped me reset. What the support group taught me was not to be afraid of my ability. After taking Kriss's amulet, something greater was unlocked inside of me."

"And after college, you spent three years in the Ministry of Green Witches, if I recall."

Gwen watched Posh's reaction. She knew it was a sensitive topic with most genies. "Yes. My degree in Field Detective Services, along with my special ability in the supernatural, placed me in a unique position. You see, green witches are natural sleuths. The Ministry came knocking right after graduation. I was naïve in my youth and enlisted. I spent one tour on the battlefield."

"You spent time in the field?"

"Just so you know, I was only there to document and observe. I had nothing to do with genies or their persecution."

Posh gave her a terse nod. "Red and yellow witches were the ones doing the killing, I know. Most genies were wiped out by them. Green witches aren't the killing type, I get it. Still…it's difficult for me."

"I understand." Gwen wanted to reach over and give Posh a hug but didn't. "The ministry ordered us to track genies' movements, crack codes, spy. But I saw things on the battlefield, abuses that my race had committed that I'll never forget. Green witches were told to ignore those atrocities, but I couldn't. I wish there was something I could do to make up for it. I guess I can start by saying I'm sorry."

Posh nodded, a bit too quickly. "Maybe we shouldn't talk about it right now."

Gwen held up her hands in surrender. "I'm happy to postpone that," she said, glad to avoid the topic. But she knew they'd eventually have to face it. She felt that Posh knew it too.

"Anyway…moving on," Posh said, twirling her fingers.

"Well, by the time I made it back to Kalispell, everything had been forgotten. I kept my history about the support group a secret, for the most part. Anyone who still remembered really didn't care. I met my partner, Daniel Harris, at a trade show right after I got back. He was a realtor, down on his luck. I didn't know what to do with my degree. After a few drinks, we had this idea to start a business. He had the realtor experience. I told him about my skills. He put two and two together, and we were off. Daniel got a kick out of the company name, Arris & Harris Realtors. As far as I know, I was the first paranormal realtor, though we kept that quiet. We bought as many haunted cottages as we could, all for a relatively cheap price. I cleansed them, then we flipped the homes for a profit. Before long, we were finding haunted homes before they hit the market, and no one was the wiser. But Harris always had a gambling streak, though I thought he'd turned that corner when we started our business together."

"Gambling streak, huh?"

Gwen sighed. "Well, that's partially why I'm here. He gambled the deed to our business away. Then, he borrowed some tokens to try and get it back. It put us in considerable debt, along with a bounty on his head with a local mountain troll named Bam Jino. I'm here to sell this castle to help him out. Just seems odd, the timing of it all. I got Kershaw's invitation on the same day."

"Doesn't it frighten you, dealing with the paranormal?" Posh asked. Gwen noticed Posh rubbing her arms, like a chill had filled the room.

"No, I guess not. I feel driven to help others, it's always been rewarding, actually. I never had a safe home growing up. Giving others that comfort in their own homes…I don't know, it just feels good."

"What's it like, when you phase, is that what you call it?"

Gwen swirled her tea, considering. "I think it's like a dream, only it happens while I'm still awake. Imagine sleepwalking, only you're conscious and aware while everything around you moves slowly. Maybe it's like being drugged, I guess."

"What do they look like, these spirits?"

"I'd describe them as floating strings."

Posh raised her eyebrows, which nearly disappeared in her blue, tufted hair. "Strings?"

"Sounds funny to say it like that, I know. As I got older, things became more defined. I could eventually see more shape, hear voices that vibrated, like a symphony of instruments."

"What do they say?" Posh leaned in, rapt with attention.

"It's random, mostly just stray thoughts like residual—a conscious stream of gibberish. Regrets…things they wanted to say or do in life and never did. Sad, if you think about it."

"Are they all like that?"

"No. There are others."

Posh waited.

Gwen could see that she wasn't going to let it drop. "Happy, sad, confused, sometimes angry."

"Angry?"

"I think it's the spirits that are upset at the things they didn't get to finish. Maybe because someone took it from them. They didn't get a chance or a fair shake in life."

"The ones that were murdered?"

Gwen shrugged. "Yes, or enslaved, imprisoned maybe."

"So, you think they're still here because they need help?"

"They need resolution, which I can help them solve. These spirits can't leave because they are caught in a perpetual ghost loop."

"Sorry, this is just so interesting to me," Posh said and leaned in, elbows on the table. "How do you even start to cleanse a place?"

"That's where my time at Encantar University and my training on the battlefield come in. Being a green witch helps, too. I find clues, sometimes in our world, sometimes by phasing into the ethereal realm.

I have to first understand what their regret was, then finish it for them. Once they have closure, they can move on."

"And you've been doing this for how long?"

"Since I took the ruby amulet."

"Sounds terrifying to me."

Gwen took a sip of tea, then leaned closer to Posh. "Most of these strings or entities don't care about us. They only care about fixing the problem. They want to move on from their loop."

"Well, Gwenevere Arris, I'm glad you're the one handling that part."

Gwen finished the last of her tea. "Anyway, I think we've talked enough about that. I'd better get back."

Before Gwen could walk out the door, Posh grasped her hand.

It took Gwen by surprise, and she looked down at their interlocked fingers.

"I…I just wanted to say—" Posh stuttered, then paused.

Gwen waited for her to continue. She felt awkward, standing so close to Posh, seeing the golden flecks in her eyes, watching the steam begin to rise from her skin. Gwen had never been so close to a genie and had obviously never had one as a friend. Their races had been taught to hate each other. Wars had been fought over genies' freedoms and control for their powers, while red, yellow and green witches had been brought up to hunt them down by governments. She didn't dislike Posh or her kind, despite what others had always told her. Yet, she felt flustered all of a sudden by this genie she barely knew.

"What is it?" Gwen said, her breath catching in her chest.

Posh looked down, finally breaking eye contact. "I just wanted to say thanks…for spending the day with me. It was nice."

# CHAPTER 12
## *TOM, THE OGRE*

IT WAS COOL and gray on Gwen's morning beach jog, the waves a bit higher than normal. She had heard from the locals that November was sea surge season. But not having lived along the coast, Gwen had no idea what that really meant. Storms in Kalispell just dumped a lot of snow. So, she assumed that meant a lot of rain here in Valeside Beach.

Gwen didn't think she'd ever get tired of the feeling of the cool, claylike sand oozing between her toes as she jogged. It helped ease her thoughts and compartmentalize her feelings. But in the back of her mind was last evening's talk with Posh. To say things had taken an unexpected turn would be putting it lightly. She didn't know where Posh was going with her questions, and Gwen was, in fact, still a bit cautious. Though Posh had seemed genuine, Gwen barely knew the genie, and she was still Kershaw's main assistant, even if she was helping Gwen. Time would tell if Posh would confide in Gwen or if she would snitch and report everything to Kershaw.

Gwen was also trying to block out her daily schedule, not just for today but for the next week. She wanted to pay a visit to the local library and do some research on the original architect for Hidden Palm Grove. Louis Holcomb, Arman had told her. She preferred to do her research from the comfort of Java House rather than brave the traffic of Valeside. But the small library at Java House didn't have the resources she needed.

When Gwen returned to Java House, she took a quick shower and dressed in one of her new outfits that Posh had gushed over: a loose-fitting blouse in white with open shoulders and matching pants. She looked at herself in the mirror and wasn't too disappointed, except for her lack of sun. She slipped into her sandals and hailed a coach.

The drive through downtown Valeside wasn't as bad as she'd expected. Then again, it was the middle of the week. Finding the library was fairly easy. It was a modern-looking building with plenty of glass and white concrete for a minimalistic aesthetic. Inside, the building was light and airy with sunlight filtering through perforated screens mounted on the large glass curtain walls. Racks of books lined a towering atrium with hundreds of steam-powered lifts zipping up and down. Thousands of people browsed and chatted softly.

Gwen located the historical architecture section and searched for Louis Holcomb. She pulled down several books, found a vacant table, and settled in. According to history, Holcomb was quite the eclectic and scandalous designer. He'd lived during the third age and practiced architecture into his late seventies, before passing away from pneumonia. Holcomb was also quite the charmer and had married multiple times, with at least a dozen children to his name. His gambling and betting had taken most of his savings. He died alone and homeless, despite being considered one of the most influential architects in Ambriel. Hidden Palm Grove was widely considered to be his crowning achievement, and it exemplified his revolutionary style of design. Just like Arman had mentioned, Holcomb worked within a modular design system and around multiples of three. He had adopted something known as the golden section, which he later combined with his own theory to create a hybrid technique of architecture that was still used in Ambriel. Soon after he began using his new theory on Hidden Palm Grove, things got a bit murky.

A wealthy land developer had commissioned Holcomb to design a castle around the landmark lighthouse. Thanks to the unique geometry of the three rock pillars that made up the castle's foundations, the site had been considered sacred by the natives in that area. Construction continued for centuries even after Holcomb's passing. Soon, streets were paved as Valeside Beach was established. It expanded quickly, but Hidden Palm Grove remained dark, secluded and mysterious.

Gwen could find very little on the castle's history, other than a handful of construction sketches and a passage written by Holcomb. The photos were old, sepia-toned images with a grainy quality. In the pictures, Gwen could see bamboo scaffolding littered with hundreds of native workers who were poorly garbed in canvas breeches, and they wore no shirts. The passage by Holcomb appeared to be a brief recount of his days on site during construction.

*I stand upon this foreign ground covered in tropical vegetation. The Green Sea is beautiful and takes my breath. Mornings are blissful and humid, the evenings covered in pastel colors. I have tried to learn the native's dialect, a hooting melody that is hauntingly reminiscent of the wildlife surrounding me.*

*The builder has gathered natives to help with the construction of the castle. The days here are long, and we work into the night. The heat in the hot months can be unbearable, and I have witnessed much death. The natives are hardy—they are pushed day and night. Beyond that, I dare not say more.*

*The longer I stay in this paradise, the more I feel as a stranger to it. I have seen many bizarre things that I cannot explain. Though I live for the day to see my design complete, this land takes on a presence of its own. Even as the castle rises before my eyes, it seems to breathe and move of its own accord. The rocky ground gives life. The great pillars of rock stand like titans for support. In my dreams, I hear the pillars. If I stay here much longer, I will go mad.*

Gwen lingered at the library for most of the day, browsing through anything she could find about the historic castle named Hidden Palm Grove. But it felt as if history did not want to remember the castle, or fate was trying to wash it away or cleanse it, perhaps. Gwen did find that the property had changed hands many times over the centuries. Rarely at first. But about forty years after completion, the owner hanged himself. The castle had sold for a fraction of its worth, and turnover was frequent after that.

Later, Gwen hailed a coach. She wanted to swing by Hidden Palm Grove on her own. She knew Posh would be upset with her, but Gwen needed to be alone tonight—she needed to *hear* the castle, and that was sometimes hard to do with others around.

When she arrived, the sun was dipping behind the palm trees. The sky seemed to come to life, a neon tangerine color that was hard to describe. Of course, Gwen had seen plenty of breathtaking sunsets in Kalispell. But along the coastline, the evening skies seem to burn a color that didn't exist in northern Ambriel.

The castle gave off a completely different vibe at sunset. The outline of Hidden Palm Grove took on a different shape with its jagged rooflines and tall minarets, its serrated rows of thorny rose nettle ringing the base. She breathed in the heady smell of saltwater mixed with the lush vegetation and grass. She noticed how the large expanse of glass reflected the sunset, making the upper portion of the castle glow. There was no breeze that evening, the tall palms silent and still. Gwen strolled across the manicured lawn and stopped at the edge of the craggy cliff. She gazed down at the Green Sea, its crashing waves a dull roar from below. Gwen made a full circuit of the grounds, taking in the castle from every angle, but nothing felt out of the ordinary.

She eventually stepped up to the large, covered veranda and fumbled around for her key. Gwen stepped inside and shut the door. The lights brightened automatically, revealing her reflection in the polished white marble walls and floors. The massive chandelier swayed slightly, as if waving to her or welcoming her home.

Gwen walked through to the kitchen, noticing again that all the décor, appliances and cutlery were still in place. Nothing had been touched since her first visit. Then she remembered Arman's warning about the lower levels and how he felt there had been something wrong with them. Curious, Gwen located the central staircase and worked her way downward. The stairs were wide and clad in the same marble, just as she recalled them. Her footsteps echoed softly around the empty castle.

The lower she went the more she could hear a scraping sound from below. She felt for her rosewood wand and brought it out. The staircase continued downward to a level she assumed was the basement. To one side, there was a massive wine cellar made of aged wood that looked to be centuries old. There was also a workroom, a mechanical room and what she guessed was the storm cellar.

Gwen poked around each space, searching thoroughly like she had during her days in the ministry. Clues were sometimes hidden in plain sight, and she wasn't leaving any stone unturned. She tapped on walls and stomped on the floors, trying to find anything of importance. But she found nothing. Furthermore, she wasn't getting the strange vibes she had felt during her first visit.

After thirty minutes, Gwen decided to leave the lower level and check the other areas on the ground level. When she reached the top landing, there was an ogre standing there, holding the handle of a mop toward her defensively.

"Who're you?" he said.

Gwen hesitated before lowering her wand.

The large ogre was middle-aged, with a feathered beret and a scraggly beard. He was dressed in a pair of old canvas trousers and a dirty leather jerkin. Below the jerkin was a stained white shirt, sleeves rolled up and showing his hairy wrists.

"My name is Gwenevere. I'm from the realtor agency…with Mister Kershaw."

The old ogre finally lowered the broom handle and chuckled. "Oh, good. Ya gave me a scare, miss. I forgot that the owner is trying to sell the castle."

Gwen placed her wand back in her satchel. "Sorry, I didn't mean to frighten you. Kershaw didn't mention there were others inside the castle."

The man waved it away. "Not to worry. I'm Tom Handry, the castle's maintenance manager." He jabbed his thumb over his shoulder in an easterly direction. "I live on the grounds, that'd be my small cottage just down the hill. It's my job to keep the castle functioning. I saw the lights on. So, you're here to sell the place?"

"Hopefully," Gwen said. She didn't say anything else, not sure if Tom knew the full story.

Tom chuckled. "I wish you well on that task."

Gwen gave him a sly grin. "I take it you know about the spirits, then?"

"Oh yes. Never met any, mind you. But seen plenty of strange things. I've heard the stories. The current owner has done a good job keeping it quiet, I reckon."

"Mind if I ask how long you've been here?"

"Hmm…" Tom scratched his chin, then started holding up fingers, starting with a large green thumb. "Let's see, I'd say maybe sixty years or so. Long enough to see a thing or two…long enough to know you shouldn't be in here after sundown, Miss."

"You can call me Gwen," she said. "Is it okay if I ask what types of strange things you've seen?"

"Best if we talk outside," Tom said in a whisper, his hand cupped around his mouth. He waved for her to follow and then left through the back door of the castle.

Gwen followed him onto the large veranda. Tom sat on the porch swing facing the Green Sea. He let out a groan of pleasure as he relaxed and the wooden swing creaked under his weight. In the distance, Gwen could see a string of thunderheads lighting up the night sky. Lightning strikes reflected across the ocean as low booms underpinned the sound of crashing waves.

"Pretty, ain't it?" Tom said with a whistle and leaned back in the swing. He waved to the storm clouds beyond in a grand gesture. "You can see everything from up here, ya know?"

Gwen took a seat on the swing, trying to place some distance between them. "It's all new to me. The storms in Kalispell just dump snow."

"Kalispell you say?" Tom said. "That'd be up north, then? Never seen snow, but it's the storm surge that'll get ya around here."

"So I've heard. I'll be careful," Gwen said. "You mentioned something about stories around the castle. Can you tell me more about that?"

Tom gave her a more serious look from the corner of his eye. "Most of it you wouldn't believe. Think I'm some crazy old kook."

"It's okay. I'm an enthusiast, you might say."

"Enthusiast? That's a bit odd. Have you been around such things?"

"You might say that."

"Well, alright then," Tom chuckled. "I guess it'd be all the typical things: doors that open and close, things that move on their own...like this porch swing. I seen it movin' back and forth every evenin', when there's no wind, mind you. Hmm...floating knives. Whispers, screams...*murder.*"

"Murder?" Gwen narrowed her eyes. "Do you mean the construction accidents?"

"Oh, aye. Most of it never got reported." Tom leaned closer to Gwen and cupped the back of his hand near his mouth and whispered. "Lot of people don't want that sort of stuff gettin' out." Tom looked over his shoulder as if someone was listening in.

"Go on," Gwen said.

"The construction accidents weren't just accidents, least that's what I think." Then he cracked a smile and began to cackle. "Gotcha," he said.

Gwen slowly returned his smile. At the same time, she was beginning to wonder if the old housekeeper was completely sane. She tilted her head in a good-natured way and snapped her fingers. "Yes, you got me."

Eventually, Tom quieted and both were silent.

Gwen stood to leave. "It was nice to meet you, Tom. Guess I'd better head back to my place."

Tom gave her a tip of his feathered cap and a nod. As she turned to leave, he cleared his throat.

"Miss Gwenevere, a word of advice for you." Tom turned toward her in the swing and planted both palms face down. "This ain't no ordinary haunted castle. If you wanna sell this property, be careful. It's a dangerous place to be after dark. Oh, this place has always been haunted, mind you. But that remodel, with all that banging and hammerin'…well, perhaps they shoulda left well enough alone. But I get paid to care for the place. I just do my work during the daylight hours. If you're gonna be poking around here, I recommend you do the same."

Gwen let Tom's words settle in. She thought of all the cottages she'd 'cleansed' over the years. This castle was shaping up to potentially be her greatest challenge. Of course, she was already anxious to tackle it head-on. After hearing Tom, she knew she would need to proceed with caution.

"So, Miss Gwenevere, does hearing that make you reconsider?" He lowered his gaze at her.

Gwen simply shrugged. "Thank you for your time, Tom. I should be heading back now."

"Will you be comin' back?"

"Yes. I'll be moving into the castle next week."

That caught good ole' Tom off guard, and his eyebrows almost tipped his feathered hat right off his bald head. "Movin' in! Oh, I don't think that's such a good idea, Miss Gwenevere. You bein' a…well, you know…it just don't seem safe."

Gwen felt her hackles go up, but she smiled at him all the same and calmed herself. "Thanks for your concern, Tom. I'll be just fine. It's just for a night or two."

# CHAPTER 13
## *A STRANGE PROPERTY SURVEY*

WHEN GWEN GOT back to Java House, it was almost eleven o'clock. She didn't bother to shower or undress. She simply kicked off her shoes and tumbled into bed.

That night, the storm that had hovered over the Green Sea made landfall and rocked the house with rain and thunder. She'd never felt such fury. A storm like that would have been a once-in-a-lifetime occurrence in Kalispell, and it felt almost supernatural, waking Gwen in the middle of the night. Unable to fall back to sleep, she decided to get up and make a pot of coffee.

Gwen sat on the lounge sofa and watched the storm's fury from the expansive windows. Near the shoreline, waves crashed along the break, lapping onto the white sands and surging inland as far as the beach grass and beach roses. The howling winds pressed on the windows. She watched the glass flex and the house creak as though it might topple around her.

Gwen pulled out the blueprints of Hidden Palm Grove to browse through the plans, more or less to take her mind off the storm. She tried to flatten out the drawings, but the edges kept curling in from all the years of being rolled up. She could see holes in the vellum from age, and the sepia print still smelled like ammonia. With Arman's words in her thoughts, and Holcomb's warnings in the back of her mind, Gwen scoured the unique pattern that the three massive chambers created. She felt like there was some clandestine secret interwoven within the parchment. Like a long-lost word just on the tip of her tongue, Gwen could almost see the elusive secret within the blueprint's unique design. It was something dark and shameful…a secret too afraid to reveal itself. Among the symbols and dimensions and architectural jargon, there was a hidden clue that wasn't ready to reveal itself just yet.

After several hours, the storm finally abated. The winds died down and the clouds dispersed. The wild night broke, and the morning sun crept just over the horizon. But Gwen was no closer to discovering what secret lay within the set of blueprints.

There was a knock on the door, and it made her jump.

She answered it to find Kershaw standing there, hands behind his back. He was wearing the same style of suit, but in a dark brown color with light pinstripes.

"Good morning, Gwen," Kershaw said and let himself in. "I see you're making yourself at home. Java House has that tendency."

"Yes, it's lovely," Gwen said and closed the door behind him. "Thank you again for the hospitality. What can I do for you?"

"I heard that you met our facility keeper, Tom."

Gwen gave him a subtle nod. She knew he was here to talk about more than a facility keeper. "He's quite the interesting fellow. A local, I take it?" she said.

"His family is one of the oldest names in the area. By the way, what did you think about your second visit to the castle?"

"I detected nothing out of the ordinary," Gwen said. "Kershaw, you're obviously here to discuss something else. What is it?"

"Ah, straight to the point. I knew I'd get nothing less from you. Our client would like an update. I was just wondering if you—"

"I need to spend a few nights at Hidden Palm Grove," Gwen blurted.

Kershaw paused his pacing and turned on his heels. "Excuse me?"

"I need to connect with the castle. I can't do that from the comfort of Java House."

"I'm not sure that's a good idea—"

"It's nothing I haven't done before. These things take time, Kershaw. You'll have to inform our client that it might take longer than anticipated."

"We have until Saint Halving Day. I've already committed to that."

"I understand."

Kershaw continued to stare at Gwen. She could see his frustration.

"I don't know what you were expecting," Gwen continued. "I can't just snap my fingers. That isn't how this works."

"I've assigned Posh to you. She's the best. What else can I do to speed this up?"

"Nothing. Just give me room to breathe and keep your client off of me so I can do my work."

"Our client," Kershaw corrected Gwen.

"Right, our client."

"Just be careful, Gwen. This castle is unlike any assignment you've had before."

"So I've heard."

Posh stood in the entryway of Java House, her hands on her hips. "You're doing what? That's crazy, Gwen."

"Calm down," Gwen said and guided Posh to the couch. "This isn't my first gig."

"But why? You have Java House. It's nice and comfy and, well…it's not haunted."

Gwen sat down next to Posh and gave her knee a pat. "Because it gets me closer. I need to understand the castle. I need to feel its vibe."

"Okay…got it. Just seems you could do that without moving in."

"It'll be fine."

"Are you sure?"

"Yes. Don't worry."

But Posh continued to shake her head, eyebrows knitted together and an index finger picking at her thumb nervously. "Well…then I'm coming along."

"No," Gwen said immediately. "Posh. This is my territory."

"And I'm assisting you."

"I don't care. You're not staying at the castle."

"Well…too bad. And if I need Kershaw to back me up, then that's what I'll do."

Gwen shook her head, then let out a long sigh. "Listen, Posh. This is serious. I can't do my job and look after you at the same time. I just need a few days."

"I don't know about this. Are you positive?"

"It's a waiting game, and this place hasn't shown itself yet, but it will. And believe me, you don't want to be there when it does."

Posh continued to look at Gwen with concern. But Gwen noticed a hint of acceptance in her gaze now.

Posh finally nodded. "Okay, Gwen. But you'll let me know at the first sign of trouble, deal?"

Gwen gripped her shoulder. "You got it."

The next morning, Gwen was up early, her mind already in overdrive as she thought about her conversation with Tom.

...the whispers, slamming doors, *floating knives.*

In her opinion, moving into Hidden Palm Grove for a few days couldn't come quickly enough. In fact, Gwen felt almost giddy at the challenge. With the mystery surrounding the castle, including the history and strange occurrences, she was itching to get started, and nothing brought home the challenge quite like staying on the property. In most cases, just a night or two, and she would have the whole thing worked out—cleansed and ready to sell. Hidden Palm Grove wouldn't be that easy, though, and she knew she would need to temper her excitement.

But before she moved in for the next few days, Gwen had decided she needed to conduct a survey of the property. Although there were several that had already been completed, she wanted to do one herself. She needed to see everything with her own eyes: the dimensions, property lines, the shape of the castle's footprint. But surveying a property worked best with two people. Gwen considered Posh. But that would come with all the nagging about being cautious. She wondered if she might coax Arman into helping, maybe offer to buy him dinner or a few drinks. Then again, he'd specifically stated he wasn't ever stepping foot on the property again.

*What about good 'ole Tom?*

But Tom had a weird vibe that Gwen hadn't yet figured out. In the end, she settled on asking Posh for help. She was, after all, assigned to 'assist' in selling the castle. Gwen would just have to deal with the genie's badgering, and sometimes sarcastic, nature. Once Gwen had the measurements, she could compare it against the information that had already been documented over the years.

Her morning jog took her further down the beach this time. As she grew more accustomed to running barefoot in the sand, her route continued to expand. She jogged past Hidden Palm Grove, Sephora Bean (which she had to resist stopping at) and more beachside shoppes, restaurants and boutique hotels. The deeper she ventured into Valeside Beach, the more she wanted to be a part of the community. The white sands and crooning sea breeze almost seemed to be luring her in. Gwen felt like she was caught in Valeside's net…and she wasn't complaining. But she also knew she'd only experienced the tip of the iceberg so far, and she was excited to venture out more.

When she returned to Java House, she showered and changed. Posh was seated on the couch, reading a magazine, when Gwen walked into the living room. She was dressed in her standard loose-fitting pants, a tank top that bared her midriff, and sandals. There was no steam from her skin, at the moment.

Posh stood and gave Gwen a long look. "You know what I'm in the mood for?"

Gwen gave her a frown. "We're not going shopping. I have enough new clothes to last me a lifetime."

"So why are you wearing the same thing you wore yesterday?"

"Because I like this particular sundress."

"What about that cute little tank top I picked out?"

"Would it make you happy if I wore it?"

"Depends on what you're asking me to do today," Posh said, and crossed her arms.

"I need your help measuring something."

"Oh?"

"You're probably not going to like it."

Posh narrowed her eyes. "Well, are you going to make me guess?"

"It's called a survey. I need to field verify the outside dimensions of Hidden Palm Grove."

Posh threw up her hands. "Seriously? There's been a dozen surveys on that castle over the years."

"Yes, and have you checked the information on them?" Gwen said. She reached for the blueprints and rolled them out. Then she found the latest survey, which had been conducted by Arman. "He said as much. None of the numbers align. Even the original floor plans have varying information."

"Okay, there are some discrepancies, I'll admit."

"It's more than discrepancies, Posh. And I'm going to find out why."

Posh pursed her lips, then gave Gwen another shrug with one shoulder. "Fine. Just ditch that sundress, and I'll go."

It took them about twenty minutes to walk to the castle. Atop the hidden stone staircase, Tom was waiting for them.

"Saw y'all coming," Tom said with a motion to the beach below. He was leaning on a shovel with one foot kicked up.

Gwen noticed he was wearing the same clothes as the day before: a dirty oxford shirt and a stained leather jerkin with heavy black boots. She began to wonder if Tom ever changed clothes and thought about Posh dragging the ogre around the department store, which brought a devious smile to her face.

"You still set on moving in for a few days?" Tom continued.

"Yes, that's still the plan. Right now, Posh and I are going to take a few measurements of the castle. Hope that's okay."

"Don't you already have the blueprints?" Tom said. "That ought to tell you everything you need to know."

"Yes, we have them," Gwen said. "I just want to verify a few things that aren't aligning."

Tom chuckled and kicked some mud off his boot. "Oh, I've heard the rumors of these halls changing sometimes. No one's ever been able to confirm it, but you two go on ahead and do what you need."

"You know about the other surveys?" Posh asked.

"Aye. Several were conducted during my grandfather's time here, one or two while my father and I oversaw the castle as well. Some say the castle 'wanders about,' which is just nonsense." He chuckled again, which turned into a coughing fit. Tom pulled out a handkerchief and wiped his lips. Gwen caught the hint of a ripe raspberry-colored smear across the cloth before he could stuff it back into his jerkin.

"Are you ok?" she asked.

Tom waved it away. "No matter. Anyway, have fun. If you figure it out, lemme know, won't you?" Tom hobbled off, talking to himself in a low chuckle.

Once he was out of earshot, Posh gave Gwen a doubtful look. "Hallways don't move."

Gwen returned her curious look. "Only one way to find out. Let's get started before the heat sets in."

Gwen and Posh used the tools from Aloe Realtors. They were older instruments, with a bit of rust. Since realtors didn't normally conduct surveys, it was all that Gwen could find, though. The measuring device used reflected daylight, which was projected onto a piece of steel at the other end. Posh would stand at the castle's opposite corner and read out the length, then Gwen would check it with the floor plans. They used another instrument, which determined the angle of the wall and the elevation of the floor's level. Each time, Posh would read out the measurements, and Gwen would check them against the floor plans and the older surveys.

Gwen and Posh spent the morning walking around the perimeter of the giant castle. They were slowed by the mass of thorny rose nettle, trampling a few azaleas during the process. Eventually, Gwen decided to use a wilting spell on the vegetation, which she hated to do.

Around noon, they finished, and Gwen stepped onto the large veranda, about to go inside for a glass of water.

"I'll just wait out here," Posh said and settled into the porch swing.

"You know, at some point you're going to have to get used to this place."

"At some point," Posh said and leaned back.

"Suit yourself." Gwen wiped some sweat from her forehead and stepped through the front door.

Inside, the ceiling fans created a gentle breeze. The sunlit polished tile looked as pristine as it had the last time she'd been there. Gwen strolled through the large chamber and into the kitchen quarters. When she walked past one of the large islands, she stopped.

On the countertop was the block of utensils. Spoons, forks, knives…all aligned perfectly except for one missing butter knife. Like a missing tooth, it stood out to Gwen in a way that made her curious.

Had Tom been back in the house?

She stood there for another few seconds, then poured a couple of glasses of water and stepped back onto the porch. Gwen handed a glass to Posh, then sat down next to her on the swing.

Posh took a sip, then gave Gwen a sidelong glance. "You alright?"

Gwen nodded. "I'm just anxious to plug in the numbers from our survey."

"Right," Posh said. "Wandering hallways…" She chuckled and nudged Gwen.

Gwen didn't laugh, her thoughts still focused on the missing butter knife.

# CHAPTER 14

## *WANDERING HALLS*

POSH HUNG OUT at Java House for the rest of the day, though she tried to talk Gwen into another shopping spree. In the end, she settled for a coffee run to Sephora Bean. Even though Java House had all the bells and whistles when it came to coffee, lattes and espressos, there was something special about Sephora Bean.

When they returned, Posh and Gwen sat at Java House's large kitchen island and spread out the blueprints and other surveys from years past. Posh read off the dimensions and other information they'd collected on their own survey, while Gwen double-checked the numbers against the other documents.

"Most of them seem to align," Gwen said. "But I do notice a few odd dimensions, around the back, where the basement sits. Look here."

Posh moved around to sit next to Gwen, their elbows pressed together.

"See," Gwen continued. "The base walls seem slightly larger than what's on the plans. I've checked it twice. It's definitely off. Not by much, but enough to be more than just a construction error."

Posh sipped her coffee, both hands cupped around the mug. "Sometimes in the field, construction drawings are revised. It might be that changes were made after the floor plans were issued. Could've been a unique site condition, or an owner request for change."

"Right," Gwen said. "But there would be a revision cloud on the drawings, which I don't see here."

It was getting late, and Posh yawned. "I don't know what to say. Maybe we can ask Arman if he recalls?"

Gwen pursed her lips. "Maybe. He seems like an architect that wouldn't have left something like that out, though." Gwen rolled up the drawings and placed the survey documents in a folder. "It's getting late."

"Is that a hint?" Posh asked, setting her mug in the sink.

"No…no," Gwen said. "I mean, you're welcome to stay as long as you like, of course. There's plenty of room."

"Okay. I'd like to hang out," Posh said. "Maybe we can sit on the deck. It's good people watching, you know?"

Gwen chuckled and grabbed a blanket. "I'm beginning to notice that. It's quite the diverse group here, not like Kalispell. In fact, I think I saw a hippogriff yesterday."

"Just wait until summer," Posh said. "You'll get the full flavor: griffins, gnomes, ogres, fairies. They all come to Valeside during vacation season."

"Can't wait," Gwen said as they stepped onto the deck and sat near each other on the lounge sofa. Gwen flicked her wand at the hearth and lit a fire.

In the distance, the sun was setting along the horizon. Pink clouds reflected the brilliant pastel sunset. The sound of waves rushing toward the beach surrounded them. Gwen watched the couples walking on the beach and thought about her friend, Kriss, and what she would make of Valeside Beach.

"You're quiet," Posh said, "not that you're always talkative, but there's something on your mind. Care to share?"

Gwen turned to face Posh. She was close enough for her to see the golden flecks in her eyes. Gwen felt the genie's skin grow a bit warmer, and some steam rose from her bare shoulders. The light created a soft halo around Posh, her blue skin a dark color in the dusky sun, almost seductive.

"I'm—" Gwen paused and shook her head. "Just a lot on my mind."

"Like what?" Posh asked. "Come on, Gwen. We're past the awkward partner phase. If we're going to get this castle sold, then we need to be able to talk, right?"

Gwen gave her a sidelong glance. "It's just all this talk about wandering hallways…Maybe there's some truth to that?"

"It sounds like crazy talk to me."

"What if it isn't? If we believe the castle is haunted, then why aren't 'wandering hallways' a possibility too?"

Posh shrugged. "Maybe. But I've never heard of such a thing in all my years with Aloe Realtors, and believe me, I've seen some strange things. If it's true, then what's your conclusion?"

"That there's something more going on at Hidden Palm Grove than just a haunting."

Posh spent the night, and Gwen was happy to have company. Java House was wonderful, but it was mostly a large and empty home. Though she could be a recluse, Gwen felt the need to bond with her new partner as much as she could—she could definitely see more sleepovers in their future. They eventually moved inside to the couch and talked about their pasts. Gwen felt like a teenager again, like she was with her old friend, staying up past their bedtime. Despite her original impression, Posh had a relaxing, calming nature that set Gwen at ease. Posh shared more information about Kershaw, and once again, Gwen found herself wondering about their true relationship. But it was after midnight, and Gwen was ready for bed.

"Feel free to sleep wherever you like." Gwen stood to go to her room.

Posh reached out and held her hand. "Are you sure you really want to spend the night at that place?"

Gwen looked down at their hands. Posh's skin grew a bit warmer. "I have to. That's the normal routine for me. I can't get a good feel of the castle at a distance. Plus, Kershaw's already asking for an update."

"He is getting anxious," Posh agreed. "Just don't rush into it, not if you have a bad feeling about it."

"I'll be fine. I've been through this many times. You can stay at Java House, if it helps. It's closer, in case I need something."

Posh sat up at that. "I'd like that. I mean, if it's really okay with you."

Gwen gave her a confused look. "Yes, of course it is. Why wouldn't it be? Besides, your company owns it. I don't see why Kershaw would care either way."

Posh stood and gave her a hug. "Thank you."

The next morning, Posh left early to get some items from her apartment. She'd left breakfast and a pot of coffee in the kitchen for Gwen.

When Posh returned later that afternoon, she had enough luggage to make Gwen wonder if she ever planned to go back to her apartment.

Posh cooked dinner that evening. "A last meal," she joked.

"It's just a few days," Gwen said. "I'll be back before you know it."

"What will you do first?" Posh asked as she dumped some noodles into a boiling vat of water.

"I'll find safe zones, try to identify hot spots. I need to set up a home base."

"What do you mean, home base?" Posh said.

"I need a place that's safe. I find that, when I phase into the ethereal realm, there are zones. Many places have what I call a 'witching hour', which just means times that are more active."

"And you think the castle will have that?"

"Probably. Most places do. But I'll determine that first, and then I'll know when it's safe to be outside of the zones I set up."

"Sounds…strange," Posh said, scooping up some pasta in a bowl. "Sorry, this is all new to me."

"It's okay," Gwen said. "It took me a while to find a system that works. There wasn't a whole lot of research out there for me to study, once I really dove into this phasing thing. But this has worked well so far."

"Zones…witching hours," Posh said. "Who would've thought any of this would apply to selling a castle?"

Posh seemed to almost dance around the kitchen. She was like a fairy chef in the confident way she moved. Gwen found herself amazed at the genie's thoughtfulness and cheery attitude now. Whatever differences there had been between them in the beginning were gone. Posh seemed like a different person, and Gwen wondered if their first few meetings had been nothing more than Posh's walls. Indeed, Gwen had a few of her own defensive walls, too.

"You're pretty handy around the kitchen," Gwen said, turning the conversation toward Posh. "Tell me how you learned it."

"Mostly my grandmother, and my mom some, too, though she was always gone, working. So, I spent a lot of time with Grandma. She loved to cook, and we were always baking pies and cookies. I remember those summer afternoons, when we'd venture into the blackberry fields and pick from the wild bushes. Everything in my small hometown was right there. We traded with the locals for the ingredients we couldn't harvest."

"Sounds like a fairytale," Gwen said, staring at Posh with her chin propped in her hand.

Posh did a pirouette on her toes, then bowed. "When this is all done, I'll take you there. I think you'd love it, Gwen. You may never want to come back."

"Speaking of, what brought you here? Sounds like your hometown was a wonderful place."

Posh turned back to the boiling water, then checked the sauce and gave it a stir. "Things didn't turn out the way I'd hoped. My mother was off at war, and I needed to find a job. Aloe Realtors had an opening, and Kershaw helped me land the gig—a favor I still owe him for. I quickly learned my way around Valeside Beach and became his assistant." Posh handed a plate to Gwen, then made her own dish and sat down next to her.

Gwen forked some of the pasta into her mouth and let out a moan. "Wow, this is fantastic, Posh. What is it?"

The genie blushed a deeper shade of blue, a bit of steam coming from her cheeks. "Thank you. An old recipe from my mother. It's called Devil Dust Delight. Dried firepot tomatoes are the secret. You just grind them up and sprinkle them in."

"Well, it's fantastic," Gwen said, "tell her I said so."

"I would, if she were still alive."

Gwen finished her mouthful of pasta. "Sorry. I...didn't realize..."

"It's fine," Posh said. She held out her hand to show Gwen a golden bracelet. It had one sapphire in the center but was otherwise simple and unadorned.

"It's beautiful," Gwen said. She took Posh's hand and examined the bracelet closer.

"It was my mother's. She gave it to me before she left. It was her last battle, she was to retire afterwards. I never saw her again. It's a memento, and I always wear it." Posh frowned and looked away. "I'm sorry, we don't need to talk about it. You've got other concerns tonight."

Gwen gave her hand a squeeze but didn't say anything.

Posh took another bite of pasta, then slid her plate to the side. She drummed her fingers on the countertop and nodded to Gwen's wand. "At least you'll have that with you."

"Won't do much good. Green witches use mostly nonlethal enchantments, not that those would do anything for me at the castle. It's really the detective enchantments that will help."

Their conversation was interrupted by a call from Kershaw. Gwen pulled out her crystal globe and waited for the image to come into focus. "What can I do for you, Kershaw?"

He was dressed in his typical suit and tie and straightened in his seat. "Ah, Gwenevere. I hope I caught you at a good time. Tom tells me that you're planning to move in tonight. Were you going to discuss the timing of that with me first?"

"No, I wasn't planning on it, since I'd already mentioned it to you."

Gwen watched Kershaw's face contort in the globe. He feathered his hair back, clearly perturbed. "I'm not sure doing this now is the best approach, Gwenevere."

"This is how I usually do it, and the sooner the better. You hired me to cleanse the castle. Let me do my job."

Kershaw remained silent for a few seconds. Gwen assumed he was considering his options.

"Why is now a problem?" Gwen continued. "No one occupies the castle currently. I won't be interrupting anything."

"I'm just concerned for your safety. Aloe Realtors has invested a lot in you."

Gwen glanced at Posh, who held a finger to her lips. She stayed hidden from the globe, petrified and seemingly afraid to say a word.

"Kershaw. I appreciate your concern, but I think now is the perfect time to do this." Gwen continued.

"I'm not sure our client would agree to this—"

"Our client doesn't need to know. What's important is getting the job done. This is what I need to do."

"Are you sure you can't do this tomorrow? It's late."

"I'm going in tonight."

Kershaw finally held up his hands. "Then I would say good luck and be careful. I'll have Tom stock the pantry for you. There's also a lady named Natalie down the road at the greenhouse. She's the grounds keeper, great arborist, by the way. Talk to her if you can't find Tom."

"Got it. Thanks."

"Oh," Kershaw said. "Tell Posh hello. And yes, she's more than welcome to stay at Java House."

# CHAPTER 15

## *NAT, THE GNOME*

IMMEDIATELY AFTER KERSHAW disappeared from the crystal globe, Gwen turned and faced Posh. "Why didn't you speak up?"

Posh hesitated, then shrugged. "I…just didn't think he should know that you and I are spending time together…after hours, that is."

"Why? Is that against company policy?"

"No, not really, I guess. I just wasn't sure what Kershaw would think about it."

"Well, apparently, he knew you were here and didn't seem to care."

"I don't know. Kershaw's tricky—"

Gwen held up a hand and stopped her midsentence. "Posh, is there something more you want to tell me about Kershaw?"

Posh raised one shoulder in a half shrug, her arms crossed.

"It's pretty obvious there's more to this. I think it's time you told me what's going on between you two. This is more than a boss-employee thing."

Posh didn't meet Gwen's gaze and finally let out a sigh. "Kershaw helped me get this job. What I didn't tell you were the terms of my agreement with him and Aloe Realtors."

Gwen waited, tapping her fingers on the kitchen island. "Go on."

Posh frowned. "I had some personal issues. He offered to help me if I agreed to be indentured to him."

"Why would Kershaw choose to indenture you instead of just hiring you?"

"I'm a genie. While indentured, I'm bound to him," Posh pulled at the fine golden chain around her thin waist. It glowed brighter when she touched it. "This binds us, and I won't be free until it's removed. He controls everything: my pay, my schedule. He essentially owns me for the next decade. Controlling a genie can come in handy."

"But genies can't use wish-magic without consequences, right?"

"Not sure Kershaw really cares about that."

"Why wouldn't he just use your magic to cleanse the castle then?"

Posh could only shrug. "I'm guessing he's probably afraid of the public outcry if he did. He also has to consider Aloe Realtor's image. Besides, a genie's wish-magic is wildly chaotic. You never know what'll happen afterwards."

That made some sense to Gwen. After all, image was everything in the realtor world. It wouldn't look good if Kershaw ensnared a genie only to use her wish-magic, especially after how unpopular the Genie Wars had been. Though a genie had strong elemental-magic, it was the wish-magic that was so coveted, powerful and consequential, if used.

"Genies were indentured for centuries," Gwen said. "Your race fought and won their freedom. Why would you ever agree to go back into servitude?"

"My grandmother was sick and needed help. She was the last of my family line. At the time, my only option was to accept his offer. But just days later, my grandmother passed away. I signed on for nothing, it seems."

Gwen felt a moment of pity for Posh. She'd apparently lost her mother in the wars, at the hand of a witch, no less. Then, Kershaw had forced her into servitude in order to save her grandmother, who had died anyway. It sounded like Posh was the last in her family line. "I'm sorry, Posh. If there's something I can do to help make things right, I'll do it." Gwen held Posh's stare and detected a moment of weakness in her expression.

"Thank you. It's nothing you did. This was our parents' war, and it was their doing. I won't hold our generation responsible. Things are different now, at least, I like to think so. Look at us, we're proof of that. Sitting here, talking and enjoying a meal together. It's something that would've been unheard of just a generation ago."

"And yet, there is still distrust on both sides. I am guilty of that."

"Well, me too," Posh said. "Let's just put that behind us."

"Pretty sure we already have," Gwen said and gave Posh a hug.

There was a moment of silence as they embraced.

Gwen finally pulled back. "Thanks for dinner," she said, her voice a bit unsteady. "Now, I have work to do."

Gwen had her things packed and ready within the hour. The sun had set when she stepped onto the back deck.

"You've got everything you need?" Posh asked, helping to straighten Gwen's green robe like some doting parent.

"Clothes, toiletries…reading glasses," Gwen patted her satchel.

"And your wand?"

Gwen pulled it out and flicked it. "Won't do much good where I'm going. I only have some basic defensive spells, and my green thumb enchantment, and there's probably not many plants inside the castle."

"Still, I feel better when you have it. Check in with me as much as you can. I'll have my globe nearby."

Tom was there, hands on hips and shaking his head at Gwen when she reached the top of the spiral staircase's landing. Gwen took a second to catch her breath, then shouldered her heavy satchel.

"I can't say that I'm glad to have company, considerin' the situation," the ogre said. "I still don't think it's a good idea, Miss Arris."

Gwen didn't say anything, tired of hearing about it from practically everyone she knew.

Tom tipped his feathered cap, turned, and led the way into the castle.

They took the large circular staircase in the center of the castle up to the bedroom level. The early evening moonlight spilled through the clerestory windows, lighting their way. To Gwen, the castle felt different at night. It wasn't the charming, light and airy feeling she got when the sun was up. Instead, there was a mysterious, dark and somewhat foreboding vibe that seemed to live in the shadows of the hallways.

Tom led her down the marble corridor that seemed to stretch for miles. They eventually stopped in front of a large pair of heavy white doors. Even though Gwen had been to the bedroom wing before, she was seeing things in a different light, now that the sun had set. The ornate trim around the door wound up and onto the walls and ceiling. It was a splendid example of past craftsmanship no longer seen in Ambriel. But as she looked closer, she could see tiny chips in the elaborate woodwork. The paint had flecked off, as if something had hacked away at it.

Tom flung the double doors open with a resounding thud, like he was trying to scare something off.

Gwen was once again greeted by the panoramic view of the Green Sea beyond. The floor-to-ceiling windows seemed to invite the ocean into the bedroom as if there were no barriers in the way. In spite of herself, Gwen felt her breath catch in her chest, like she was seeing it for the first time all over again. "Well…I don't think I'll ever get tired of this view."

But Tom glanced around, almost skittishly. The large ogre seemed spooked.

"Everything alright?" Gwen asked.

Tom avoided her gaze. "The kitchen's stocked. There's plenty of fuel for the torches. Soap and towels are in the bathroom here. I assume you'll only be staying in the master suite. I haven't stocked any of the other rooms. Anything else?" Tom looked nervous as he rolled back and forth on the balls of his feet.

"What can you tell me about Natalie, the groundskeeper?"

"Oh, Nat?" Tom said. "She's a bit…peculiar." He made a circular motion around his ear with his finger. "Lives down yonder." He nodded his head to the side and clicked his tongue to his cheek. "Go see her if you want, but I wouldn't waste my time. If you do go out, I'd be back here in the master suite before midnight, though."

Gwen lowered her gaze, then furrowed her brow. "Why do you say that?"

"That's when all the activity starts, at least, from what I've noticed. Oh, and you'll be needin' these…should get you access to every room, I think." Tom pulled out a large rusty ring of keys. There were a few dozen skeleton keys, the type with an old bit that resembled missing teeth. They jingled as he handed them to her. "Good luck, Miss Arris." Tom tipped his feathered cap and promptly left.

Gwen watched him leave and smiled. Tom had just given her two very valuable pieces of information.

The master suite was one of the castle's safe zones.

Also, the 'witching hour' started at midnight.

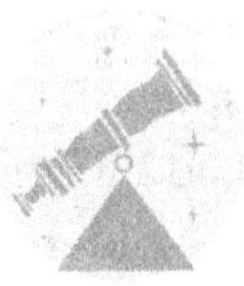

Once Gwen had unpacked, she decided to pay a visit to Natalie, or Nat, as Tom had called her. She checked the time to see there were still several hours until midnight, plenty of time to pay a quick visit to the groundskeeper.

Hidden Palm Grove was a twenty-acre estate, which was plenty of space to get turned around, considering all the landscaping and trails. Lush tropical plants clung low to the grounds, along with the pink and green thorny rose nettle that seemed to be everywhere. The emerald-toned grass was immaculate beneath the large palms that swayed gently in the breeze. Gwen could hear the sound of the sea, even over the wind through the trees. It was like a persistent whispering in the background that was both soothing and haunting. She strolled along the gravel paths, her boots crunching as she followed the twists and turns. She hit a few dead ends before finally stumbling upon a small cottage.

It had white stucco walls, with patches of brick poking through where age had worn the façade away. A large greenhouse was attached to the back of the cottage. The thatched roof had a steep pitch with a stone chimney jutting through it. There was a small porch on the front with several glowing lanterns perched along the railing. To say it was cozy was an understatement.

Gwen stepped onto the porch and rapped the door knocker. A few seconds later, a short garden gnome with white hair, dark green skin and hazel eyes opened the door. She squinted, then tilted her head as if trying to remember something. Eventually, a smile eased across her weathered face.

"Ah…you must be Gwenevere," she said and shook Gwen's hand. "Kershaw mentioned we'd have a guest in the main castle. Please, come in."

Gwen stepped into the cottage and waited for Natalie to lead the way. It was a modest space with a patchwork of furniture in different colors and styles. Gwen guessed that Natalie was probably a hoarder, clinging to everything like some valuable piece of her own history. There was a fire in the stone hearth, a few cats roaming in the back, and several plaid-patterned blankets on the backs of the sofas and chairs. Even the curtains were mismatched. But somehow, it all worked in a way that leant to the cozy feel of the space.

"Have a seat," Natalie said. "Can I get you something to drink?"

Gwen sat in one of the old recliners. "Tea, if you have some, Natalie—"

"Please, Gwenevere. Nat will do."

Gwen smiled. "Okay. And please, you can call me Gwen."

Nat already had a pot of green tea on the hearth and poured two cups.

"Do you live here by yourself?" Gwen asked.

"No, there are others in my family, but they choose to live in nature. I tend to the cottage, but we all work together to keep the estate in good shape. My family has been here for ages, starting with my great-grandmother, who was the first garden gnome to immigrate to Ambriel. When the castle was being built, the owner asked us to stay and help. He offered housing and food. Eventually, my ancestors built this cottage. I've lived here my entire life."

"What can you tell me about the castle?"

Nat set her teacup down. "Probably nothing you haven't already heard from Tom." She shook her head. "That castle…" She made a motion with her hand, like she was warding off some evil spirit. "It hasn't been the same since the remodel, though I think it's always been an odd place. Honestly, I never go near it."

"You say you don't go near the castle, but I imagine you've seen a thing or two."

"Oh yes, but Tom's the one you want to talk to about stories. I try to avoid him."

"You do?" Gwen said and tilted her head.

"We respect each other's privacy," Nat said, but then smirked. "Oh, that's an excuse. Our feud goes back a while. Tom…well, how should I say this? He doesn't like my kind. Apparently, neither did his parents."

Gwen, unfortunately, could relate. Though she'd never known her parents, the ongoing quarrel between witches and genies sounded similar to what ogres and garden gnomes were dealing with.

Nat seemed to read the look on Gwen's face. "Yes, it's common, here in this part of Ambriel. That's one reason why I don't mind being secluded in my cottage. I have nature to fulfil the void. I'm also aware of the ongoing strife between genies and witches."

Gwen gave her a brief, somewhat forced smile. "Yes, there is that."

Nat eyed her over the rim of her teacup, steam rising in the firelight. "Hmm. I hear Kershaw keeps a genie on his team. Not many genies around these parts."

"No, there aren't. Her name is Posh. She's…helping me—" Gwen gulped down the rest of her tea, coughed a bit from the burning sensation in her throat, then set the cup on the end table and stood. "It was nice to meet you, Nat."

Nat stood and looked up at Gwen. "My apologies if I have offended you—"

"No, it's okay. I just..." Gwen paused again, not sure that she wanted to share everything with someone she'd just met. "It's getting late. I need to get back to the castle."

"How long do you plan to stay?"

"Only a few days, I hope."

"You're welcome to come visit. I could use some company on occasion. If things get too dicey in the castle, you can stay here in the spare room."

"Dicey?" Gwen said.

"Not that you can't handle it, of course," Nat said. "Good night, Gwen."

# CHAPTER 16
## *PAST CURFEW*

GWEN TOOK HER time walking back to the castle, letting the fireflies light her way. Twilight had settled in, and the stars above shone brightly amidst the swirling clouds. The sound of crickets blended with the crunching gravel beneath her boots as she tried to remember the route back to the castle, but she kept getting turned around. The campus grounds were large, and Gwen wished there was some directional signage. Low torchlit bollards helped light the area, but after thirty minutes, Gwen was no closer to finding her way. It was almost like the campus trails had shifted, and she had no recollection of the current path she was on. Gwen felt a moment of panic when she thought about what Tom had said—*don't get lost in the castle past midnight.*

But when Gwen finally made it back to the castle, it *was* close to midnight. She hurried up the stairs two at a time and stepped into the master suite's massive walk-in closet. She forced a chuckle at the few clothes hanging there, which reminded her of missing teeth. Her two outfits in the otherwise vacant closet were ones that Posh had picked out. But Gwen wasn't looking for a change of clothes. She needed Kriss's amulet, and it was hanging at the end of the closet.

Gwen picked it up, feeling the weight of the tarnished metal and bright ruby. She grasped it in her palm and closed her eyes. It felt like a shockwave flowed through her veins. She placed the amulet around her neck and let the ethereal feeling sink into her bones. Then she dropped the crystal globe and wand into her leather satchel, grabbed an extra sweater, and made her way downstairs toward the castle's basement.

The vibe in the castle increased. Like the approach of a storm, the air felt alive, and her senses were heightened by the amulet's power. When she wore the amulet during the witching hour, it always felt like a wash of colors was covering her vision. Like looking through a stained-glass window, the time to phase was near. But it only worked when she was outside of the safe zone, which in this case was the master suite.

But right now, she wasn't in a safe zone. Here, she was in danger, and only the amulet protected her. But that protection came with a price, and Gwen would likely spend most of tomorrow recouping her energy.

With the amulet's aura surrounding her, the castle was a russet color or a muddled amber, perhaps. Haunting whispers enveloped her, threatening to infiltrate her mind. Gwen continued down the circular staircase, the moonlight reflecting off the marble tile. When she made it to the bottom, she paused to listen.

Gwen could feel a strong current running through the basement. The color was darker here, reminding her of a house in Kalispell on the northern edge of town. That old cottage had been on the foothills of the Cascade Mountain Range, and it'd had a similar energy—one that had frightened her. She rarely felt fear; most places didn't possess such energy. But Gwen knew instantly that this castle held more than one spirit, many more. The challenge she had yearned for was right in front of her. She was starting to second-guess her wish.

Dealing with a place that held multiple spirits was always tricky. The danger level went up considerably. It would leave her vulnerable, unlike dealing with a single spirit. Even though the amulet would still protect her, its energy would drain much faster.

The basement level was just as Gwen remembered it from her last visit. Mostly, it was an unfinished space reserved for storage, food and other essential items. Beyond was a corridor that led to several spare bed chambers with restrooms. There was another kitchen, for what purpose Gwen couldn't imagine, with all the kitchen space upstairs. Near the center were several dumbwaiters, or small elevators for hoisting food and supplies to the main level.

Gwen decided to set up near the kitchen, since it was the largest open space. She laid out a blanket, placed her wand across her lap, and set her crystal globe in front of her. Gwen sat cross-legged and settled in. Soon, she could hear the whispers and grasped the amulet in both palms. The amulet began to heat up, a soothing wave that calmed her nerves and centered her energy. She thought of Kriss…

…then she whispered her name.

Slowly, Gwen's essence started to phase into another plane.

The ethereal realm was full of colors, despite what others believed. Gwen's first trip into the nether region had shocked her. She still remembered that day, witnessing all the colors that had no names…colors that weren't meant for mortals' eyes. And every time she 'phased' into the ethereal realm, she felt stronger, more experienced. That feeling never grew old to her.

Gwen stood from her physical form and steadied herself. She was merely a shadow that had a shape, like her true self, but her shadow had no matter. Still, she wasn't like a spirit: she couldn't just walk through walls. Even as a shade, Gwen still had to follow certain rules.

Her surroundings looked the same, though everything pulsed and vibrated, blurry in her vision. But it was the burst of colors that stole her breath. If Gwen had to guess, she was only a visitor in this world. If she broke the rules, she somehow knew she'd be expelled—*forever.* The biggest question was, what exactly *were* the rules?

One of them, she did know. There was to be no communication, only observance. Mostly, she would listen and follow the spirits, hoping to find a clue as to why they were stuck in both worlds. Gwen began to see multiple shapes around her, which were more like blurbs of light or gossamer strings floating in the wind. They weren't fully defined, more memory than form. Some of the spirits could sense her presence, though. These were the ones that were usually stuck. Gwen had to use caution so that she didn't get too close to them, or she could get caught in their ghost loop.

She walked through the basement and moved into another space she didn't recognize. There were dozens of spirits smushed together, and Gwen could hear them chanting. It sounded fuzzy and muffled in her thoughts. She heard the sound of pickaxes and chisels. She could smell the sweat and dirt of the laborers here. She could hear the crack of a whip and cries of agony…

…and she could sense their anger.

Gwen rushed through the area, searching around and listening, hoping to find a clue. But before long, she could already feel the amulet's energy waning. Its power was getting dangerously weak, and she'd be vulnerable if she wasn't in a safe zone. There were more spirits here than she'd realized, based on how quickly the amulet had drained.

As much as she hated to, Gwen decided to pull her essence back. She felt frustrated at having barely explored the basement, but she had no choice.

Her shadow form slowly merged with her physical being. Gwen settled into herself, finally returning to the land of the living. But since the flow of time was different in the ethereal realm, the night was nearly spent.

Once Gwen regained her equilibrium, she stood and raced up the staircase. The whispers closed in on her as she sprinted, and angry thoughts threatened to infiltrate her mind. There was still enough energy in the amulet to get back to the safe zone if she hurried.

When she made it to the upper level, the amulet's ruby light flickered, and the metal grew cold. Gwen plunged through the doorway of the master suite and slammed the doors shut just as the amulet's light extinguished.

# CHAPTER 17

## *THE DEPARTMENT OF PUBLIC RECORDS*

THE STROBING LIGHT of Gwen's crystal globe brought her world into focus.

She sat up and tried to steady her spinning head. She was lying on the floor, where she'd collapsed from exhaustion. Her wand and globe had tumbled out of her hands and lay next to the massive bed's pedestal post.

Daylight poured through the large windows, and the sound of the Green Sea could be heard from beyond, accompanied by the cawing of sea gulls. Gwen sat there for several seconds, trying to recall what had happened the night before. Then the pulsing from her globe drew her attention. She had several missed messages, all of them from Posh.

She finally stood to her feet, immediately reaching out for the bedpost and thought about vomiting. Reentry into the living realm was usually hell on her system. Gwen sat on the edge of the bed and gazed into her globe, then sent a message to Posh. She answered on the first casting.

"Are you okay?" Posh was sitting on the sofa, a cup of coffee in both hands. She looked a bit tired, her hair a tangled tuft of blue.

"Yes, I'm fine. Just a bit loopy."

"Good," Posh said softly. Then she yelled into the globe. "Why didn't you call me last night? You said you would."

Gwen held the globe at arm's length and turned her head. She placed a hand to her forehead, trying to ease the pounding. "Easy, Posh. I just lost track of time," which was the honest truth.

"Okay, okay. Sorry," Posh said, settling back into the sofa. "I just kept thinking something bad had happened. I almost walked over around midnight—"

"Posh. You have to let me do my job. Trust me, I'm fine. Relax."

A few seconds of silence passed on Posh's end. "Alright. But you have to call me next time."

"I'll try to do a better job. Just understand that when I'm phased into the ethereal realm, you can't do anything for me. It really isn't safe here at night."

"How unsafe is it?"

"More than I originally thought."

"Care to elaborate?"

"No, at least not right now. Not over the globe like this. Maybe later we can talk."

"How about we meet at Sephora Bean? You can tell me about it over a latte?"

"Maybe," Gwen said, still rubbing her forehead. Her migraine was fading, but Gwen wasn't sure if she really felt like company at the moment.

"Come on," Posh persisted. "I could really go for one right now, partner." Posh said the last bit with a wink and a smile.

Gwen frowned into the globe as she held it closer. How could she say no to that? "Give me about an hour and I'll meet you there."

"Well," Posh said, propping her chin in her hand, elbow on the table. "Let's hear it."

Gwen blinked at her from across the booth. It was a bit humid that morning, and the way Posh's blue hair dangled in front of her made Gwen visually trace the highlights of her face. The gold flecks in her eyes seemed to glow in the morning light while her toned shoulders reflected the sun. Gwen had to admit she'd missed Posh, and it had only been one day.

"Give me a minute to catch my breath," Gwen said and took a sip of her latte. Despite her exhaustion, she'd elected to jog all the way to Sephora Bean, a decision she'd regret by midday. She could take a nap later, though. She leaned back into the wicker lounge sofa, savoring the taste of her mint latte while trying to sort her thoughts.

"I take it last night was a doozy?" Posh said.

"You could say that."

"How bad?"

"Worse than I thought it'd be," Gwen said. "I also met Nat, the head groundskeeper."

"I heard the castle got to her years ago," Posh said.

"That's interesting," Gwen replied. "She didn't say anything about that. Who told you?"

"Kershaw, but I don't know where he heard it. Maybe it was our client. Anyway, it was said that Nat got locked inside the castle one evening...*lost*, I think Kershaw said. She was found passed out on the floor."

"Maybe there's some truth to those 'wandering walls' after all?"

"She would only say that she got lost, nothing more. Since then, she seems to have almost erased it from her memory."

Gwen pursed her lips in thought. "I'll look into it. Maybe tonight. It is a big place."

"Will tonight be your last night?" Posh asked in a hopeful tone.

"I can't say. Last night took a lot out of me. I didn't find much."

"Nothing at all?"

"Well, it wasn't a total loss. I did learn one thing." Gwen paused and lowered her voice. "The reason my amulet drained so fast was because there was so much energy in the castle. We're talking about dozens of spirits, maybe hundreds. When there are that many in the same location, it usually means one thing. Something really bad happened to a lot of people."

Gwen and Posh walked back to Java House together. Gwen showered, feeling as though she needed to wash the castle's scent from her skin. Afterwards, she took the coach to the Department of Public Records. With Arman's words stuck in her head, she wondered if the accidental deaths had been reported. If so, they'd be on file, and maybe she could find a clue.

Along the way, Gwen pondered last night's events at Hidden Palm Grove. She'd established there were multiple spirits within the castle. This meant there was a possibility that each spirit had its own 'unsolved' residual. If she had to unravel each case, it could take her years. She didn't know if she could accomplish that, even with the amulet. But if she'd learned anything in all her time as a paranormal realtor, it was that there was usually a common thread. And with so many spirits in one place, she was betting their demise was connected. But finding that common thread wouldn't be easy.

Furthermore, it appeared she would struggle to get any meaningful investigation done. The amulet's power had drained so quickly, she'd barely had time to phase, then make it back to the safe zone. She was going to need to work faster or find a more resourceful method.

When Gwen arrived at the Department of Public Records, she found the information counter.

A dark-skinned fairy hovered behind the counter and batted her eyes at Gwen. "Oh, a green witch. We don't see many of you here in Valeside. What can I help you with?"

Gwen felt an awkward moment as the fairy blinked her eyes in a seductive way. "I'd…like to see the records for accidental deaths at Hidden Palm Grove."

The fairy smiled, then looked into a large crystal globe. She read something to herself, then her expression changed. "I'm sorry. That information is no longer public knowledge."

Gwen furrowed her brow. "Are you saying that it once was, and now it isn't?"

"Maybe," the fairy said. "I don't think I can tell you that."

Gwen shook her head. "That's kind of ridiculous, don't you think?"

"Oh, yes. It's very ridiculous. But still, it's classified now."

Gwen considered for a few seconds. She hated to drop Kershaw's name, but she needed to see that information. "Well, I've been commissioned by Lorenzo Kershaw. Does that help?"

The fairy tilted her head toward the ceiling, thinking. Gwen got the impression that, as cute as the fairy was, intelligence wasn't one of her gifts.

"Okay, that will work." The fairy clapped and giggled. "I just love sharing classified information, and with such an attractive witch…" She handed the large crystal globe over the counter and lowered her voice. "Please hurry."

Gwen cupped her hands around her eyes and peered into the globe.

Inside the crystal, there were pages of parchment that had been stored within. It was thick with documentation of injuries and deaths surrounding the old castle. The records went back nearly eighty years. Gwen read through all the different accidents: slips, falls, drownings, a couple of crane malfunctions. The list went on and on. Arman had mentioned only a few, but there were many more, according to this record.

But as Gwen continued to read through the documents, something else bothered her. During her investigation the night before, she had sensed that the spirits were well beyond the age of the dates in this article. She knew that the original incident—or common thread—was something much older.

# CHAPTER 18

## *RETURN TO ETHEREAL REALM*

GWEN HURRIED BACK to Java House, hoping to spend some time with Posh before heading back to the castle. Somehow, Posh could sense Gwen's uneasiness and tried to find out what had happened at the Department of Public Records. But Gwen sidestepped her questions, saying she'd talk about it later. Instead of pushing the topic, Posh tried to keep things light by suggesting a game of cards. Gwen wanted to kiss her for that. She desired to share everything with Posh lately, but she also needed to relax before heading back to Hidden Palm Grove. She'd need all her focus tonight, and talking about the castle wouldn't help. Posh seemed to respect that.

They managed to get a few rounds of cards in, then they watched a movie over dinner.

Gwen chatted with Posh throughout the night, while grudgingly keeping an eye on the time. At sunset, Gwen and Posh sat on the deck and watched the last rays of sunlight disappear behind the Green Sea.

"It'll be fine," Posh says. "Just search for the details."

Gwen studied Posh and the curving silhouette of her neck. She reached out and brushed her azure-colored hair away, and a bit of steam rose from Posh's shoulders. At that moment, Gwen saw her old friend, Kriss, and realized just how much she missed her.

"You'd better move along…before we get carried away," Posh said with a mischievous grin. "I'll talk to you in the morning."

Gwen hurried along the beach, practically sprinting up the stone pillar's staircase and not stopping until she stood at the castle's veranda.

She heard someone approach from behind. The sound of gravel crunching in the dark made her pause. Finally, Tom appeared from the shadows. The ogre made an attempt at a smile, but his fanged grin looked more menacing than kind.

He tipped his feathered cap, "Back for more, Miss Arris?"

Gwen stepped forward and nodded. "Guess I didn't get enough last night."

Tom took a seat on the wooden porch swing, which creaked under his hefty frame. He took off his hat and armed some sweat from his bald green forehead. "Spent the day down at the grounds shed, bumped into Nat. She said you paid her a visit last evening."

"That's right. She seems like a very nice lady."

"Well, that depends."

"On what?"

Tom rocked the swing a bit faster. "Garden gnomes…can't trust 'em. Especially Nat. She never quite recovered from the castle incident, wandering walls and all. A shame what happened to her."

"I just heard about that today, in fact. Sad, and strange, if what she said is true. Odd, don't you think?"

"What's that?"

"How she seemed to *magically* get locked in the castle."

"I suppose she should've been a bit more careful."

"Am I correct in saying that the housekeeper controls all the keys for the property?"

Tom stood to his full height and glared down at Gwen. She felt for her wand.

"That'd be correct," Tom growled. "I hope you're not insinuatin' that I locked her inside."

"Of course not," Gwen said. "That would be ridiculous, just like all that talk of wandering halls, right?"

Tom eased, as if reconsidering his attitude. Then he raised a bushy eyebrow and hooked his thumbs into his leather jerkin. "Well, what do I know? Only been here my entire life. Still not sure 'bout shifting halls, but something's leechin' out of that castle. Been doing it for a long time, too. Poisoned the grounds, if you ask me. But again, what do I know?"

Gwen took a deep breath and relaxed her grip on her wand. She had no desire to take on an ogre the size of Tom. But the tense moment had abated, and Tom didn't seem to want trouble either. She guessed that Tom understood Kershaw was part of this venture, and he probably didn't want to upset him.

"How many owners have you seen come and go?" Gwen asked.

Tom scrunched up his left eye in consideration, then started tapping a large finger on his lower fang. "Ah, hell. I lost track after the first dozen. This castle never stayed occupied for long."

"That matches what I saw at the County Assessor's records. This castle seems to be on the market every other year."

Tom smirked. "Figures. This castle has a dark history. Wasn't goin' to stay a secret forever. You didn't hear that from me. I imagine our client wouldn't like it. Otherwise, this place is a tough sell."

Gwen thought about Kershaw and his 'business first' attitude. She had to agree with Tom. No, Kershaw wouldn't want that information floating out there in the public. The NDA he'd made her sign proved that. But Gwen wondered how it had all been kept so quiet for so long—*like it had been brushed under the rug over the years.*

Gossip. Hearsay. *Legends perhaps.*

To Gwen, it seemed like a lot of effort…or a lot of steam tokens. Sure, this old castle was worth a fortune just because of the property's location. But she was beginning to see there was a much bigger secret hidden within the walls of Hidden Palm Grove.

Tom chuckled as he studied her expression. "I know what you're thinkin' cause I've been over it a thousand times myself. But hey, just do what you're told, don't ask any questions," Tom said in a dismissive manner. He glanced up at the moon, which was rising in the night sky. "I'd better let you get to work, Miss Arris. Kershaw will have my hide if I get in the way. Besides, the spirits'll be missin' you."

"Tell me something, Tom," Gwen said as the ogre moved toward the steps of the veranda. "Have you ever stopped to wonder how many spirits are inside this castle?"

Tom turned toward her, his towering frame a bit more hunched than when he'd first walked up. "Oh…who can say? Hundreds? Hell, maybe thousands? Nighty-night, Miss Arris."

When Gwen stepped inside the castle, she couldn't stop thinking about Tom's last statement.

Hundreds? *Thousands?*

Of course, she'd known the castle was filled with multiple spirits. But she hadn't considered there might be thousands. If each one was an individual case to be resolved, she would never cleanse Hidden Palm Grove. Again, she had to hope she could find the 'common thread' connecting them. If there had been one defining event—and assuming she could identify it and solve it—then she could possibly cleanse the castle by Saint Halving Day and pay Harris's debt to Bam Jino.

Gwen hurried up to the master suite and prepared for the witching hour. She took out the ruby amulet and draped it around her neck. The metal began to heat up, and the ruby flickered to life. Almost immediately, whispers seemed to emanate from the woodwork. Color flooded her vision. Gossamer strings floated outside the master suite, like spiderwebs on a summer morning. Each strand was caught in a ghost loop, and it was up to her to find out why.

Even though it was her second visit into the ethereal realm here, it felt more alive than just the night before. Gwen had been expecting this, though not so quickly. Once she began an investigation, the site became more receptive. The amount of energy within the castle seemed to be accelerating, even from the night before. The pace caught her by surprise.

Since Gwen couldn't phase from a safe zone, she needed to be outside of the master suite. Even though being in the basement put her closer to the activity, she was worried about being caught too far from a safe zone—last night she'd barely made it back to the master suite in time. Instead, she stepped into the closet and sat cross-legged, waiting for the witching hour, which was just seconds away. With the ruby amulet draped about her neck, Gwen was ready. But just before the witching hour struck, she heard something bumping outside the bedroom door. It sounded more like tapping, like someone or something was chipping away at the door.

Gwen checked the time. Her skin had already faded into a shadow, translucent and vague. She was nearly phased out of the physical world now—a shade of her former self.

She rose to her feet and felt like she was floating. Gwen approached the door.

The ticking noise grew louder.

She grasped the doorknob and gave it a slow twist, and the door swung open.

What Gwen saw was something she'd never seen before.

A floating knife struck the door, pulled back, and repeatedly struck it again.

It was the missing butter knife from the kitchen below.

# CHAPTER 19
## *SPELLBINDER*

IT WAS A fine utensil, the pommel fashioned from high-quality pearl and pewter with green emeralds, though the blunt tip of the blade was slightly bent. Gwen could hear a whisper from the butter knife, a phrase that repeated over and over.

*...they didn't deserve this...*

She recognized it as a residual pattern, and a potential clue. The problem was that she couldn't make contact with the spirit. That was forbidden while she was in the ethereal realm.

Gwen stood near the knife, watching in fascination. She'd never seen such an occurrence—*a haunted butter knife?*

But then the knife stopped, turned and reoriented toward her.

This was another first. *A sentient haunted butter knife?*

It hovered a few inches from her face, and she wondered how it could even detect her. Most entities normally didn't notice her shade while she was phased.

Gwen stood still, hardly daring to breathe. But as the knife inched forward, she sensed its uncertainty.

She thought about stepping back into the safety of the master suite. Instead, she held her ground and waited, curious now.

But the knife stopped, pivoted, and floated down the corridor as if it was looking for someone in particular.

Gwen let out a sigh of relief. She wasn't frightened, just a bit unnerved. She'd never seen such a strange occurrence, but she was betting it wouldn't be the last within this castle.

She hurried down the circular staircase, avoiding the gossamer spirits as she ran. When she reached the bottom landing, she paused. She could continue down another flight and reach the basement. But she didn't want to go to the basement tonight. If she did, it would drain her amulet quickly, due to the amount of spirits there. Besides, something seemed to be pressing her toward the ground level.

Gwen walked into the living chamber, which was one of the three large rooms that made up the ground level. Moonlight from the clerestory windows landed on the large mural she'd been so impressed with during her first visit.

The angle of the moon seemed to align perfectly, highlighting the painting and beckoning her in closer. She recalled Kershaw had bragged about it, an up-and-coming local artist—*what was his name again? Rodrick Tanzier?*

The Friar's Inferno and the Three Rings of Hell.

Gwen noticed the paint strokes and how they glimmered in the moonlight. It was a spiraling, swirling technique, as if a ghostly wind pushed the paint strokes around the canvas. Gwen could almost hear those strokes, speaking to her as if the wind was trying to tell a story. The longer she stared, the more she felt as one with the painting. Gwen could envision herself within the scene, voyaging into the pits of hell and seeking out the secrets of the Friars.

Maybe it was because she was phased, but the jumble of shapes and geometries were organized in the semblance of a tall spire or turret…

…or a lighthouse.

Like a ray of sunlight, inspiration hit her.

"It's the lighthouse," she whispered. "That must be the next step in this madness."

Gwen raced toward where she thought the lighthouse might be. It was already getting late, and she was concerned that the amulet's power would run out soon. The last place she wanted to get stranded was the lighthouse. It was probably filled with spirits, but she had to get there tonight.

The hallways of the castle meandered and twisted and turned. Gwen had to guess a few times, but eventually she found the long winding staircase that led up to the lighthouse.

She climbed the spiral staircase, which seemed to take an eternity.

Finally, she dropped to her knees on the top landing. In front of her stood a set of rusted doors that led into the ancient lighthouse. Gwen remained doubled over on her knees, trying to catch her breath. Eventually, she stood and fumbled for the key ring that Tom had given her. She sorted through them, cursing with each wrong guess and wishing good ole' Tom had labeled them. She finally found the right one, which happened to be shaped like a lighthouse, and placed it in the keyhole. She had to jiggle it a few times and put her shoulder into the large iron door to turn the key. It groaned from decades of disuse as a cloud of dust plumed out, reminding her of a crypt that hadn't been opened in ages.

Gwen used her heavy boot to prop the door open. She poked her head through the crack and tucked the wide brim of her hat to one side.

All was silent beyond.

After a few more seconds, she stepped into the lighthouse, letting the iron doors shut behind her with a thud.

Since she was still in her phased form, everything was colored in chaotic shades. But the view from this height was majestic. The cloud tops looked like cotton candy, swirling and shifting colors like an undulating rug. Pops of pastels lit the cloudscape, even in the dark evening sky, which had a calming effect on her. She stepped up to one of the large, curved windows and knelt on the sill. Through the cloud breaks, Gwen could see the land formations below like a colorful quilt. The rooftop of the castle sprawled out below, and the beach looked like a dark blanket. Beyond was the Green Sea—a darkened mass that reflected the moonlight in thousands of tiny eclipses.

The lighthouse was a large circular chamber with a full panoramic view. Gwen was surprised to see a massive telescope at the center instead of a beacon, though. There was a curving staircase leading up to it. She thought that odd, considering this was originally a lighthouse, not an observatory. At the base of the stairs was a plaque made of brass that read: *SPELLBINDER*.

Gwen guessed that the telescope was about ten meters in length. It was a large cone-shaped tube that tapered down to a small eyehole or oculus on the closer end. At the far end was a massive lens, and the metal was some strange, golden-hued alloy that shifted in her vision. It was set on a pyramid-shaped pivot like a ball bearing fulcrum. Gears, cranks, and cogs surrounded it, all connected by chains with steam pumping gently from beneath it like the strange contraption was still functional. Etched into the floor surrounding the telescope were charts and coordinates and other golden symbols that looked like some arcane language. Gwen knelt to get a better look and saw that around the perimeter was something like a circular ruler. If she had to guess, it seemed like a stargazer's map. She thought she recognized some constellations woven around the sigils. But when she looked closer, she noticed they were actually shaped like ordinary objects. They were animals or trees or buildings. But there were perhaps hundreds of sigils, all embedded within the floor. However, there were several missing, and she had no idea what it all meant. But in that moment, Gwen knew two things for certain.

First, there were no spirits within the lighthouse, which made it a safe zone.

Second, she knew her next step in solving the mystery behind Hidden Palm Grove was gazing into the telescope called Spellbinder.

# PART TWO

## SPELLBINDER'S GAME

# CHAPTER 20

## *THE GOLDEN RULES*

AFTER A FEW more trips around the circular chamber, she slipped her amulet off, and her physical form solidified, bringing her body back into the realm of the living. Then, Gwen climbed the staircase up to the telescope. Upon closer inspection, the casing of the telescope was engraved with thousands of incantations. Gwen had seen a few magical artifacts over the years and understood that this one had been imbued with some mystical attributes. But what those were was beyond her arcane knowledge.

When she reached the top of the staircase, she gave the telescope a gentle nudge. The ten-meter-long tube rotated on the pyramid fulcrum with ease. Thinking again about the three missing sigils, her detective instinct took over, and she turned the telescope in the first one's direction. Then, she peered into the oculus.

What Gwen saw was an island, far away from Valeside Beach. It was a lush green dot in the vast sea. At the very center of the island, the telescope zoomed in on one massive tree. It was a bright golden color, almost too bright to be real. Spellbinder continued to reveal the huge tree in greater clarity. Gwen watched, captivated. She could see every leaf with exquisite detail, even down to the veining. She watched as birds built nests or squirrels rummaged for acorns. She could see the wind ruffling the leaves in a mesmerizing way. Amongst the thousands of other trees, this one stood out. Gwen knew it was a special tree.

She pulled her gaze from the oculus, flabbergasted.

*How is this possible?*

Somehow, this magical telescope, Spellbinder, seemed to be leading her to the next clue. Was it coincidence that she had stumbled upon the painting that had led her to the lighthouse, which had, in fact, housed this artifact?

How things had taken a turn.

It seemed that the answer to solving the mystery behind Hidden Palm Grove—and in turn, freeing all the spirits within—was by way of

Spellbinder. She knew then that this challenge was beyond her ruby amulet, beyond her own ability.

Someone, or something, was leading her on a scavenger hunt, it seemed.

Gwen tried to turn the telescope toward one of the other missing sigils. But it seemed to be locked in place now. She leaned her shoulder into it, pushing with all her strength. She even turned some of the gears and pulled a few levers. But nothing seemed to work. It appeared that the telescope had given her marching orders, and it wouldn't budge until that task had been completed, at least, that's what she assumed. Whatever she was supposed to do would be revealed at the special tree on the island, it seemed.

She stepped down from the telescope.

In her curiosity, she had lost track of time. She was still within the witching hour, but at least she was in a safe zone there in the lighthouse. But Gwen really didn't want to sit around until dawn. She felt anxious now. She took the stairs down the tall spire and to a window at midlevel, where she propped it open and worked her way along the castle's rampart. In the moonlight, she eventually found a drainpipe and shimmied her way down to ground level unscathed.

It was a cool night, and, unfortunately, there was no way of getting back to the master suite. She could walk back to Java House, but Gwen really didn't want to disturb Posh. So, she decided to go for a walk around the estate to ease her racing mind. Eventually, Gwen found herself standing in front of Nat's cottage. There was a light on and smoke lifting from the stone chimney.

Gwen walked around back and saw the garden gnome sitting in a chair, gazing up at the stars. Nat saw Gwen and waved her over.

"Why, what brings you out so late?" Nat asked. She patted the spot next to her.

Gwen walked over and sat down, thankful to be off her feet. Nat immediately offered her a blanket.

"Cup of lavender tea? I have a pot on the hearth."

"Thanks," Gwen said. "That'd really hit the spot."

Nat went inside, and a few seconds later, handed Gwen a steaming mug.

Gwen took a sip, warming her hands on the mug and breathing in the aroma.

"Why are you wandering about?" Nat asked. "Couldn't sleep?"

"You could say that." Gwen chuckled. "Actually, I lost track of time."

Nat hummed. "Oh, you mean you got too far away from the safe zone."

Gwen arched her brow in surprise. "Excuse me?"

"I know about the zones, more than I care to."

"I keep forgetting about your experience in the castle. I'm sorry."

Nat leaned back and looked up at the stars again. She seemed to shrink into herself as she spoke, like she was reliving a horrifying experience. "I was lost for several days within the castle. Those walls shifted, like the castle didn't want me to leave. It was the lighthouse that saved me."

Gwen perked up. "What? You know about that place?"

Nat gave her a knowing smile. "Ah, I see you stumbled upon our friend, Spellbinder."

Gwen sat back in her seat. She looked at Nat with narrowed eyes. "It appears you know more than I do. What can you tell me?"

"Spellbinder called to me, as it did to you, it would seem. The way is hidden to all unless it deems you worthy…as a friend."

Gwen chuckled again. "Well, Nat…you're full of surprises. You have my attention."

"It will grant what you most desire, which in your case would be solving the mystery of Hidden Palm Grove. But do you know why you desire that so much?"

Gwen thought for a moment. She craved a good challenge. She'd taken the job from Kershaw because she couldn't resist trying to solve the mystery. But in the back of her mind, she knew there was more to it.

"I want to set those spirits free."

Nat smiled and patted Gwen on her shoulder. "It is a worthy desire. That is why Spellbinder calls to you. That is why it will show you the way. And…that is why you must follow. These are its golden rules."

Gwen didn't know what to say. She held the mug of tea close to her lips and simply stared at the tiny garden gnome. If things had taken a strange turn with the magical telescope, then they had gone even further off the tracks with Nat.

"And why did Spellbinder call to you?" Gwen asked.

Nat held Gwen's gaze for an uncomfortable minute. "Because I wished to free someone from their regret."

"Sounds worthy. Who?"
"Tom. For locking me inside the castle when I was a child."

# CHAPTER 21

## *LEGEND OF THE SIGILS*

SO, TOM DID lock you in?" Gwen asked.

"He did," Nat said. There was no hesitation in her response.

"But he sounded pretty confident that it wasn't him when I asked," Gwen said.

"That's because his memory of that moment was erased when I forgave him. That was my desire. I hold no grudge against Tom, and neither should you. He has a stubborn personality, but deep down, there's a good person in there. Hopefully, I can help him find that someday. Though it was a traumatic time in my life, we were both young. He's no longer like that."

"So, you didn't want him to bear that guilt for the rest of his life?" Gwen said. "That was very gracious of you. I suppose that's why Spellbinder called to you?"

"Precisely. The enchantment it grants only works that way."

"Do you know its history?" Gwen asked. "I mean, how did it end up there? I thought it was a lighthouse, but inside it seems to be designed to house the telescope."

"As best I can tell, it was always meant to disguise the telescope. The wandering halls are another enchantment used to keep the uninvited out. The selfish would find a way to exploit Spellbinder."

"Though…I seemed to find it with no problem. I guess that's because I was invited."

Nat nodded her head, then clasped her tiny hands in her lap. "Now, as far as its history, there isn't much written about Spellbinder. It does seem to have a conscience. What it truly is and where it came from, I do not know. But I have kept its location a secret and so should you."

Gwen shook her head in disbelief. "How does it work?"

"You must collect three sigils, or keys, if you will. They must be returned in sequence to see the next clue. Only then will it grant your desire."

"So, let me get this straight. A magical telescope will grant me a wish of what I desire the most, as long as it's considered worthy, and only *if* I find and replace the three golden sigils it has chosen for me?"

"Correct. Spellbinder only offers this challenge to the ones it deems worthy. It has called to you, even though you didn't know it."

"And...now that I know, I must follow through?" Gwen asked with some incredulity.

"It seeks your desire, if that makes sense. There is no turning back."

"Okay, that's interesting," Gwen said. "Not that I would turn back even if I could. I just think it's odd that I wasn't given a choice."

"You were given a choice when you made the decision to take on this challenge of cleansing the castle."

Gwen thought back to her agreement with Kershaw. She'd felt a bit guilty about taking on the commission now, mainly because of the salary attached to it. Though she needed the tokens for Harris, deep down, there had always been the hope of freeing the spirits within the castle. That thought made her feel better about her decision, knowing it had been grounded in a worthy desire.

"My amulet isn't powerful enough, I'm afraid," Gwen said. "It seems Spellbinder showed up just in time."

"And yet, I sense that you still have questions."

"Well, yes. I am curious if you remember seeing a butter knife while in the castle."

"Oh yes. I did meet her," Nat chuckled.

"Her?"

"Matilda. She was the head chef a long time ago. That's when some sort of incident happened."

"So, there *is* a common thread, then?" Gwen said and clapped her hands together. "I knew it. Usually, when there are this many spirits in one location it means the spirits' fates are tied together. If I can unravel what that was and find a way to fix it, I think I can free them all at once. Do you think it has something to do with Matilda?"

"I don't know exactly, but I think she might be a good place to start."

Gwen nodded. "Makes sense, only I can't interact with spirits." She set her mug down and stood to leave. "Thank you again. I'll let you get back to your stargazing."

Nat stood and clasped her hands together. "You are welcome to stay. I know it's a long walk back to Java House."

Gwen thought for only a few seconds. "Actually, that would be nice."

Gwen stayed the night in Nat's guest bedroom. It was a cozy little room with a corner hearth and a small bed. On the walls were paintings of some unique and sought-after flowers and trees in Ambriel, all signed by Nat. Gwen recognized them, having been well-versed in the lore of herbology. It reminded her of those days at Encantar University, where she'd minored in the arcane study of plants and how to utilize them properly. There were all kinds of ways to kill with plants: asphyxiation with the Carotyd Flower, strangulation with the Python Vine, eternal hallucination with the Serebel Nightingale. Even a large tree could be commanded to uproot and fight. But her favorite had always been thorny rose nettle. She loved the plant and the beauty of the roses' minty green and pink colors, which had always drawn her in, along with their fragrance. The nettle portion could be used in many ways, including its healing properties. But the thorns could be deadly. It was a versatile, strong, beautiful and mysterious plant, which was why she felt drawn to it. If she could choose a single plant, it would be thorny rose nettle because it represented her principles in life better than anything else. She'd even fashioned her rosewood wand from it.

Being able to enchant and control the flora and fauna of the forests and woods was one of her abilities, known as *phyto-mori*, meaning plant death. Thankfully, she'd never been inclined to do such things. And, thankfully, she hadn't experienced many of those situations during her three years with the ministry. Only on one occasion, when she'd stumbled upon a crew of ogres, had she been forced to turn a stand of rose nettle into a barrage of thorny projectiles. She hated destroying plants or trees, which was always the result after controlling them. Where red witches were aggressive and looked for opportunities to use their elemental magic, and yellow witches, who were more haphazard with their animal magic, Gwen was thankful that green witches were more controlled in their use of magic. Otherwise, Ambriel would be a far less peaceful place to live.

In the morning, she spent a little time with Nat over a cup of coffee, but she was in a hurry to be on her way to the castle. She thanked Nat again and promised to stop by on occasion to chat, which Nat was very thankful for.

The air was sultry that morning on her walk back to Hidden Palm Grove. She waved at Tom, who was working around the castle. He tipped his feathered hat and went right back to work. Gwen entered the castle's lobby. Although Posh would be expecting a call from her soon, Gwen had a few things she needed to check out, now that the witching hour had ended. Primarily, she wanted more information on the magical telescope named Spellbinder, though Matilda and her butter knife were still in the back of her mind.

Hidden Palm Grove had its own library, and she might find some answers there. Although it was a massive library of old tomes, it wasn't as large as the downtown Valeside library. Still, she was betting it had information that wasn't privy to the public, maybe even arcane knowledge on magical relics. Gwen wondered if this private library might have some forgotten historical data about the castle itself.

She brought out her rosewood wand and used a luminance spell to light the way through the castle, searching for the library. She was still learning her way around, and remembering which passages felt obscure in her mind. She recalled passing by the library only once.

She walked through corridors, finding many side rooms and vacant storage closets she hadn't noticed before. After what felt like hours, Gwen finally turned a corner and paused. Before her was the castle's private library, though she could've sworn it had been in the east wing.

Its main hall was wide and tall, soaring some fifteen meters perhaps. Heavy timber trusses spanned the vaulted ceiling, intricately carved in oak and stained a deep amber color. She could see cobwebs between the trusses, pulsing and swaying in rhythm with the low breeze. The walls were limestone with a light patina, and the shelving reached near the bottom chord of the trusses. The width of the library filled the entire floor of the wing, maybe twenty meters. And in the middle were islands of shelving lined with thousands of dusty tomes. Gwen looked at the sea of books, her hand to her forehead. *How was she going to find anything in all of this?*

Maybe there was a card catalog system or something that could help her track down what she needed? She walked down the aisles while searching through the files and drawers. Near one end, she noticed a counter and worked her way around the books. Behind the counter were dozens of drawers, most of them locked. She used her wand and a simple rummage spell to sift through them until she found several dusty scrolls. One was labeled 'ancient artifacts.' The label had **6A** on the top.

Gwen took the scroll and marched down the aisles until she found the one labeled **6A**, then walked among the tomes, letting her fingertips brush the spines. There was something charming about books to her. Growing up through her college days, she'd found a fascination with libraries. Maybe it was the vibe, or the quiet atmosphere, or maybe just the fact that the knowledge written within was power. It made her feel giddy, especially the older tomes.

She found a section with several leather-bound books, most of them very large, and stopped at one labeled, "Mystic Artifacts.' She had to use the step ladder to get it, then found an old wooden table and sat down. As she leafed through the old tome, the information page claimed the book had been written in the 8th age, which had been hundreds of years ago. The author had been none other than the wizard named Speartine himself. Gwen recalled him from legend as a misguided sorcerer who'd designed many strange artifacts, some of his inventions more successful than others.

Gwen flipped gingerly through the pages, which were dry and cracked. When she turned to chapter nineteen, it was titled: *Spellbinder.*

Gwen settled into the old wooden chair and read the entire chapter.

According to the codex, Spellbinder only revealed itself to those it felt were worthy, which aligned with what Nat had told her. That made Gwen smile. However, the mythical telescope worked in a way that seemed a bit awkward. It would weigh the user's desire, then it would reveal the path to achieving said desire through a series of quests—three to be exact. Once the special keys, or sigils, were found and returned to Spellbinder, the subject's desire would be granted.

Gwen remembered seeing the flooring of the lighthouse where Spellbinder was housed. It had been missing several of those keys or golden sigils. Nat's theory and this tome were starting to align. Gwen had already accepted that freeing the spirits of Hidden Palm Grove was beyond her ability. Here was this powerful tool, which had revealed itself to her, no less. Though her pride had taken a hit at not being able to solve this on her own merits, she wasn't one to stare a gift horse in the mouth.

Gwen thought about stealing the tome. There was no one around, and anyone who cared was probably long dead. She started to replace it on the shelf but then slipped it into her satchel. If no one believed her about the telescope, she could use the book as proof. Then Gwen made her way out of the library and back to the master suite, where she showered and changed into a fresh set of her green robes. There was a message in her crystal globe from Posh when she finished—*meet me at Sephora Bean.*

The beach stroll was pleasant, as usual. Couples meandered along the shoreline and lounged on the white sand, soaking up the sun. The beachfront restaurants were in full swing, preparing for the lunch crowd. Gwen removed her boots and walked barefoot, letting the sand ooze between her toes and soothe her. Soon, she was approaching Sephora Bean. The strong smell of coffee hit her and sent her head abuzz.

Posh was seated in the normal booth with one arm draped over the back and steam rising from her blue skin. She gazed calmly out across the white sands.

Gwen slid in across from Posh, a mint latte waiting for her on the table. Gwen could clearly see she was upset.

Posh let out a disgruntled sigh. "Guess what you forgot to do last night?"

Gwen took a tentative sip of her latte, bracing herself for Posh's verbal onslaught.

"Not talking?" Posh prodded. She leaned onto the table. "Gimme something, Gwen. An excuse, make something up, I don't care. But don't ignore me."

"Okay, I'm sorry, Posh. I got carried away, again. But this is how things happen sometimes. If I can check in with you, I will. I need you to understand that."

Posh continued to stare at her for a few more seconds, then frowned. "Well, what was it that kept you from calling?"

Gwen shook her head, not sure where to begin. "I guess the night started with the paintings."

"Paintings?" Posh said. "Which ones?"

"Remember the mural in the living room, Rodrick Tanzier?"

"Right, the up-and-coming local painter. *The Friar's Inferno.*"

"When I was phased into the ethereal realm, I seemed to see it with more detail. Long story short, it led me to the lighthouse."

"Okay…" Posh muttered in an uncertain tone, her voice trailing off.

"Turns out, the lighthouse was never designed to function as one."

"No? You're certain?" Posh said, leaning in.

Gwen lowered her voice. "That's right. It was designed to house a magical artifact."

"Alright, I'm intrigued."

"Gwen pulled the old tome from her satchel and laid it on the table. She thumbed to chapter nineteen and rotated the book so Posh could read it."

"Spellbinder?" Posh whispered. It was hard not to notice the look on her face. Her eyebrows lifted with intrigue and nearly disappeared into her blue tufted hair. Even the steam pouring off her skin seemed to thicken. "Ooh, it's shiny." She traced the picture with her fingertips, her golden eyes glinting.

"That's right. Spellbinder's a magical artifact that just so happens to be stashed inside the lighthouse."

Posh flipped the book back around. "Alright. I assume it's important?"

Gwen dropped her voice even lower and read the passage that described how Spellbinder worked. After she finished, Posh's eyes were wide.

"So, it called to you?" Posh said, a bit of doubt in her voice.

"As strange as it sounds, this thing has offered to grant my wish, or desire, I guess. But only if I can retrieve three golden sigils and return them to the lighthouse."

Posh looked at the book again. "So, you're going to believe everything written in this book? Seems like we should verify this."

"Well, I kind of already did that with Nat."

"The groundskeeper?" Posh said. "You trust a garden gnome's word?"

"Yes, because she actually had a similar quest from Spellbinder. Everything she told me checks out with this book."

Posh still looked doubtful and rubbed her chin.

"Come on, Posh," Gwen said. "I'm at the end of my ability, even with the ruby amulet. Hidden Palm Grove…there are just too many spirits. But with this artifact, I might be able to do this."

Posh chuckled. "A magical telescope. Who would've thought?"

Gwen waited patiently, taking small sips from her latte.

"Okay, well, looks like we're going on a quest. I just didn't see this twist coming. Where do we begin?"

Gwen placed the codex back in her leather satchel. "When I looked through the telescope, it revealed an island in the Green Sea. It focused on a massive tree. I think that's where we will find the first sigil."

"Was it a golden tree?" Posh asked.

"Actually…yes, it was," Gwen said. "Do you know of it?"

"It's called the November Tree, in the Autumn Forest."

"Do you know how to get there?"

"I know the general direction," Posh said. "It's said that the November Tree only appears once a year, and not many know when and where. The Autumn Forest is vast and ancient."

Gwen thought it odd that she, a green witch, had never heard of the Autumn Forest or the November Tree. "I feel like we need to go visit this place," she said.

"And what then? No maps exist to the November Tree, and I don't know anyone who could guide us there."

"We'll just have to figure it out once we get to the Autumn Forest," Gwen said. "Have a little faith."

# CHAPTER 22
## *LINHEM*

GWEN HAD SOME direction now, though it was a bit muddled. At least, Posh was on board with this new quest, which Gwen was thankful for. Deep down, she wondered if there was more to Spellbinder than just quests for golden sigils. Gwen's intuition warned her that this magical telescope had a deeper story to tell, and before it was all said and done, she intended to find out what it was.

The next day, Gwen and Posh booked two tickets to the Autumn Forest Isle, which was west of Valeside Beach in the Bay of Fireflies. Gwen wasn't too fond of travel, especially across water. Though she was nervous about the sea voyage, Posh, who'd traveled by sea many times, assured her it was a safe mode of travel.

Their voyage would take place aboard a large vessel named *The Sea Grazer*. The vessel was several hundred feet in length and perhaps fifteen or so levels deep. Great sails and steam-powered engines propelled the vessel. As they boarded, Gwen felt the ocean spray on her face and the thrum of the propulsion system beneath her feet. The trip would take a full day. Tickets aboard the luxury cruiser weren't cheap, but Kershaw's account covered them—*perks of the job*, Posh had trilled.

Posh had brought along a magic purse, which she had stuffed most of her possessions into. To say she traveled light was an understatement, considering the compact nature of the purse. Gwen, however, had little to bring: one extra robe (she always brought an extra robe), a backup wand, an extra pair of boots—one for inclement weather—and of course her journal and the codex from the castle's private library.

Their sleeping quarters were near the top deck at the front of the ship, giving their two rooms a spectacular view. The top deck had plenty of areas for lounging or soaking up the sun. There were also a few pools, soakers and steam saunas. Below was a workout facility and spa, which Posh immediately visited after they'd unpacked.

Gwen found a lounge chair on the top deck and opened the codex book to skim through it again. As she'd noticed before, the sorcerer named Speartine had created many additional artifacts: spears, swords, spellbooks and even wands. It was a very intriguing tome, one that she found herself evermore drawn to.

As Gwen lounged in her robe (green skin was, in fact, susceptible to sunburn), the shadow of someone loomed over her. She shielded her eyes and looked up.

A large male griffin sat on its hind haunches and stared at her with its eagle eyes. The sharp beak was yellow and downturned, like a dangerous hooked weapon. Even seated, the griffin was seven feet tall, its eagle feathers bright white and reflecting the sun. The creature tilted its head as she sat up.

"Hello," Gwen said, sliding her robes down from her knees a bit. "Can I help you?"

"Indeed," the griffin said. "I just noticed your reading material. I haven't seen one of the great codex tomes in many years. Of course, being a librarian, I had to introduce myself. My name is LinHem."

Gwen returned his gaze, a bit curious now. She'd never heard of a griffin librarian. Most griffins were soldiers, seen in wars or militias. Even the retired ones were hired as mercenaries or sometimes generals. The towering griffin stood majestically. Its lower body was that of a lion, and it rippled with power and strength, though its spectacles were bent and patinaed in several places.

"My name is Gwenevere Arris," she said. "Sorry, I don't mean to stare. It's just that I've never met a griffin librarian before."

"Not to worry," LinHem replied. "I must admit, it is a bit of a paradox. I've been drawn to books my entire life, though. Naturally, I gravitate toward others who read. It's hard to miss, for me at least, and especially something as unique as what you're reading."

"Sure," Gwen said slowly, still at a loss. "I'm intrigued by knowledge as well. If you would like, you're welcome to have a look. I don't mind sharing."

The look on LinHem's face was one of surprise and genuine shock. "Hmm…actually, that would be amazing. Thank you. Though I might recommend we take the codex inside. The sun's rays could damage the book. It is very old, to be sure. Sorry, this is the librarian coming out in me."

"No, it's a good point. I think I've had enough sun for today. Where shall we go?"

"There's a great reading room on the level just below us."

The two of them left the upper deck—Gwen felt she was starting to burn anyway—and they located the reading room. LinHem was right, the space was large, open, and airy. The indirect sunlight was perfect for reading.

They found a common table and settled in. The griffin barely fit into the chair, which obviously hadn't been designed for larger creatures. But he seemed content to sit on his hind haunches anyway as they read through the old tome.

Gwen flipped the pages for him, since his clawed talons were a bit unwieldy, though in truth, she thought he did just fine. He was very dexterous, and she could see he was a gentle beast, his love for books evident in how he tapped the pages.

"What brings you on this voyage?" Gwen asked.

"Actually, I'm heading to the Autumn Forest," LinHem said. "I'm on a sabbatical, and the forest is my favorite place in Ambriel. Might I ask how you came across this book? It is in impeccable condition, considering its age."

Gwen wasn't sure how much she should share. There were confidentiality concerns regarding her agreement with Aloe Realtors. She decided to play it down. "I know a friend with a private collection. He…let me bring this along for research purposes."

"I see. And where are you heading with such an elaborate codex, if you don't mind me asking?"

"Actually, the same place as you. The Autumn Forest."

"Alone?" LinHem squawked, ruffling his feathers. "You know, there are dark places in that forest. You don't want to be traveling alone after dark."

"Oh, is that so?"

"Yes. You should have a guide, at least. The forest is vast and easy to get lost in, and I know my way around it."

"I have a friend with me," Gwen said.

"Has she experienced the forest?"

Gwen considered as she gazed at the griffin. She thought it was odd timing, meeting this winged beast who happened to like ancient tomes and also happened to be heading to the same place. "I'm not certain if she has, but I think we can manage."

"Well. I don't mind accompanying you, if you are open to the idea. Seems we are heading in the same general direction."

Gwen narrowed her eyes. "I'll consider it. I'd like to talk to my partner first."

"I understand," LinHem said. "In the meantime, may I continue to inspect this fine specimen of a book?" LinHem straightened his glasses and leaned over to gaze at the tome again. "Hmm…yes. Oh, I see here a sketch of the famous telescope, Spellbinder. Very interesting. Wands, swords, speaking amulets—"

"Really?" Gwen said. "Speaking amulets, you say?" She leaned in to look at the book. "Odd that I hadn't seen this one yet."

"I'm somewhat familiar with those," LinHem hummed. "The sorcerer named Speartine was said to create sentient jewelry quite often. Amulets were popular with him."

As LinHem leaned in, Gwen's amulet slipped out, and she clasped a hand over it, tucking it back into her heavy robes.

"Pardon?" LinHem said, cocking his head. "What was that?"

"Nothing," Gwen said abruptly.

LinHem gave her an odd look but continued reading. "Well, again, a very intriguing book. I should like to have more time to study it, for educational purposes, of course." He scooted back and folded his wings. "You mentioned a partner? Does this person have a name?"

"She does," Gwen said, and turned to face the griffin and crossed her arms. "But first, I'm curious, LinHem. Why are you so interested in me and this book? Seems very odd that you happen to be here at the same time, don't you think?"

"Oh, goodness. I apologize, Gwenevere. It seems I've overstepped my boundaries. I didn't mean to impose upon you. Maybe I should leave."

LinHem stood to walk out of the reading room.

"No, wait." Gwen cleared her throat. "There's no need for that. It's probably fine. At least let me introduce you to my partner, Posh."

LinHem paused, then gave a gentle bow. "That would be wonderful. Thank you."

"I think she's in the spa. Let's go up top and wait for her."

They made their way to the upper deck, sat under an umbrella, and enjoyed the breeze. There were all manner of creatures milling about and sightseeing. It was great peoplewatching: fairies, ogres, gnomes, and even a few yellow witches. In the distance, they could see some mermaids and sea serpents cutting through the water.

Gwen lay back and closed her eyes as LinHem continued to look through the book. It wasn't long before Gwen felt someone's presence and opened her eyes to see Posh standing next to them, her arms crossed and a scowl on her face.

# CHAPTER 23

## *GRINDLE-TOP*

POSH GLARED AT LinHem, then Gwen. "What exactly is this about?"

Gwen sat up and pulled the brim of her hat down a bit lower. "Umm…Posh. This is LinHem. He has an interest in the book, and he happens to be headed in the same direction as us. Thought he might tag along." The look on Posh's face told Gwen she wasn't interested, though.

The genie continued to glare between the two of them, a bit of steam coming from her skin.

"Come on, Posh," Gwen continued. "Lighten up. We could use the company—"

"Really?" Posh said wistfully. "Already tired of *my* company?"

"You know that's not what I meant."

Posh remained silent, arms still crossed.

Gwen stood and pulled Posh by the elbow. "Excuse us just a moment," she said to LinHem and led Posh to the far railing. They leaned against it, and Gwen lowered her voice. "What's wrong with adding to our team?"

"Seriously?" Posh hissed. "That's a griffin."

"Yes, I noticed. So?"

"Have you ever seen one of those things get riled up?"

"Well…no. Does that happen often?"

"That's what I've heard, and it's not pretty if it does."

"Okay. I can see how that might be an issue. But LinHem seems pretty tame; he's a librarian, not some mercenary. I don't sense any aggression in him."

Gwen looked over her shoulder at the griffin, who was lying on an oversized lounge chair now, his lion's paws and eagle claws kicked up, a smile stretched across his beak.

"I mean, look at him. Does he look dangerous?" Gwen continued.

Posh frowned. "All I see are claws and that sharp beak."

"He seems fairly knowledgeable about the book, the telescope and the forest we're heading to. And, now that you mention those claws, it might be nice to have him around, just in case. Who knows what we'll find in the forest?"

Posh finally uncrossed her arms and leaned her head. Gwen could see her starting to come around to the idea of adding a griffin to their team.

"Anyway. If he does go berserk, you're a genie. You could handle him, right?"

Posh squinted one eye at Gwen. "You really think I'd use my wish-magic on him?"

"Well, I still think it's a good idea to invite him along," Gwen said, not budging.

Posh glanced over her shoulder at the basking griffin. "Alright, Gwen. This is your show anyway."

"Wrong," Gwen said, and gripped Posh by the shoulders. "It's our show, alright?"

Posh held Gwen's gaze, her golden-flecked eyes steady. "Okay. Let's go talk to him."

They both walked over and stood in front of the griffin as he lay on his back, paws and claws still pointing skyward. Gwen cleared her throat.

"Ah," LinHem said and cracked one eye open. "There you both are." He rolled over and sat on his haunches, waiting.

"We have discussed it," Gwen said, "and we'd be happy if you accompanied us, that is, as long as you're heading our direction."

"Excellent." LinHem bowed low. "I am on my way to study the November Tree on my sabbatical, anyway. But I would very much appreciate the chance to research the codex along the way. Thank you." He bowed low again.

"Great…no need to bow," Gwen said, a bit flustered as she tried to pull him up. "Posh, would you like to say something?"

Posh stood in front of LinHem, looking up into his eagle eyes. "I've heard about the 'berserker rage' from griffins. Can you give us any assurance that you will not do such a thing?"

The griffin brought one of his eagle wings to his feathered chest as if he might faint. "Heavens, no! I have never been under such bloodlust, and I never will. Unlike other griffins, there is very little military training in my lineage. My father and mother were both scholars, though my elder brothers did join the marksman brigade. Well, I can assure you no such thing will happen."

Posh finally nodded. "Then I feel better about your company."

The griffin bowed again, not nearly as low this time. "Very well. I shall meet you at the gate tomorrow morning." LinHem spread his wings and leapt into the air and flew off, searching for dinner, Gwen assumed.

Later that evening, Gwen and Posh settled into their quarters. After a full day in the sun, Gwen felt exhausted and was ready for some downtime. Posh, still uncertain about adding LinHem, found her magic purse and immediately whisked herself into it without a word.

Gwen lay in her bed, looking out the portal-shaped window. In the distance, she watched the sun set, a splash of pink and magenta soaked across the rolling Green Sea. As she watched the sun sink into the ocean, she wondered again about their chance meeting with LinHem. It was almost too coincidental to be ignored, which made her think immediately of Spellbinder and its strange enchantments. Could it be that the artifact, which had been referred to as a 'sentient object', was looking out for her best interest? Or was this simply a chance encounter?

Early the next morning, Gwen and Posh had their things packed and ready. Of course, Posh simply left everything inside her purse and then placed it into her backpack. Gwen placed her things in her rolling suitcase, then waved her wand and sent the suitcase into Posh's magic purse for safe storage—with Posh's permission, of course. Fifteen minutes later, they were standing on the gangway, waiting for LinHem.

It was a sultry morning, more so than Valeside Beach, which was saying something. The waves lapped across the stony riprapped shoreline of Autumn Forest Isle. Gulls cawed in the distance, and a light breeze ruffled Gwen's greenish-tinged hair as she waited next to Posh. She could tell that Posh was still doubtful about the griffin. But Gwen felt better about her decision, having slept on it overnight.

Eventually, they grew tired of standing on the gangway and moved to a park bench in the busy port city of Emerald Grotto, which was the northernmost city on the island. The emerald tones of the dense tree line and water reflected off the pearly seafoam waves, giving everything in the vicinity a vibrant aura. It was easy to see where the namesake of the island had been taken. Gwen felt alive just standing there. After all, green was her favorite color.

LinHem eventually showed up. He swooped down amongst the tourists and trotted over to meet them.

"Ah, there you both are. Greetings again," LinHem said with a bow. "Are we ready for an adventure?"

Posh stood, ignoring him, and hurried along.

Gwen followed with a brief smile. "Yes. I'm curious to see what this November Tree is all about."

"Excellent, you won't be disappointed," LinHem said and fell in beside her.

Gwen noticed how walking seemed to be a bit awkward for LinHem. His long talons clacked on the cobbled paving, like a tap dancer's shoes. He continually ruffled his neck feathers as he looked from side to side, snapping his eagle's beak on occasion. She assumed he felt more comfortable flying, and indeed, he had looked as much when she'd seen him in the air.

"It sounds as if you've seen it before?" Gwen asked.

"Oh yes. I try to come every autumn. Though I have missed a handful of times, and it always makes me sad when I do. I think you'll find this to be a worthy pilgrimage for you and your friend. Thousands make the trip every year. Once you've seen the tree, it's hard not to come back."

"That's interesting. But all of this for a tree?"

"It's not just any tree. It holds a power over one's emotions that cannot be explained. Since my first visit, the tree has called to me, even when it isn't autumn. I liken it to a siren's call from across Ambriel."

Gwen nodded, not sure what to say. Regardless, she was even more curious to see this tree now.

"How long do you plan to stay?" LinHem asked.

"I'm not sure," Gwen said, still careful about how much information to give. "We're…looking for something. So, as long as it takes, I suppose."

They found a tram, which was a series of coaches strung together. Posh paid for the fee out of Kershaw's account, and the three of them settled in among the other tourists.

"We should check into our hotel first," Posh said. "I've made the arrangements. We'll have to see about a third room, I guess."

"Oh, it's no concern," LinHem said. "I do not require lodging. I prefer to fly at night and dine on fish."

Posh only nodded, though Gwen could see she was satisfied with that.

The tram wove its way through the Autumn Forest. The palm trees surrounding the shoreline gave way to larger deciduous trees: oaks, elms, and willows. The trees in the area were massive. Gwen felt at home amidst the forest, which looked to be ancient with girthy trees hundreds of years old. Trunks as large as a castle turret stretched up and out of sight. The tree canopy filtered the sunlight into pastel pinks and deep purples. Shadows stretched across the cobbled road, and beyond was mystery and intrigue—Nat would have been impressed.

As Gwen took in the sights, she could hear nature whispering to her. But she had trouble understanding this forest's ancient dialect, which sounded like the wind in its motion and cadence. One of her abilities as a green witch was communication with nature, the fauna and flora. She guessed that, due to the age of these trees, they'd lost (or forgotten) some of their native tongue. Consequently, she knew she wouldn't be able to talk to the Autumn Forest, which saddened her. There was so much history here, and it was at risk of being lost.

Regardless, Gwen loved the woodland realm, and it brought her back to her youth. As a child, she would run and play in the nearby forests. The vibrant hues of green haunted her memories in a good way. Perhaps the forest was responsible for setting her on the path to becoming a green witch. Though witches were all born neutral and didn't have to decide until the age of seven, Gwen had always liked the color green. But deep down, she understood that her personality was responsible for the direction she'd chosen. She desired peaceful, intuitive and inquisitive learning. She preferred fact-finding, mystery and upholding the truth. Above all, she loved nature, which was one reason she refrained from using her green-thumb spells. Once a plant was enchanted, it would eventually perish after the spell had run its course. Red witches had no such restrictions, since their main enchantment was elemental, which matched their aggression. And yellow witches, (who identified with creatures), their attitudes fell somewhere in between the greens and reds. She'd had no desire for a middle-of-the-road stance either. Being a green witch suited her just fine.

They eventually made it to the station, where the masses of tourists unloaded. Wedged within the thicket of green vegetation and built into one of the largest trees she had ever seen was their hotel.

Posh stepped off the tram and held out a hand for Gwen. She took it and stepped off with her gaze still focused on the amazing hotel.

"Grendle-Top Hotel, right this way," Posh said, in a tourist guide-like voice.

They held hands and walked up to the hotel with LinHem following behind, swishing his lion's tail.

The hotel was nothing short of incredible. It seemed to be built into and around the massive tree's trunk and limbs. Gwen lost count of how many levels there were. The hotel's walls were clad with wood siding, shaped like fish scales and painted in playful green and brown tones. The roofs were also built with wood siding and sloped to a steep pitch to help shed rainwater. Little chimneys poked through, wafting a bit of smoke. The windows were large diamond-shaped pieces of colored glass that refracted the sunlight like a prism. The hotel continued up and disappeared into the trees' canopy far above.

A doorman waited at the base. "Welcome to Hotel Grendle-Top. Please, this way." He directed them toward the interior of the massive tree trunk.

Inside, there were several elevator banks. They stepped into one of the wooden elevator cabs, and the grate slid closed before whisking them up to the higher levels. When it stopped, they moved into a lobby, which was tall and airy with birds flying in and out of the open-air space. They made their way to the check-in desk, and Posh paid with Kershaw's account.

"Well, LinHem," Posh said, a bit curtly. "I suppose we'll see you in the morning then?"

"Ah, yes. The day is getting on. We'll make our adventure tomorrow."

"That sounds good," Gwen said.

LinHem turned and launched over a balcony and disappeared into the setting sun.

Posh faced Gwen. "I still don't know how I feel about him."

"It'll be fine," Gwen said.

"There's still something strange about that bird."

"Then I'll leave you in charge of finding out what it is. Come on. Let's check out our rooms."

Posh and Gwen made it to their rooms, which were near the top of the hotel. Posh had purchased adjoining rooms with a wooden door between them, which Posh insisted on keeping open. The bed in Gwen's room was large with soft down comforters and stacked with lacy pillows in gold trim. Off to one side was an exquisite bathroom, a black granite tub cut from a boulder sat in the middle, warm water already drawn for her. The room smelled of cinnamon and sage, and the wall of windows along one side was open, letting the fragrance of the forest filter into the space, along with a gentle breeze and the sounds of nature. The chirping of birds at this height was soft, and outside the wall of windows was a large balcony.

She stepped out to take in the breathtaking view. Gwen leaned against the railing, propped her chin in her hands, and closed her eyes. She let her senses take in the forest. It was something she hadn't known she needed until now. Soon, she felt Posh's cool skin brush up against her own.

"I can see you're taken by the view," Posh muttered, and Gwen could hear a slight hesitation in her voice.

"I think I could get used to it." Gwen turned to look at Posh. "I can tell you aren't, though. Everything alright?"

"Honestly, forests aren't my thing, even though I'm part elf," Posh said. "I much prefer the open beach."

"Hold on," Gwen said. "You're part elf?"

"Surprise, surprise," Posh said, her hand to her forehead in feigned dismay. "My father was elven. They raided the genies often, taking what they wanted and who they wanted. It was the early days when my mother was raped."

Gwen's shocked expression made Posh smirk. "Don't act so surprised. Witches know all about raids." Posh paused and waved a hand. "I'm...sorry. That was uncalled for. We're past all that."

"It's okay," Gwen said quickly. "You have every reason to feel that way. It's unfortunate, what happened between the witches and the genies. I saw so many horrible things in my time with the ministry, so many unspeakable acts during my investigations. There's enough hate on both sides of our races to fill a continent. I don't blame you, and I'm not proud of what happened. If being here in the forest is too much, you don't have to stay. I think LinHem and I can find the sigil—"

"No way," Posh said immediately. "I'm not leaving you with that bird until I know more about him. Besides, I can cope with it. Maybe this time I can find peace with the forest. Perhaps we're not that different, in that department."

"What do you mean?" Gwen asked.

Posh gave Gwen a meaningful look. "At some point, you're going to tell me about your childhood. I can sense the pain within you. I'm a survivor of abuse. I know when I'm around another person who's been through it too."

"We may be partners in this venture, but that doesn't mean you get to know everything about me."

"Even though I'm finally trying to open up to you?" Posh asked.

Gwen sighed. "I'm sorry. I just need time to think about it." She wasn't sure what else to say at that moment. Though she felt a pang of pity, knowing that Posh had probably been put through many unfortunate things. After all, genie owners were known to be ruthless. If Posh was anything, she *was* a survivor, and Gwen respected her for that. Gwen gave her a brief smile and gripped her gently by the shoulders. "Now that I know you, I see a kind, gentle and caring person. I want to share everything with you, Posh. Just give me some time, okay? That part of my past is difficult."

Posh finally nodded. "Guess I can wait a bit longer. When you're ready, I'm listening." She turned and left the balcony, closing the adjoining door behind her.

Gwen stared after her, wondering if she should let their conversation end on that note. But she didn't want to think about her childhood tonight, or Posh's, for that matter.

Gwen eventually stripped down and soaked in the large obsidian bathtub. She let the hot water and fragrant soap wash away her troubled thoughts. The sounds of nature wafted into the suite, calming the noise inside her head. Thirty minutes later, she felt relaxed enough to towel off and get ready for bed.

Just as she was toweling off, she heard the flapping of large wings from the balcony.

# CHAPTER 24

## *THE GHOSTLY BALL*

THE SOUND OF flapping wings thrummed through Gwen's hotel suite. It was a deep thumping sound that reverberated around the room. Gwen felt a split second of panic and reached for her wand. Still half-naked and dripping from her bath, she stepped out to the balcony to see what the commotion was.

Standing there with wings folded back was LinHem. He reached a talon up and straightened his glasses, then looked around to see Gwen half-naked and hair still wet. Gwen wasn't even sure if it was possible for a griffin to blush, but LinHem seemed to turn a shade of red.

"Oh, goodness," he said and averted his gaze. "I must apologize. I didn't mean to intrude during your bathing hour."

Gwen pulled her towel tighter, then lowered her wand a bit. "It's fine. I was just finishing up—"

The adjoining door burst open, and Posh rushed into Gwen's suite. Her thumbs and forefingers were touching, and a golden glow lit her eyes. Gwen could see she was ready to dispel some magic.

"What's the meaning of this?" Posh blurted.

Gwen held up her hands, which nearly caused her towel to drop. "Easy. It's just LinHem."

Posh slowed then straightened, the golden glow from her eyes diminishing. "Well, there's a doorbell, you know."

"Oh, right," LinHem said. "Well, for someone my size, the hallways are a bit cramped. Sorry, again."

"It's fine, LinHem," Gwen said. "But why are you here? Is it something important?"

LinHem clawed at the wood balcony, and Gwen thought he was being bashful. "Actually, I have something I'd like to confess."

Posh gave Gwen an 'I-told-you-so' look, then crossed her arms. "Go on."

"Mind you, I'm not supposed to speak about this, because I'm actually under a contract—"

"LinHem, just say it," Posh said.

"Well…I've been hired by a third party."

Gwen's eyebrows arched upward in surprise. "A third party?"

"One who claims you owe him," LinHem continued.

"Okay," Posh said. "Now I'm confused."

"Oh, what's another way of saying this?" LinHem said, considering. "A mob boss, I believe."

Gwen gritted her jaw, then slapped the wall. "Bam Jino. I knew it! Doesn't surprise me. Of course, that mountain troll would want to keep tabs on us. What exactly has he asked you to do?"

"Honestly, he just asked that I spy on you two, then report back to him. Well, this I cannot do now."

"How did he get to you in the first place?" Gwen asked.

"He found me through my university library connection. He thought that I might have luck finding common ground with you. When I saw the codex, I assumed that might work. But, after thinking it through, it was too unethical. Let me apologize."

"What was he paying you?" Gwen said.

"Oh, it was a considerable number of tokens. But I haven't taken payment yet, so I don't feel bad backing out now."

"You'd better watch your back, LinHem," Gwen said. "Bam Jino doesn't look kindly on rejection. He'll be out for revenge."

"I am not concerned, Miss Gwenevere. I can handle myself, if it comes to that." LinHem pawed at the balcony again with his talon.

Gwen could see that he was still embarrassed, and perhaps a bit ashamed as well. "Is there something else you'd like to say?" she asked.

"Well, yes. I'm afraid I've not been very forthcoming about my background either. My parents weren't librarians. They served in the military, amongst the ranks of commanders in the last war."

Posh and Gwen looked at each other. Gwen held out a hand for him to continue.

"I was estranged from my home. I didn't have what was required to join the military marksman brigade, like my two siblings. You see, I was an embarrassment to my family and lineage. I am a griffin who has no desire for battle. Well, it's unheard of, in our race. So, as you can imagine, I was belittled and bullied by other griffins. My parents thought it would toughen me up, so to speak, and they allowed it to continue throughout my upbringing. Eventually, I could take no more and fled my homeland. I could not bear to bring more shame upon my family's name. I do love my parents, despite their harsh nature, but I cannot return to them until I've proven myself worthy."

"I'm sorry to hear that, LinHem," Gwen said. "I wish there was something I could do to help."

"Well, my ladies, there might be. I need to prove myself, and it seems your quest for the November Tree might be something I can aid with. I may not be of the caliber my brothers are, but I am able to protect. And I am honestly an excellent guide. I know the Autumn Forest well. Perhaps our paths have aligned? With that in mind, would it be too much to ask if I continue on with your quest?"

Gwen glanced at Posh and shrugged. "Well, he seems to be telling the truth this time."

Posh continued to glare at LinHem, then her mood softened. "Okay. Fine."

"I am at your service," LinHem said and bowed his eagle head.

"Of course, this is all subject to change," Posh said.

"I understand," LinHem said.

Posh sighed, then turned and walked back into her room, leaving the door open.

LinHem still looked a bit flustered but stretched his wings. "Well then. First thing in the morning? Have a good evening, Gwenevere."

LinHem flew off with Gwen looking after him. She couldn't think of an odder grouping than a genie, a green witch and a librarian griffin…and she had no idea if this was going to work out.

The next morning, Gwen and Posh met LinHem outside of the main lobby.

The trip to the November Tree was about a two-day hike, and they loaded their backpacks. LinHem had brought a packed lunch for them: figs and berries, along with a few fish. Gwen and Posh politely declined.

"Tell me what you know about this magical tree," Gwen said as they struck off.

It was a muggy morning, though there was a cool breeze in the lower valleys. Some early morning fog clung to the lush ground cover while birds and the sounds of nature filled the air. Sunrays shone through the fog as Gwen breathed in the earthy scents of the flora and fauna.

"Hmm, let's see," LinHem hummed. "Well. It's a bit of a mystery, the November Tree. Obviously, it only becomes visible late in the month of November. But its location changes year to year."

"And, do you know where we're heading?" Posh asked.

"Yes. Through local chatter, I've tracked it. This year, the tree has been appearing in the southern reach, along the Red Gulch area."

Posh looked at Gwen. "Kershaw's not going to be happy about this little excursion."

"Well, he'll have to deal with it," Gwen said. "Just keep him occupied so we can follow the clues."

"I will, as much as I can. I just know how he'll respond. Saint Halving Day really isn't that far off."

LinHem seemed to be lost in his own world as he hummed along, speaking to the butterflies and stopping occasionally to taste a few berries or marvel at some rare tree.

"You think you should be eating wild berries?" Posh said, her nose scrunched up.

"Posh, my dear. Apparently, you've not heard about a griffin's digestive system."

"Can't say that I have, nor do I care to," she responded.

"Then you wouldn't know that our gut is essentially made of iron," LinHem stated.

"Well, good for you," Posh said, a sarcastic smirk on her face. Then she leaned in closer to Gwen. "Not sure our friend knows where he's going."

"It'll be fine," Gwen whispered back, though she, too, was a bit worried.

They continued to traipse through the forest, listening to LinHem point out other types of berries, trees and forest creatures. Occasionally, they passed by cottages, the smell of baked bread wafting through the late morning air. Gwen took in the sounds and smells. The massive trees seemed to grow larger in size the deeper they ventured into the mysterious woodland realm.

Soon, they came to a stone bridge that spanned a large ravine with a river far below.

"This is the Greenleaf River," LinHem said. "Ah, listen to the roar of it!"

The griffin reared back and let out his own roar. It was impressive, and aggressive sounding, coming from the bespectacled griffin. Both Gwen and Posh stared at him, their mouths hanging open.

"Oh, pardon me," he said. "Sometimes the desire takes me. Hopefully, I didn't frighten you. Anyway, on we go." LinHem stepped onto the bridge, and they followed.

Once on the other side, they came to a stone keep. It was a large fortress with round windows and jagged ramparts. The drawbridge had been lowered, and the keep seemed to be in a state of disrepair, with some of the stone block crumbling around the base.

"We can either go through it or around it," Posh said. "What'll it be, oh great leader?"

LinHem missed the sarcasm and scratched his beak with a talon. "What's this? I don't recall a fortress here." LinHem sat on his haunches and pulled a book out of his satchel. "Hmm…says here that this keep doesn't exist. Yet, it looks real enough to me. I guess we'll have to go inside. He stood and walked through the portcullis."

"Uh, hold on a tick, Great Mane," Posh said and pointed after him. "I'm not too keen on just inviting ourselves into some spooky keep."

"Posh, the wall goes on for a ways, and the woods are too dense here," Gwen said. "Why not take the road through the keep?"

Posh gave her a concerned look. "We're not invited guests. Besides, I try to avoid spooky keeps in the middle of nowhere."

Gwen looked at the fortress. "Well, I don't think anyone's home."

"Come along, my colorful friends," LinHem said and didn't look back as he strolled into the castle.

Inside, the air was thick. Dust and cobwebs lined the walls and ceiling and pulsed in the low crooning breeze. There was a grand staircase that led up to the top level of a ballroom. An eerie music box melody played from the upper reaches of the soaring ceiling. A mirrored ball spun, reflecting the filtered sunlight, which cast a surreal glow about the space. Prancing about the ballroom was a large panther. Surrounding it were several dozen dancing ghosts.

Gwen, Posh and LinHem stood looking in shock at the bizarre group of dancers.

"Uh, I think maybe it's time to go," Posh said.

"Nonsense," LinHem hooted. "We need to stay and observe this event."

"Hold on, Posh," Gwen said. "There, in the middle. Is that a panther...with plaid fur?"

Posh shook her head vigorously. "I don't care about the cat. Did you happen to notice the four dozen ghosts?"

"It looks like the panther is being held captive, though, see?" Gwen pointed at how the large cat seemed to be in a trance, waltzing in the middle of the ghosts.

The panther was massive, maybe as large as LinHem. Its fur was several shades of gray, but in a plaid pattern. It also had green glowing eyes with its lids half open.

"I think we should try to free it," Gwen said.

"Hmm, very intriguing," LinHem murmured.

Posh twirled her blue hair nervously. "I don't know. Do we really need another misfit in this group?"

LinHem stared at her, his feathers ruffled. "I take offense at that, I think." He tilted his eagle head, and his eyes narrowed.

"Well, I'll do it myself then," Gwen said. Though she didn't know any good release spells, she had a distraction spell that she thought might work well enough. She pointed it at the spinning mirror ball above and spoke the right combination of enchantments. A wispy, thin fog shot from the tip of her wand and hit the spinning ball. The mirrored glass exploded, and the ball shot sideways. It continued to swing back and forth before finally dropping to the ground. When it hit, there was a loud explosion and glass chunks shot in all directions.

The ghosts stopped moving, their attention now on Gwen, Posh and LinHem.

But before they could move, the ghosts instantly surrounded them. Gwen felt her head begin to spin. Her thoughts went suddenly calm, too calm. In her mind, she seemed to be falling backward and down into a deep grave. The spirits reached for her, their ethereal fingers grasping at her from all directions. She managed to turn her head and saw Posh and LinHem doing the same. They were caught in some ghostly loop.

Gwen lost all sense of time. In her vision, she could see her friend Kriss. They were at archery practice the day before her death. Kriss was smiling, her arms about Gwen, showing her how to properly draw the bowstring with a nocked arrow. *My little secret*, she whispered.

Gwen reached for the magic amulet at her neck, but it was missing. Had she misplaced it? Had the ghosts simply stolen it?

She started to panic.

Though she was still falling, she tried to twist and look for the ruby amulet.

*What will I do without it? It's all I have left of Kriss.*

But suddenly, Gwen's falling slowed. She felt suspended within the strange, inky void—some foreign universe that the living shouldn't be in. Then, everything reversed. It made her head spin in the opposite direction like she was sitting on some macabre merry-go-round. It almost felt as if time was reversing. Her world spun faster until she thought she would be thrown sideways and out of the mysterious void altogether.

Then, it all stopped.

Gwen sat on the cold stone floor of the dim ballroom. All was silent around her. The eerie music box melody was gone, though the candles around the space still flickered and danced in the mottled sunlight.

Surrounding Gwen were her friends. LinHem sat on his haunches, shaking his head, his eagle beak shone in the light of the candles, and his piercing eyes glinted in the dark. Posh sat cross-legged, her hands extended palm up and her index fingers and thumbs pinched together like she was about to incant some magical spell.

Not part of their group was the strange, gray and black plaid-patterned panther. The giant cat traipsed around them, circling them like it was about to pounce. Missing now were the ghostly apparitions that had been dancing around the ballroom.

Gwen sat frozen, not daring to move. She thought about reaching for her wand, already knowing she had no spell that would ward her against such a large beast. It seemed like LinHem and Posh were frozen with fear as well.

Then, the panther rushed at Gwen, its jaws open wide. She braced herself, finally raising her arms and hoping for the best.

# CHAPTER 25

## *BALLY WHO?*

WHEN GWEN FINALLY opened her eyes, she was greeted by the whiskers and wet tongue of the large panther. She was still in shock as she looked on, feeling the weight of the enormous cat on her. She tried to sit up, but the panther continued to pin her down and lick her face.

"Okay, enough," she said, and the big cat stopped and moved to the side.

Gwen was able to finally stand up. She wiped her face with the sleeve of her robe. "What is this? Who are you?"

The panther sat on its hindquarters and stared at her with its large green eyes in the dark. "I am Bally, a ghost panther."

The other two finally began to wake, as if from a trance. LinHem looked at the cat and immediately stood and reared back, raising his front talons. Posh moved toward Gwen and raised her hands, ready to use some of her magic.

"Wait!" Gwen yelled, then turned to the panther. "Explain this."

The panther remained calm, though, his eyelids drooping low as he looked at the three companions. "I've been caught in a trance for a century. I stumbled upon this keep and fell into the ghosts' loop." The big cat purred, and Gwen could almost hear the relief in its growl.

"So, you've been caught in a ghost loop for a century?" Posh said.

The big cat nodded, then began licking its massive paw. "I've not had a bath in so long."

LinHem lowered his talons, now that things had settled down. "Oh, a ghost loop. How very interesting. I've read about such things. It must have been a fascinating voyage."

The cat eyed LinHem, and Gwen thought she saw the panther roll its eyes at the bespectacled griffin.

"You're a ghost panther," LinHem continued. "I've studied your kind. Very rare, not many have been seen in these parts. Nearly extinct, I believe."

"So, it was you who knocked us out of the ghost loop?" Gwen said. She was tall for a witch but still didn't even reach the panther's chest as it sat, licking its front paw.

"Yes, only after you freed me from their loop. It was the least I could do. I am indebted to you." The panther bowed low, allowing Gwen to pet him on the head, which Gwen did after LinHem gave her a nod.

Bally stood on all fours and addressed Gwen. "Allow me to accompany you. It is the right thing to do—"

"We probably don't need any more mythical creatures," Posh interjected.

"Hold on, Posh," Gwen said and looked at Bally. "Why would you want to accompany us? You don't even know where we're heading."

"I am indebted to you," Bally said. "And yes, I know exactly where you are heading. The November Tree."

"How would you know that? You've been in a trance for a century," Posh said.

"I know, because that's where I was heading before I got sidetracked."

Gwen glanced at Posh and LinHem; both had uncertain looks on their faces. "And…why were you searching for the November Tree?"

"Because that's where the first golden sigil is hidden."

Gwen cracked a smile. "Is this some joke? How could you know about the sigils?"

"Because, for my quest, it was also the first sigil from Spellbinder."

Gwen's mouth practically dropped open at hearing that. This ghost panther, who'd been trapped for over a century, had also been searching for the same sigil she was?

"It is why you are all here," Bally said. "Is that not so? It's the same reason that I was here a century ago. I am now going the same way as you, it seems."

"What is it that Spellbinder showed you?" Gwen asked.

"For now, I will keep that to myself."

"I find it odd that you would even know about the telescope," Posh said. "Care to elaborate?"

"I know of it because my master built it," Bally said.

Once again, the three companions stood in shocked silence.

Gwen wondered if it was just a coincidence that they had stumbled upon the strange keep, found the ghost panther and released it, only to learn that Bally had also been on a similar quest from Spellbinder.

"Well, it would seem that some benevolent luck is in play," LinHem said. "What do you say? I see no reason we can't take on another furry companion."

Posh pulled Gwen to the side, where the other two couldn't hear her. "Gwen…I don't like this!" she whispered. "We already have the griffin and now this panther? What if that thing goes rogue? Did you see the size of its paws?"

"I know, Posh. It seems almost too coincidental. But what are the odds? I mean, it seems like fate is calling us here. I don't see how we can walk away from it. I believe that Bally was caught in that loop, and something led us here to free him."

"Okay, I agree that it is strange. But Kershaw isn't going to like this one bit—"

"Well, Kershaw isn't here," Gwen said. "He appointed me to do this. I say we at least let the cat tag along. I don't think there's a malicious intent in the thing. Remember, he didn't have to free us from the loop. Besides, he's kind of cute, don't you think?"

Posh sighed. "Don't kid yourself, that thing is dangerous. If the legends are true about ghost panthers, we need to be on our guard."

They walked back to the panther and griffin.

LinHem was strutting around Bally, checking out the cat's black and grey plaid-patterned fur while humming to himself. "Ah, very intriguing," LinHem said. "Look here, Gwenevere. Its pattern shifts in the shadows. I never read about that, though I'll admit there is very little information on ghost panthers. In fact, I don't think a live one has ever been studied—"

Gwen held up a hand. "Alright, Bally. You're coming with us. We are seeking the sigil to the first riddle of Spellbinder, as you said. Maybe you can give us a little more background on the telescope along the way."

Posh still looked uneasy but crossed her arms and stayed near Gwen and LinHem as they left the keep. Bally strolled behind them, purring his approval as they walked.

"It feels exquisite to be back in the living world," Bally said.

They stepped out onto the dirt path on the backside of the fortress. Once they moved a bit further, the castle began to dissolve, and with a final pop, it disappeared.

"Good riddance," Bally said. "Until the next unfortunate adventurer comes along."

"Well?" Posh said. "Let's hear about this telescope and the man who created it."

"Ah, he was a great wizard, Speartine," Bally began. "He was my master, and he adopted me. Back then, ghost panthers were more common among royalty, more so with wizards. We exhibit traits cherished by wizards and sorceresses."

"Like what?" Posh said, still keeping her distance.

"We don't sleep for one. We make excellent guards, since we can move in and out of the dream realm, too. This provides good protection for important artifacts."

"Like magical telescopes?" Gwen asked. "Is that why you were with the wizard?"

"Yes, indeed. It was my job to protect his family and Spellbinder. Over the years, I would watch at night as my master slept. I began to grow intrigued by the telescope, though. We had many long conversations—"

"Wait." Posh stopped the panther. "The telescope can talk?"

"Spellbinder's speech is different than ours. It communicates through memories, which might be the easiest way to explain it. It called to me, and I peered into it. The telescope seemed to know my strong desire, and it gave me the answer on how to achieve it. When I had served my tenure with Speartine, I was granted leave. I was on a quest for the November Tree when I fell into the ghost loop a century past."

"Where was your family?" Posh asked.

At that, the panther remained silent, though, and only the padding of its enormous paws answered on the dirt path.

Gwen and LinHem looked at each other, and Posh shrugged. "Okay, I see that's a topic we won't discuss right now. I can only assume it has something to do with your quest?"

Again, there was no answer from Bally.

"I must apologize for my friend's stubbornness," LinHem said.

"Oh, sure, LinHem," Posh blurted. "So, why are you here again? Seems like we all want something, doesn't it?"

"Might I ask the same of you, Posh?" LinHem hooted, sounding a bit perturbed for the first time. "A genie's power is unrivaled. Could you not simply wish Gwenevere's desire into existence with a simple incantation?"

Posh glared at the griffin. "It doesn't work like that. You should know that a genie's wish-magic comes at a steep price." Posh pointed at the vertical scar over her left eye.

Gwen spoke up, trying to settle the group. "Look, maybe the real reason we're here together is because we were meant to be. Why can't fate draw us together for a greater cause? I'm hopeful that I can help others, and I think that you all feel the same way. All I ask is that we work together. Can we do that?"

Posh, LinHem, and Bally remained silent for a few seconds.

Then Posh nodded to LinHem and scratched Bally behind the ears. "Yeah, I think we can do that for you, Gwen."

# CHAPTER 26

## *THE NOVEMBER TREE*

THE FOUR COMPANIONS eventually decided to settle in for the night. They found a wooded clearing and LinHem pitched a few tents from Posh's magic purse (she'd thought of everything). LinHem continued to pull items from the purse while Gwen wondered how in Ambriel it all fit. Soon, their campsite was furnished with a fire, benches, cooking utensils and other essentials.

"Not really roughing it, I'd say," Posh crooned as she sat near the fire and warmed her hands. The icy steam from her skin seemed to glimmer in the firelight.

"Oh, I don't like roughing it," LinHem said. "Not my style either, Miss Posh."

The evening air cooled, and low fog clung to the ground as they settled in around the campfire. Gwen heard the sounds of the forest come to life, but now she wasn't too worried about being attacked by woodland creatures, thanks to the griffin and panther.

LinHem began to fry up some fish, which he'd stored in a portable ice chest of some sort—Gwen was becoming increasingly impressed at his plethora of inventory and gadgets. This time, Posh and Gwen, both ravenous, accepted the fried fish along with Bally. There was also baked bread, and for dessert, they popped popcorn.

LinHem sang a few songs from his youth, from the Isle of Myrnn. As it turned out, Bally was a fantastic storyteller, which, after Gwen thought about it, made total sense because he was, after all, a ghost panther from the dream realm. Of course, he'd made some spirit friends, not to mention all of the time he'd spent trapped in the ghost loop. It was an entertaining evening, to say the least.

Gwen and Posh slept in the girls' tent, while LinHem and Bally slept in the boys' tent. Gwen was amazed that two full-grown mythical creatures, like a ghost panther and a griffin, could fit in the tent, let alone agree to be near each other the entire night. Not that they disliked one another, from what Gwen had observed so far. But LinHem's hoity-toity attitude seemed to annoy the composed ghost panther, based on Bally's body language.

Early the next morning, the quartet had a quick breakfast, took care of nature, and stowed everything back inside Posh's magical purse.

"We should reach the November Tree today," LinHem said, glancing up at the morning sun.

"Assuming we don't run into any more mythical creatures," Posh grumbled with a bit of sarcasm.

But to Gwen, things seemed to be going well, considering how different they all were. Posh's lack of patience, LinHem's overly curious nature, and Bally's quiet and reserved attitude, along with Gwen's need to keep things steadily progressing forward, seemed like a perfect recipe for a storm. Hopefully, they could avoid any quarrels until they made it to the fabled November Tree. After that, she didn't much care what happened.

By midafternoon, Gwen's feet were throbbing. Her tall leather boots weren't much for hiking, and she was about to call for a break when something ahead glimmered. Gwen heard what sounded like a rattle, then there were several more rattles sounding off. Suddenly, they were surrounded by the strange noise.

The gravel path was fairly wide but surrounded by thick trees. The closer she looked, the more she could see glowing eyes in the darkness beyond.

Gwen pointed into the thicket. "What is it?"

Posh quickly turned her back to Gwen. "LinHem, Bally, back-to-back, now! The genie held her thumbs and forefingers together, ready to dispel an incantation.

LinHem stood beside Posh and Gwen. "Oh, grattler vipers," he said in a whimsical tone. "I have not seen these before. Very poisonous. Deadly as well. Do not make any quick movements."

Posh remained still, but whispered to the others, "Where is Bally?"

Gwen craned her neck around slowly, only to see that the ghost panther had literally vanished.

*Great!* she thought. *Has the ghost panther abandoned us already?* She'd had such a good feeling about him too, like destiny had brought them together.

But the sun was dipping below the treetops now, and dusk gave away to night. There was a golden glow in the air that was fading quickly to a deep purple. The grattlers inched closer as the darkness loomed.

Gwen saw their sinuous bodies, powerful with gold and green scales. As darkness fell, she could see there was nowhere to go. They were trapped on the trail.

Gwen held out her rosewood wand, trying to think of an effective spell or enchantment that might ward the grattlers off. There were a few defensive spells she knew, but none that could protect all three of them. She couldn't use her green-thumb spell to enchant the trees or plants, thanks to the forest's ancient language. LinHem was large and powerful, but what could one griffin do against the dozens of grattlers surrounding them?

The grattlers were growing bolder as night set in. Their sinewy bodies looked like flames in the fading sunlight. She watched their heads bob as they moved closer, their fangs glinting in the dull light.

Posh closed her eyes, her skin began to grow icy cold, and a sizzling sound began to emanate from her fingertips. Gwen could see that she was about to discharge some of her crucial wish-magic.

But suddenly, one of the snakes stiffened and went into some sort of slithering dance. Then another and another. Gwen could hear a low rumbling noise from somewhere among the trees. Before long, all the grattlers were moving the same way, as if in a trance. They began to back away. Then, without another rattle, they slithered off into the dark woods. The sounds of the forest returned, and Gwen let out a long, slow breath.

Posh relaxed, the glowing light from her fingers dissipating. "What in Ambriel is going on?"

A pair of luminous green eyes blinked from the forest's edge.

It was Bally.

The enormous ghost panther seemed to magically solidify from the shadows and stepped onto the path.

"How did you manage that?" Gwen asked.

"I've learned a thing or two over the centuries," Bally purred.

Posh rushed over and threw her arms around the large cat and buried her face in his thick fur. "Oh, I knew you wouldn't leave us, you big furry teddy bear!"

Bally bared his teeth for just a second, but then he closed his eyes and purred a bit louder.

The group didn't face any more grattlers or other strange creatures that night.

But it was getting late, and Gwen began to wonder if they'd need to stop again and make camp, even though LinHem had said they'd reach their destination before day's end.

But then, LinHem let out a high-pitched squawk. "There, I see it," he whispered. "Near that stand of evergreens." He lifted his front talon and motioned to it.

Gwen cupped her hands over her brow, trying to peer through the dark thicket of trees beyond. At first, she saw nothing. But then, as if by magic, something materialized. It was a small tree, one that she might even describe as a dwarf tree. It appeared frail and diseased; perhaps it had been struck by lightning. The stunted thing looked more like a sad Saint Halving Day tree. Either way, it certainly didn't resemble the majestic tree she'd seen in her vision.

"That's it?" Posh said. Then she dropped to the ground and roared in laughter. "I'm sorry. I just…is that really what we came all this way for?" She rolled in the underbrush, wiping tears from her cheek, which had already frozen because of her cool skin.

LinHem looked at her from behind his spectacles, disapprovingly. "Now, now, Miss Posh. Don't judge the tree by its looks."

"Let us engage with it," Bally said and led the way forward.

The others followed, almost using the panther as a shield.

To Gwen, the tree looked beyond dead. It was perhaps two meters tall and deciduous with rust-colored leaves that were dry and cracked. She considered using a spell to heal the poor thing but waited for Bally.

"The tree's appearance is meant as a disguise," Bally whispered. "Be silent, lest it whisks itself away."

"What is this madness?" Posh said in a low voice.

"This tree uses deception and illusion to throw off would-be seekers," LinHem said. "Bally speaks the truth."

The four companions tiptoed up to the tree. Gwen could almost see its leaves quivering, like the frail tree was alive and frightened. When they were within reach, the tree suddenly changed. It lit up in an explosion of color. The leaves changed to a golden hue, and the sound of bells filled the air.

Then the branches stood up straight, and the tree began to grow. Slow at first, then increasing with tremendous speed. It happened so quickly that Gwen, Posh, LinHem and Bally had no time to move out of the way. One of the golden branches dipped down, like a giant's hand, and scooped the four of them up.

Gwen managed to roll to her feet and grip her wand as they shot skyward. She could hear the tree singing in her mind. Like a strange and ancient lullaby, the words made no sense. Within seconds, they were high above the tree canopy, and Gwen could see the entire forest below, like some green carpet. Beyond that, she could see the island's shores and the Green Sea.

Posh and Gwen looked at each other, bewildered, while Bally and LinHem seemed a bit more relaxed. Gwen wanted to ask questions, but the rush of wind made it difficult to speak. So, she gripped the branch and decided to hold tight until they arrived, wherever their destination might be.

Eventually, they slowed, and the rush of clouds and wind diminished until the branch stopped with a sudden jolt. Posh had gripped a handful of Bally's fur and buried her face into his neck. LinHem had his wings fluffed out and around the group for protection.

"Uh…I think we're here, wherever *here* is," Posh said.

Bally stepped off the limb and onto the next one. "Follow me."

He led the way with everyone falling into a single file line. They hopped between the golden branches, Gwen careful not to look down. The soft sound of bells continued to chime through the tree branches as the leaves fluttered in the breeze.

"Stay focused," Bally said. "The music is also meant to deceive you. We can't have anyone falling off."

The branches seemed to create a pathway, like some organic spiral staircase made of gold, which led them upward. When they reached the highest point of the tree, Gwen saw a mountain top she hadn't noticed before.

"Where'd that come from?" Posh asked. "It wasn't there a moment ago."

"Just follow and keep silent till we reach the end," Bally whispered.

The mountain top was narrow and steeply pitched with gravel paths. There were many forks in the trail they took, and Bally paused occasionally to sniff out the right path. Gwen wanted to ask what possible scent he was trying to pick up. If they were hunting for the sigil, why would it have a scent? But she kept quiet and followed directly behind the large cat.

While Gwen and Posh struggled up the gravel path, LinHem and Bally were much more surefooted, and they had to stop occasionally to help out. The trails continued to slope, pitch and dead-end. It was dark and ominous atop the strange mountain top. Gwen noticed several other trees, similar to the November Tree, but they were a different color and shape or species, though they were also stunted and dead. In fact, she saw one that was a Saint Halving tree. She saw another that looked like a palm tree. There was a dragon wood trying to bloom pink flowers, like it was spring somewhere in Ambriel.

"One for each month," Bally whispered in a low growl. "For our region, we only get the November Tree."

Soon, the trails grew too perilous. Posh hopped on Bally's back while Gwen climbed aboard LinHem. Gwen felt her palms grow clammy at the thought of hitting a loose spot of gravel and sliding over the cliff's edge.

They followed the trails for most of the night, and soon the sun began to rise over the lip of the cloud bank. It grew cold with the higher altitude, and Gwen tried to cling tighter to LinHem, using his feather coat to fight off the chilly mountain air. She could feel LinHem's muscles ripple below her as he leapt and climbed.

Finally, the sun crested the clouds and exploded in a burst of pastel colors of pink, tangerine, and teal. The colorful display was almost too intense to register, and it brought tears to her eyes. When she glanced back at Posh, she noticed the same expression of amazement on her face.

"Ah, such beauty," LinHem said in a low squawk, which drew a growl from Bally to hush.

"There it is," Bally said. "Just beyond the peak."

To Gwen, it was like some Greek temple. There was a plinth or base, with fluted columns and ionic capitals. A heavy frieze sat on top with a pitched roof, carved from white marble and goldleaf. The sun hit the temple at just the right angle, sending rays of sunlight across the pastel sky. It felt like some heavenly epiphany, as if the planets were aligning.

Gwen started to climb down from LinHem.

"No!" Bally said in a low growl. "We must wait."

LinHem looked on, also confused. Apparently, even his vast knowledge had reached its limit. They were relying on the ghost panther now and whatever information he knew about the November Tree.

Gwen guessed that Bally's time under the tutelage of Speartine had given him some inside knowledge.

"Well?" Posh said impatiently. "Are we waiting for a sign from the gods or something?"

Just as the sun crested the top of the temple, hundreds of symbols along its frieze lit up. Their reddish amber color cast golden rays onto the ground. But there was one that shone brighter.

"That's it," Bally said.

Gwen felt LinHem's muscles flex as the griffin bounded forward with Bally leading the way. Her head snapped back, unprepared for the great leap. She gripped LinHem's feathers and held tight.

They covered the distance in just seconds. Bally sprinted for the area of ground that was highlighted in golden light. But the November sun angle was already changing, and the golden rays were beginning to fade. At the last second, Bally reached the spot and swiped one of his massive paws at a patch of dirt. His claws ripped a furrow in the ground, and something popped up just as the light faded.

Their group slowed and gathered around a budding golden tree in the dirt. The tiny sapling was thin and delicate. As they stood around the golden trinket, it continued to blossom. But just as quickly, it turned brown and wilted.

The sapling peeled and withered away, leaving a golden sigil in its place.

# CHAPTER 27

## *THE FIRST GOLDEN SIGIL*

GWEN KNELT AND plucked the golden trinket from the ground and held it up to the sunlight. The morning sun spilled over the Greek temple and flooded the area. Now the four of them stood in a golden field of wheat with stalks waist high and swaying rhythmically in the breeze.

The sigil was heavier than it looked, deceptive in weight like a waterlogged piece of wood. Gwen flipped it over a few times, noticing its shape and golden hue. Like the void inset within the floor of the lighthouse, the outline was that of a tree, which she understood now to be the November Tree.

Posh took the sigil and looked it over, then handed it to LinHem.

"Ah, exquisite," he said, holding it in his talon. "Not many have held one of the sigils, let alone seen one. Spellbinder does not hand these out to just anyone."

Bally padded forward and held up a large paw, claws poking from beneath his fur. LinHem set the golden sigil on his paw, and Bally sniffed it. Gwen noticed how his eyelids closed slightly, his green glowing eyes rolling back in undeniable pleasure. She wondered again what noble desire it was that Bally was so driven to rectify.

"The sigil is a bespoke, one-of-a-kind object," Bally said and handed it back to Gwen. "Once it is replaced within the lighthouse, it will disappear forever."

Gwen placed it in her satchel, then looked at her three companions. "Thank you, all three of you. Should we explore, or head back?"

"I think it wise to head back," Bally said. "Places such as these are easy to get lost in. I would not tarry here."

LinHem seemed ready to disagree but finally nodded. "Very well."

"Bally, what is your destination now?" Posh said. "You've been waiting for a century to find the sigil. Do you have other plans?"

"I wish to continue with you, Gwenevere. Our paths are intertwined."

Posh leaned over and whispered to Gwen. “Actually, I think the ghost panther might be an asset to bring along.”

Gwen didn’t need any prodding, though. “Bally, of course you are welcome to accompany us as long as you like. There is plenty of room at Java House for everyone.”

The panther bowed low, his long furry tail lifting high. “I would be honored. Thank you.”

The group found their way back to the massive November Tree, located a large branch and settled in. According to LinHem, they had to wait until sunset. Gwen relaxed, enjoying the view, and she even managed a quick nap while leaning against Bally.

At dusk, the tree began to reduce in size. It wasn’t long before they were descending back through the cloudscape and into the Autumn Forest. Once they made landfall, Bally led everyone back to the main path. As night settled in, they readied their camp and sat around a blazing fire. They were in a cheerful mood that evening and stayed up late into the night telling more stories. Bally shared tidbits about his upbringing and his origin, which Gwen found interesting. He’d been brought to Ambriel from across the Green Sea several centuries ago as a cub. He’d been raised by a surrogate family and worked in a circus of sorts, where he had perfected his trips into the dream realm. In his travels, he had been introduced to the great wizard Speartine and was eventually recruited into his security detail. Bally had then moved into the wizard’s castle and learned about the magical artifacts, which included the telescope known as Spellbinder.

The next day, they made their way back to Grendel-Top Hotel, where they spent one last night on the island—Kershaw’s treat, of course, though he had no idea there were two new companions. Gwen and Posh roomed together while LinHem and Bally shared a suite, which was a little larger. The looks they received walking into the hotel were priceless. A green witch and a blue genie (who were supposed to be bitter rivals), along with a griffin and a rarely seen ghost panther, were likely something most people had never witnessed before.

The next morning, they all stood in the hotel lobby, waiting for Posh to check out.

"What now?" Posh asked as she walked up.

"Back to Java House, where we'll regroup," Gwen said.

"I'd like to visit Spellbinder, if that's acceptable," Bally said, and LinHem perked up as well. "We'll need to replace the sigil to attain the next clue."

"Sure. I can take you there," Gwen said. "But the way is hidden. Hopefully, I can retrace my path back to the lighthouse."

"If you cannot, then I shall map the way," Bally said.

They boarded the Sea Grazer and ferried across the Bay of Fireflies.

They all stood on the bow, though LinHem preferred to fly above and scoop up fish. Before long, Gwen could see the main harbor, and their cruise ship docked at the pier. The gangway lowered, and they made the short trek along the beach back to Java House.

"Up there," Gwen said, and pointed to the overlook above the beach. "That's Hidden Palm Grove."

Stars twinkled, and the fireflies began to descend around them as they strolled along. Gwen had removed her leather sandals and walked barefoot in the sea wash, letting it pool around her toes.

"Ah. So, that is where Spellbinder is hidden?" LinHem asked.

"Yes, at the top of the lighthouse," Gwen said.

LinHem flapped his wings. "I could simply fly everyone up there and avoid the wandering halls within."

"It does not work in that manner," Bally said. "You would find nothing inside if you did so. Spellbinder can only be found from within."

"You are sure of this?" LinHem asked.

"Absolutely. Only then will Spellbinder reveal itself. As I said, I shall map the way."

"Be careful, Bally," Gwen said. "There are restless spirits inside. We should visit the castle outside of the witching hour, when the spirits are at rest. I think it would be dangerous, even for you."

The panther nodded, lowering his eyelids. "Can I assume that your noble desire is to free the spirits? This is why Spellbinder has spoken to you?"

Gwen realized then how intuitive the ghost panther was. He'd already made the connection about her mission and goal. "Well, it seems you've already figured it out," she said. "Yes, Posh and I are working to sell the castle. In order to do that, we must first cleanse it, so to speak. But my real goal is to free the trapped spirits."

"And this is a commission from the castle's owner, who hired the man named Kershaw?" Bally continued.

"You think that selling the castle is a bad idea?" Posh said.

"It is not my place to decide the castle's fate," Bally said.

"Let's just get to Java House," Gwen said. "We'll decide what to do first thing in the morning."

"Right after my morning coffee," Posh said.

"Oh, of course," Gwen replied good-naturedly.

"Coffee?" Balley said, a curious tone in his voice.

"It is a scrumptious drink, my good Bally," LinHem said, and clapped his talon on the sandy beach.

"Hold on," Posh said and stopped the griffin. "You drink coffee?"

Gwen could see that Posh was about to burst into laughter.

"Oh, yes," LinHem said. "As often as I can."

"Well, it's settled then!" Posh exclaimed. "We're going to hit Sephora Bean first thing in the morning."

Once they made it to Java House, the sun had settled low over the horizon, its bright rays cutting a swath of gold across the Green Sea.

Posh stepped up to the back patio door and punched in the code. She moved inside and flopped down on the leather sofa and stretched out. "It feels so good to be home again."

LinHem and Bally both had to duck in through the doorway. Gwen followed them inside.

"Hmm, very nice," LinHem hooted and walked around the kitchen, wings folded back and his talons clicking on the marble tile.

Bally sat on his haunches but didn't bother to venture around.

"Don't you want to see your room?" Posh asked.

"No. Right here will do." The ghost panther closed his eyes and instantly fell into a state of meditation.

The others looked at him, shocked at how quickly Bally had gone into his trance.

Posh walked over and waved her hand in front of the panther. "Wow. He may not need sleep, but he's serious about his meditations. Guess that means LinHem gets to choose which room he wants."

In the morning, Posh and Bally were up early. Gwen walked into the living room to see that LinHem was missing.

"He must be out fishing for breakfast," Posh said.

When LinHem finally showed up, the group set off to Sephora Bean.

It was a humid and somewhat breezy day, the sun peeking over the sea. They drew numerous stares as they walked along the beach. When they got to Sephora Bean, they were quickly seated at their typical booth.

It was quite the sight, seeing a ghost panther lap up a buttermilk latte. Gwen didn't think she'd ever witnessed anything so bizarre as Bally and LinHem sitting in the booth of a coffee shoppe and enjoying a drink together.

Bally purred as he finished his fourth latte. "Why have I not heard of such a drink?"

"You've been asleep for a century, remember?" Posh said. "Anyway, better take it easy, or you'll be bouncing off the walls."

Gwen was anxious to be on her way, though, and paid the tab and left.

They found the hidden spiral staircase within the rock outcropping and climbed up to the castle grounds above.

Gwen used her key to enter Hidden Palm Grove, and they walked inside to see Kershaw waiting for them.

# CHAPTER 28

## *BALLY'S WAY*

KERSHAW STOOD FROM the sofa and set his morning paper on the credenza. He calmly placed his hands behind his back and eyed the four of them. "I see you've picked up a few companions."

Gwen glanced at Posh, then faced Kershaw. "Is that a problem?"

"No, I suppose not. You know what my goal is. However you accomplished that is up to you. Are these other two...*creatures* to receive part of your commission?"

Gwen glanced sidelong at LinHem, then Bally and shrugged. "Perhaps."

The four of them stood facing Kershaw while an uncomfortable silence filled the vast foyer. Posh started shuffling her feet, and Gwen could sense her nervousness. Posh still felt compelled to defend Kershaw, no doubt. But Gwen had no desire to talk to the man. Her attitude had changed since the night Posh had admitted that Kershaw had forced her into servitude.

Kershaw finally clapped his hands and moved to the exit. "Have it your way, Gwenevere. I just hope you can finish this on time." He turned to leave, then stopped. "Oh, I bumped into a troll this morning. He claims that you owe him a large sum of steam tokens. Is there something you're not telling me?"

Gwen held his gaze. "That's my business, Kershaw."

He shrugged, "Just don't let it get in the way." He gave them one last look before pushing through the front doors.

Gwen let out a long breath. *Bam Jino was in Valeside?*

LinHem glanced at her. "Am I missing something?"

Gwen shook her head. "Nothing to be concerned about."

"Seems like that gentleman could use a long sabbatical," LinHem said.

"He is a bit uptight," Posh agreed. "Anyway, shall we begin?"

Bally stood and paced around the floor of the foyer. He bent low occasionally to sniff the marble tiles, like he was searching for a scent. "You are correct, Gwenevere. There are many spirits here indeed. Trapped, I might add. They are here against their will, and they are not happy about it."

"Which would explain why the witching hour is not a time to be down in this area," Gwen said.

"Show me the safe zone," Bally said.

Gwen led them up the circular stairs and to the bedroom wing. They walked down the long corridor and past several suites where the high clerestory windows spilled morning light off the polished floors.

"It is quite the regal estate," LinHem said.

"It is. You'd love the private library, too," Gwen replied.

"Library?" LinHem squawked and stepped up next to her. "You don't say? Why, I'd love a chance to peruse it, assuming that's alright with you?"

"Yes, of course. As soon as we get Bally moving on his mapmaking, I'll take you to it."

When they reached the master suite, Bally stopped to sniff the heavy wooden doors. He reached up and pawed at the deep gashes in the wood. "What made these marks?"

"Oh…that's—" Gwen paused and scratched her head. "Uh, it's a ghost named Matilda. She seems to have imbued a butter knife."

Bally narrowed his green eyes. "Interesting. I'd say she has some unfinished business."

"As do these other spirits," Gwen said.

"Has Matilda come after you?" Bally asked.

"No, not exactly. Though it tries to get into this room every night. There must be a powerful ward on the door. So far, so good."

Bally sniffed the door for a few more seconds, then turned. "So, we have several things to do before nightfall. I shall begin."

"We'll leave you to it," Gwen said. "It's a large castle. Be careful you don't get lost. I'm taking LinHem to the library."

"I'll tag along with Bally," Posh said. Gwen could see she had little interest in the library.

Bally glanced at Posh and gave her a long look. "I will go places you may find unacceptable. Can you keep up?"

"Sure…" Posh said a bit hesitantly.

"Very well. Let us begin."

Posh and Bally left for the lower levels as Gwen led LinHem to the private library.

Gwen had difficulty finding the library. It still amazed her that she couldn't seem to get her bearings inside the castle, like the compass kept changing direction. But she eventually found it and pushed through the massive oak doors.

The library was the same as she'd left it. A thick layer of dust sat on all the surfaces, along with some diluted sunlight filtering in from the large stained-glass windows. They sat at a nearby table, and she kicked her feet up. "The library is all yours, LinHem. Have fun."

She thought the griffin was about to hop up and down in excitement.

"Oh, what a treat," he said. "Thank you, Gwenevere."

LinHem rushed off while Gwen sat in the leather chair and thought back to everything that had happened over the last several days. Then she thought about Kershaw and what he'd said down in the foyer. It had almost sounded like a threat. Kershaw's attitude toward her had definitely changed since they'd first met. Was he beginning to notice that her attitude had also changed? Most likely, yes. She needed to be cautious. Though she wasn't frightened or intimidated by Kershaw, there was no reason to upset him. She still had a contract to fulfil, and he was, after all, her employer now.

Still, she liked him less with each passing day, especially when she thought about Posh and how he'd essentially been holding her captive. In fact, Posh was more or less his servant, and that's what upset her the most.

Regardless, the clock was ticking, and her only hope now was Spellbinder. She needed to be efficient if she wanted to free these spirits, and her ruby amulet had reached its limit.

Gwen sat up with a start.

She tried to focus on her surroundings.

The sun was no longer pouring through the stained-glass windows, and all was quiet inside the library. She felt a moment of panic as she stood and hurried down one of the dark aisles.

"LinHem?" she called out. "Oh no," she whispered. Gwen sensed that the witching hour was near, and the griffin was nowhere to be seen.

Gwen pulled out her wand and lit the room with a luminance spell. She searched the entire library but found no sign of LinHem. She rushed out of the library and down the dark corridors. Her wand lit the spaces, shadows leaping away as she sprinted into the foyer.

"Posh! Bally!"

The sound of her voice echoed around the large chamber as she waited for a response.

Then she felt the space come to life.

The witching hour was near: Hidden Palm Grove was waking.

Gwen grasped her amulet and held it. She sat down right in the middle of the large foyer and began to chant. Her amulet lit up, a red light from the ruby. Gwen fell quickly into a trance, and soon, she was standing outside of her body. She placed a protective ward around her physical being, knowing she had only a few hours to find her friends.

Gwen ran around the lower levels, her ethereal form wispy and gossamer-like. She searched the hallways, then the butler's pantry and kitchen. All the while, spirits began to float aimlessly around her. Soon, the space was littered with the ghostly string-like figures, phasing in and out of the walls and ceilings.

After a full search of the ground level, Gwen came up empty, though. There was no sign of Posh, LinHem or Bally. Gwen was about to start a second loop when she stumbled upon the large central staircase. She decided to go down a few levels and try near the basement.

Gwen called out in her ethereal form, trying to get to the others. She felt that perhaps she could reach the ghost panther, knowing that he could see into the ether realm as well.

Eventually, she heard the panther respond. They were down one more level…only…there wasn't another level.

Gwen stopped, confused. But it was clear—the others were one level below her. They must have found a way down.

She searched the circular staircase, letting her ethereal hands float over the smooth white stone until she felt something inside one of the grout joints. It was an engraving, something she'd missed before. She pressed it, and the stairs spiraled downward. Like an optical illusion, when she walked around to the other side, it disappeared. Yet when she stood at the top landing and placed her foot on the stairs, it was solid.

Trusting her instincts, she placed her other foot on the next step. Gwen continued downward. Before long, she was descending into a lower level she didn't know existed.

At the bottom of the hidden staircase, Gwen paused to listen.

She was at least two levels below the basement now. It was much warmer down here, even in her ethereal form. It felt heavy, the air was still and somewhat stagnant. There was an ominous feeling that she couldn't explain. Though the main level had that same feeling, this was much worse, and it made her wonder what the others would be doing down here.

She focused on Bally again. He seemed to be the one she could somehow track. She was guessing that he could sense her too, and maybe they would bump into each other. But she had to hurry, her protection ward would run out soon, and she could easily lose track of time when she was in her phased state.

The corridors were more rudimentary, like carved stone from some cave. It was obvious that the remodel hadn't extended to these levels, probably because the owner wasn't aware of this hidden basement. There seemed to be some strong magic on the place, and Gwen began to wonder why. What was hidden down in these depths?

The floor was paved with rough blocks, which were hewn stone with a worn sheen on the surface from years of foot traffic. Many people had once traversed these corridors it seemed.

"Bally?" she called out, her voice barely more than a whisper.

It continued to grow warmer as she moved through what she now assumed were catacombs. As she glided along, she could feel Bally's energy tugging at her core. She let her form follow it.

Then she saw them.

There was Posh, sitting with her forefingers and thumbs together, as if she was about to dispense some of her magic. But for some reason, she was frozen in place. Then she saw LinHem reared back on his hind legs in a frozen state as well. Bally was missing, though.

Gwen stood behind them and focused some energy from the amulet. She could hear it speaking to her in Kriss's voice.

*Free them*, Gwen whispered.

The amulet lit up with a red flash, and something like a fog moved to encompass Posh and LinHem. Suddenly, they were moving again.

Gwen tried to talk to them, but in her ethereal form, she had no substance or sound. LinHem and Posh stood, looking around. Gwen could see a bit of panic on Posh's face as she pulled at LinHem, forcing him back down the stairs.

"We have to find Bally," Posh said.

"There's no time," LinHem said. "He's gone elsewhere."

"He wouldn't leave us behind."

"We must go. Bally can look after himself."

Gwen watched them move up the stairs.

She turned and continued looking. But soon, she got the sense that Bally was no longer on this lower level. He'd already moved up and out of the catacombs. She followed Posh and LinHem up the spiral stairs and away from the basement.

Gwen used her amulet's power to make sure that her friends were safely into the master suite's safe zone. Then she returned to her form and settled back into herself. When she awoke, the amulet's energy was nearly spent. Gwen sprinted up the staircase and down the corridor, barging into the master suite. She slammed the door behind her, then turned to see LinHem and Posh staring at her, both looking a bit rattled.

Gwen breathed in relief. She felt exhausted and knelt to the floor on one knee.

Posh and LinHem gathered around her.

"What happened?" Gwen said.

LinHem looked at her a bit bashfully. "Forgive me, but I heard Posh yelling and left the library. Bally had gotten trapped on the spiral staircase. Posh and I went after him. I suppose we got stuck in a ghost loop while searching for him. Bally was there one instant, then he was gone. I have no idea where he went."

"He was looking for a path to Spellbinder," Posh said. "He stepped onto the stairs and disappeared. That's when I called for LinHem."

There was a sudden tapping on the door.

Posh looked at Gwen. "What's that?"

Gwen waved it away. "Matilda, the butter knife chef. Just ignore it."

"Ignore it?" Posh said. "Seriously?"

"She's not after us," Gwen said. "Apparently, some residual essence looking for a specific person." Gwen continued to pace while Posh and LinHem waited. She walked through the double doors and onto the balcony, letting the moonlight wash over her. The sultry breeze wafted up from the ocean below, helping to calm her nerves.

"What are you thinking?" Posh said as she stood beside her.

"Nothing, at the moment. The amulet's energy is gone. Bally is on his own now."

"I get the sense he'll be fine," LinHem said. "He's had a century of practice around spirits."

"We'll have to wait till the morning," Gwen said. "Might as well settle in for the night. Not much else we can do."

The three of them brought some blankets and pillows out to the spacious balcony, mainly because of the constant banging from Matilda. They circled around and talked about the day's events while gazing up at the stars. But Gwen couldn't stop thinking about Bally and hoped he'd be okay. At some point during the night, she finally dozed off.

The warmth of the sun on Gwen's face woke her. She sat up and stretched to the sound of gulls in the distance and the low crooning of the ocean below. Posh was curled up next to her, but LinHem was nowhere to be seen. Gwen had a suspicion he was out fishing for his breakfast.

She gently shook Posh awake. "Let's go see what we can find."

When Gwen opened the door to the master suite, Matilda's butter knife was stuck in the door.

Posh gave Gwen a wide-eyed look. "It's a sign."

"A sign?" Gwen asked. "What are you talking about?"

"Take it," Posh said. "I've seen this before."

That made Gwen narrow her eyes. "Since when did you become a sleuth?"

"I'm not. But I've been around for a while and seen a thing or two."

Gwen almost started laughing. "You've seen a spirit leave a knife stuck in a door?"

"Well, no. Not a knife. It was actually a sword. And it was wedged in a tree."

Gwen placed her hands on her hips, waiting.

"It was an executioner who'd been wrongfully killed," Posh continued. "His spirit latched onto a friend of mine and left the sword behind."

"Are you saying that Matilda has selected me to take up this…butter knife?"

"Yes, I think so," Posh said. "And I also think you'd better take it. A spirit blade is extremely rare in Ambriel."

Gwen took in a long breath, then walked over and pulled the butter knife from the door. It made a dull 'thunk' sound, and she held it for a second, as if to say, *Fine, are you happy now?* Then she stuck it in her satchel. "Satisfied?"

The two of them walked down the spiral stairs and to the ground level, calling out for Bally and trying to listen for any movement.

"Should we check down in the catacombs?" Posh asked.

Gwen shook her head. "Let's just stay here for the moment. I have a feeling he'll show up soon enough."

They went to the kitchen and scrounged up something for breakfast. Tom must have recently stocked the pantry with fresh eggs and bread. Posh brewed a pot of coffee, and they sat in the breakfast nook.

"Not sure where Bally's gotten to," Posh said. "You sure he hasn't just left us?"

"He'll be back."

"What makes you say that?"

"Because he wants the sigils as much as I do, Posh. Remember, Bally's desire is somehow aligned with mine."

"And I wonder why he's so reluctant to tell us what that is?" Posh mused.

Gwen could only shrug. "It must be deeply personal. I assume he'll share it when he's ready."

"Isn't it odd, though? I mean, just when we need someone who can map a way back to the telescope, Bally shows up. He also knows the history behind Spellbinder."

"Yes. I noticed that. The only answer I can come up with is that Spellbinder caused it."

Posh shook her head, though. "I don't see how a magical telescope could do such a thing, Gwen. I've witnessed some strange things in my life. But never a sentient telescope."

"Well, call it a witch's intuition, but there's something bigger going on."

"But why would it be trying to help us?"

"That's the big question," Gwen said.

"I don't know. It just doesn't make sense—"

"It makes complete sense," someone said from behind them.

Both Gwen and Posh jumped as Bally suddenly appeared from the opposite side of the breakfast nook.

Posh leaned over the table and threw her arms around the large cat's neck. "Where did you go! You can't just leave us like that."

Bally ignored them. "I've found the way."

"So, you've mapped it out?" Gwen said. "You're certain?"

"Indeed. And I have it memorized. A ghost panther never forgets its way."

# CHAPTER 29

## *THE SECOND GOLDEN SIGIL*

WELL, WHAT ARE we waiting for?" Posh said. "Let's get on with it."

Bally led the way. It was a path that Gwen somewhat remembered, though it was fuzzy and gray in her mind's eye. She'd only stumbled upon it by chance, and it still felt like a dream. Of course, her theory now was that Spellbinder had made the way clear because it had wanted her to find it. But without Bally, she would never have found her way back.

As they strolled through the main living area, LinHem joined them. He'd finished his breakfast, or fishing expedition, and fell in next to Gwen.

"Can I assume that Bally's return means he's found the way?" LinHem said.

"Yes," Posh replied. "And he's mapped it as well."

"Marked it on the walls, did he? Ah, very smart. Excellent idea," LinHem crowed.

Gwen watched as Bally rolled his eyes in subtle annoyance.

Bally moved through the maze of corridors that seemed to magically shift. What Gwen remembered was now completely different. Bally stopped occasionally to sniff the walls, then his eyes would light up to reveal a large pawprint on the wall, as if it had been traced with invisible ink. Then it faded just as quickly.

"Stay close," Bally said. Posh was nearly riding on Bally's back as they moved deeper into the maze of corridors.

The limestone corridors were mostly vacant. There were no portraits or any other decorations on the walls. With no distinguishing marks, it didn't take long before Gwen was completely turned around. She knew if she got separated from the group, she'd be forever lost in the wandering halls of Hidden Palm Grove.

Bally continued to use his glowing eyes to reveal the invisible pawprints. They seemed to walk for hours, and Gwen felt like she was caught in some nightmarish maze. But eventually, they climbed a curving set of stairs.

Finally, Bally stopped in front of a large iron door.

"I recognize this door," Gwen said.

Bally stood in front of it, blocking the way. "Before we enter, know that Spellbinder thrives on positive energy. Negative thoughts are discouraged. Be careful what you say and do."

Posh nodded, along with LinHem and Gwen.

"Very well, let us enter," Bally said and led them into the lighthouse.

It was just as Gwen recalled from her first visit. The lighthouse was a rotunda-shaped space with a full view of Ambriel. The clarity of the vista felt like an illusion. She seemed to be able to see the entire continent in all directions. There were intermittent clouds in a puffy pink color just above them, and beyond was the glint of sunlight off the Green Sea. The sigils embedded into the floor glittered at them like golden points of light. Overhead, she could see stars and galaxies, which gave the lighthouse an even more dreamlike vibe.

Of course, the telescope in the center was the main attraction. Like a giant contraption of steel and gears and cogs, its metallic colors of brass and copper blended to create some sort of steampunk anomaly.

Gwen noticed the missing golden sigils, which she knew now to be the keys to her quest.

Posh and LinHem walked around in awe as Bally rubbed against the telescope like he was greeting some long-lost friend.

Gwen stepped onto the massive staircase that encircled the telescope and walked up, letting her hand glide over the aged, patinaed handrail. She made a full circle before reaching the top. The long tube of the massive telescope tapered down to the eyepiece, and on the opposite end was the enormous lens.

"Before you seek the next sigil, you must replace the first one," Bally said.

Gwen felt for the trinket in her satchel and drew it out. The golden sigil was glowing now, a dull shine that pulsed like a heartbeat. "Right, of course," she said and descended the staircase.

The four companions circled the cobbled floor, searching through the plethora of golden sigils until Posh found the void.

Gwen knelt and traced the tree-shaped void with her fingers, then placed the golden sigil into it.

The space around them seemed to hum in response, and the air inside the observatory grew heavy, filled with positive energy. If Gwen didn't know any better, she sensed that the telescope seemed happy.

"Now," Bally said. "You may gaze into Spellbinder."

Gwen made her way up the staircase again and approached the telescope. She oriented it toward the next sigil, took a deep breath and peered into the eyepiece.

Spellbinder took control of her vision. It guided her across the landscape of Ambriel, like she was riding on the back of a dragon and speeding over the mountains and lakes and pastures. Greens and blues and purples shot by so fast that it made her feel disoriented. Finally, her visions slowed and solidified. Below her was a single puffy cloud. It was separated from the others, like a kingdom apart from the neighboring clouds. Poking through the top of it was what appeared to be a city of gears chugging away. It reminded her of the telescope with all the parts and assorted metals and alloys, glistening in the misty sunlight.

Then, her vision reversed, as though time was rewinding. She was catapulted backwards before finally connecting with her physical form. Gwen stumbled away from the telescope, her head spinning. Posh raced over and caught her by the waist and held her upright.

Gwen held a hand to her forehead. "Well…that was quite the experience, a bit different than last time."

Posh helped her down the stairs, where the four of them gathered around.

"What did it show you?" Posh asked.

Gwen sat down on the cobbled floor and leaned back on her hands. "I…I saw mountains, and there was a cloud. It was pink, and it floated above one of the mountaintops."

"A pink cloud?" Posh said. "Anything else you remember?"

"There were gears and gadgets inside the cloud, like a clock. There was plenty of snow. That one cloud, though, it almost didn't seem real."

Gwen looked at Bally and LinHem, but both shook their heads.

"I apologize," LinHem said. "Geography is not an area of expertise for me. But perhaps we can look over the maps. The castle's library might have some information."

Since there was nothing else to be gleaned from Spellbinder, they left the observatory. But it was growing late, and they had no desire to spend another night in the haunted castle.

Bally led them back to the foyer, which took a while to navigate the shifting walls. By the time they made it back, it was getting close to dusk. The group had a bite to eat, scrounging something from the butler's pantry of dried goods. Thankfully, Tom had once again stocked the castle's kitchen. It turned out that LinHem was a fine cook and whipped up some oats with figs and berries. Gwen thought she'd seen it all, but watching a griffin cook seemed to defy logic.

They finished their meal just as the sun dipped below the Green Sea and quickly left the castle.

As they walked along the beach toward Java House, Bally paced next to Gwen.

"Your amulet," Bally said, nodding to the ruby around her neck. "It is a special item to you?"

"Yes. It belonged to a close friend of mine. She was murdered when we were in school."

"And she gave it to you?"

Gwen tilted her head, wondering where Bally was headed with his questions. "Not exactly. I stole it." She noticed the look on Bally's face and quickly added, "...though I think she wanted me to have it."

"Why do you believe that?"

Gwen shrugged as she continued to walk next to Bally. "It's just a feeling that I get. I confronted her mother about it and confessed. She forgave me and said that her daughter would have wanted me to have it. The amulet speaks to me in my friend's voice. I imagine you've had similar experiences?"

By giving Bally more explanation, Gwen was hoping the panther might open up about his own past. She sensed that he was beginning to trust his new companions. Maybe now was the time to press him a bit.

Bally's green eyes flashed in the dark as he padded along. Gwen noticed his long tail whipping about in a playful way. "When I was a cub, I lived in a land across the Green Sea. A jungle environment filled with my kind. I was happy there with my family. My mother and father led a community of panthers. But when the traders came to our jungle, they trapped and shipped off our kind until we were mostly depleted. I was taken captive and sent away from my family. A group of gnomes adopted me, once I reached Ambriel. I worked in a traveling circus, where I caught the attention of the great wizard, Speartine. He had created a preserve for other wayward creatures."

"You must miss your family."

"Yes, very much," Bally said. "Over the years, I gradually gained the wizard's trust and became his assistant. Since I had the ability to travel into the dream realm, he had a need for me. I protected his magical relics, which is how I came to know Spellbinder."

Gwen listened to the panther, rapt with interest now. When she glanced over her shoulder, she saw a frozen tear stuck to Posh's cheek, and LinHem sniffled. But Bally didn't seem to notice and continued with his story.

"One day, the same traders came after Speartine. Though my master was very powerful, he was also kind and naïve. Unfortunately, he believed that everyone was peaceful in his land. Perhaps this was his one great flaw—he trusted others too much. He couldn't fathom the evil that dwelled in the hearts of some people. It cost him that day. The animals in his preserve were rounded up and shipped off. I watched as Speartine was killed by a simple trader. A great loss to the land of Ambriel…all because of greed. I was enslaved for the second time that day. However, my master did have the foresight to hide many of his relics. The lighthouse at Hidden Palm Grove was built with strong wards to protect it."

"Is this why you are seeking Spellbinder's sigils?" Gwen asked. "For revenge on the traders?"

Bally looked at Gwen. "Have you learned nothing about Spellbinder? It does not grant desires based on negative energy. Only noble desires can be attained through its sigils."

"Then, what is it you seek?" Gwen continued.

"The same as you, Gwenevere. Many of the spirits within the castle are my family and friends, creatures who were forced into labor or murdered by the traders. It is and has been my goal to free them."

# CHAPTER 30

## *A LITTLE SAINT HALVING SPIRIT*

GWEN, POSH AND LinHem all stopped walking. Only the sound of the waves crashing onto the beach broke the silence.

"Now you know my story," Bally said, "and now you know why I must accompany you. Our desires align, Gwenevere. 'Tis not happenstance that you found me. I will travel with you until the end…until the castle at Hidden Palm Grove has been cleansed and every single spirit set free from its chains, including my murdered family."

Posh rushed forward and threw her arms around Bally's neck and buried her face into his plaid fur. "I'm so sorry, Bally. Why didn't you say something sooner?"

"I was not ready, and the time was not relevant. Now that I know the three of you are invested in this quest, I have no qualms in sharing my story."

Gwen stepped forward and placed her hands on Bally's shoulders. "Thank you for trusting us and sharing your story. I will do everything I can to help free your friends and family who were wrongfully murdered."

Early the following morning, Gwen and Posh sat on the deck at Java House and talked. The morning sun was rising, and the air pushing in from the south was drier and cooler, though she felt a slight crispness in the breeze.

"We're going shopping," Gwen said.

Posh sat up, and the golden flecks in her eyes lit up. "Shut up. Are you kidding me? Since when do you care about shopping?"

"I guess it's a recent development."

"Are the others coming along?" Posh said with a bit of giddiness in her tone.

"No…gosh no," Gwen said and feigned shock. "Can you imagine a panther and a griffin in Rothmar & Vine?"

Posh giggled at that. "But wouldn't it be fun?"

Gwen only shook her head and laughed. "Honestly, I need to do some Saint Halving shopping for them. I feel like it will lighten the mood a bit, especially after yesterday."

"Of course, you don't have to twist my arm," Posh said.

LinHem had already snuck out to do his morning fishing, and Bally was still meditating, which was one thing Gwen noticed about the panther: he could stay in that state for long periods. She wondered if he was making up for centuries of lost time.

Gwen left a note on the kitchen island asking LinHem to go back to the castle and return with any maps he could find from the library. Then Gwen and Posh made a quick trip to Sephora Bean for a morning latte. Gwen wanted to stay and lounge the morning away and enjoy the sea breeze. But Posh was anxious to hit the shoppes, and soon they were on the coach to the market.

Their first stop was to Rothmar & Vine, of course, which was Posh's favorite store. Gwen felt she was starting to enjoy shopping. Whether it was the Saint Halving Day spirit or something else, she didn't know. But she found something she thought LinHem would enjoy, which was a hunting satchel for keeping fish fresh. Posh was specifically shopping for Bally, though (a set of hiking boots to keep his paws warm), and Gwen could tell that the genie was building a certain fondness for the ghost panther.

Soon, they were moving on to other shoppes. Gwen let Posh lead the way, and the genie was practically hopping up and down with enthusiasm. She pulled Gwen by the hand across the market and into each shoppe.

Before long, they'd hit practically every store in Valeside's downtown area. The ornaments and holiday lights added to the festive spirit. The crowds were out in full, and everywhere they went, it was packed with shoppers. In the afternoon, they took a quick break to eat. Posh introduced Gwen to some fusion food—a honey-roasted nut with blackberry marmalade, which had a sweet, but bitter taste. Gwen was experiencing so many new things with Posh that it made her head spin.

Eventually, Posh asked to split up for an hour or so. *We can get more done if we split up*, she said. Gwen agreed and used that time to get some shopping in for Posh. She browsed through the stores, trying to think what a genie might want. She hadn't really considered it. In fact, she'd never really thought about shopping for others because she'd never had many friends or family. It was all new to her, something she was trying to get used to.

Gwen stopped in front of a jewelry store with golden trinkets in the windows.

She stepped inside and browsed through the rings, necklaces and bracelets. If there was one thing she had noticed about Posh, it was that she liked jewelry, whether it be gold or platinum or precious gems. Posh had mentioned a few of her jewelry items in passing, referring to them as mementos or reminders of certain times in her life. Maybe Gwen could give Posh a reminder of their new friendship, an item symbolic of the barriers they'd overcome?

The clerk walked up and greeted Gwen, a younger lady with a kind but tired look on her face. Her name tag read Dorris.

"How can I help you?" Dorris said.

"I'm shopping for a friend."

"Okay. Can you tell me more?" Dorris asked.

"Well, she's a genie, if that helps."

"Oh, a genie? Well, we don't see many of them around. Genies are quite fond of gold jewelry. I have a few things over here..." Dorris walked off, and Gwen followed.

"This is our Heritage Collection. These items are relics from the Holland Empire. Very sought after, I might add."

Gwen walked around the large, circular rack. It was shaped like a tree with metallic branches that held dozens of shiny necklaces, rings and bracelets. Gwen could see that each piece had a story to tell, perhaps reminders of love, heartache or celebration. She found one in particular that looked very similar to her own ruby amulet. In fact, it was the same style and shape, but with a turquoise sapphire instead. It was a close match to the color of Posh's skin. Gwen picked it up and looked at the price tag, then nearly dropped the amulet.

"This one is from the early Holland Empire, and it's several hundred years old. It's said to have belonged to the princess." Dorris held it up; the pale blue jewel glinted in the light. "Notice the motifs? Rumored to hold special enchantments, perfect for a loved one. Old jewelry never goes out of style," Dorris said and handed it back to Gwen. "Shall I wrap it up?"

Despite the price, Gwen knew it was perfect. She had the steam tokens in her account from the stipend anyway.

"I'll take it."

Dorris brought it to the counter. "Would you like it engraved?"

"You can do that?"

"Certainly. What would you like it to say?"

Gwen thought for a moment. "How about…"

*Freedom.*
*Your friend,*
*Gwenevere*

Dorris took the sapphire amulet to the back, then brought it out to show Gwen.

"It's perfect," Gwen said.

The shoppes were starting to close down for the night when Gwen found Posh. With their arms full of gifts, they boarded the coach. It was dark when they made it back to Java House. Thankfully, LinHem and Bally weren't there, and Gwen and Posh quickly hid the gifts and started making dinner.

Soon, LinHem returned, followed by Bally. LinHem had several rolls of parchment in his beak and dropped them on the kitchen island. "Behold, I return with maps. And my goodness, what is that smell?"

Bally's tail perked up when he smelled the food. Gwen noticed his eyelids droop in satisfaction at the scent, and he began to purr loud enough to shake the dishes.

"I'm cooking tonight," Posh said, gliding around the kitchen. "Well, what did we discover today?"

"Might we discuss after dinner?" LinHem said. "It is difficult to talk strategy on an empty stomach, after all."

Everyone agreed, and soon the four of them gathered on the patio. Posh set the outdoor table, and they sat and had wine, roasted veggies, and LinHem's favorite, grilled fish. It was like the family dinner that Gwen had always wanted, and she felt grateful for her friends.

Eventually, they finished and sat back, looking at the ocean glinting in the moonlight. The fireflies floated like embers on the breeze and lit the entire bay area in a green and yellow bonfire of color.

"Mind grabbing the maps now?" Gwen asked.

LinHem brought the rolled pieces of parchment out and flattened them on the table.

"So, what do we know?" Posh asked and clapped her hands.

LinHem cleared his throat. "Though I am not familiar with the northern regions or the mountains, Bally and I have made a few determinations. Based on your description, and after talking to some librarians, we are looking at this area." LinHem pointed a talon at a lone mountain in the northeastern range of Glacia Falls called Steamtop Mountain.

"Steamtop Mountain?" Gwen muttered. "I've not heard of it, though I'm familiar with the Glacia Falls Mountain Range."

"Nor have I," LinHem said. "But the images we found seem to match the vision you described. I think it is a good place to start."

Gwen thought for a moment, then sat forward. "Agreed. We're running out of time. I say we get there as soon as possible."

"How soon?" Posh said.

Gwen gave her a pat on the shoulder. "We leave tomorrow."

# CHAPTER 31

## *THE GREAT STEAMPUNK ADVENTURE*

THEY PACKED EARLY the next morning and took a coach to the nearest skyport, which sat atop several of the taller skyscrapers. The sprawling port was fancy, which was saying something, being in downtown Valeside. Posh paid for their airfare with Kershaw's account, and they found the correct terminal and boarded the strange craft.

Gwen had never been aboard a blimp, nor had she ever seen one up close. It was a long-range vessel, and there were hundreds of passengers boarding it. Its outer skin was a silvery metallic that glowed like platinum in the sunlight. It was long and elliptical, the outer skin stretched around an inner skeletal framework made of a lightweight alloy. It had a dorsal fin, reminding Gwen of a whale, though there were also several fins along the bottom side too. Once on board, Gwen noticed that there were multiple levels inside the hull, built between the alloy frame. It almost felt like sitting inside an arena.

On the middle levels, there was entertainment, like movies, plays and musicals. The upper level was an observation deck with miniature telescopes and hammocks for relaxing while taking in the dreamy cloudscape. It appeared that there was plenty to do aboard the massive airship, which was good, considering that the trip wasn't short. Gwen felt some trepidation when she boarded: airflight probably wasn't going to set well with her. But she placed her trust in the engineering of the craft and tried to relax.

Their seats were located on the lowest level, which gave them a good view of the ground below. Through the tiny glasslike portals, Gwen could see the ground in purples and earth tones like a quilt. She settled in next to Posh with Bally and LinHem forced to sit in the aisles, due to their size.

LinHem huffed. "Well, the audacity. How embarrassing."

The other passengers were starting to give him dirty looks as he tried to wedge his lion's rump into the plush felt seating anyway. Bally was also trying to get comfortable, but as he tried to sit in the chair, it began to separate, and eventually, it collapsed with a loud crash.

"Uh, fellas," Posh said. "Maybe you'd be more comfortable on the top deck? There's plenty of fresh air and more room."

LinHem still looked upset while Bally just walked up the narrow steel stairs and disappeared. LinHem gave them a frustrated look, as if he was about to report the inconvenience to the stewardess. But instead, he stood and marched up the stairs after Bally.

Posh gave Gwen an exasperated look and lowered her seat to a flat position. "I'll cover the ruined seat. Kershaw's going to want an explanation for that one."

Gwen shifted in her seat, still trying to relax. Her hands gripped the armrest a bit tighter, and Posh noticed.

"Thought you'd be right at home in the air, being a witch…broomsticks and all. Come to think of it, how come I've never seen yours?"

"Don't own one, never did. Truth is, green witches don't use brooms like reds and yellows do, since they're made of wood. Killing trees to ride a stick? That's just unethical."

"Oh. Well, that's interesting," Posh said and leaned back. "I wouldn't worry. There hasn't been a blimp crash in a few months."

"Few months?" Gwen said. "They happen that often?"

But Posh had already pulled a mask over her eyes and didn't answer.

The blimp began to lift. It bumped and hissed, causing Gwen to grip the armrest even tighter. It banked at a slight angle, then nosed upward. The wings on the sides began to flap, making the entire vessel thrum. Soon, they were moving at a good pace, the soft white clouds zooming past Gwen's window. But Gwen couldn't get relaxed enough to sit still, and she decided to go find LinHem and Bally.

The upper observation deck was amazing. Gwen could see all around her in every direction. It was quiet amidst the clouds, and the stillness was breathtaking. There was an outer railing made of brass, with telescopes stationed around the perimeter, and a few passengers lounging in the sun. It almost reminded Gwen of the cruise liner they'd taken to the Autumn Forest, but with the tables and chairs.

LinHem and Bally were seated up front, chatting with one of the employees.

"…so the gear system uses how many cogs?" LinHem was asking.

"Over one thousand in total, quite the engineering feat," the employee bragged. "Would you like a tour?"

"Oh, that would be fascinating," LinHem said. "Gwen, are you coming along?"

In truth, Gwen wasn't interested in seeing the internal workings of the airship. She preferred to stay up top in hopes of settling her nerves. "Umm, maybe Bally can accompany you?"

Bally was stretched out on one of the lounge sofas, eyes closed. "I have no desire to see the internal system," he said flatly.

LinHem waved him off. "Come, Gwen. This should be very educational." LinHem pushed her with his beak toward the stairs.

They followed the deck hand from the observation level to the engineering level down below. The engineering section was hot and steamy with loud hissing and chugging noises. The gears were made of bright metallic parts that spun and glittered in the dull light.

"These gears keep the interior hull inflated, while also propelling the wings," one of the engineering officers stated to a group of passengers. "The air inside is lighter than the outside air, which keeps the blimp buoyant enough to float."

"Fascinating," LinHem said. He began a conversation with the engineer on the synchronization of gears and the perpetual motion of the motor.

Gwen quickly lost interest, though, and found the young deckhand who'd led them down to the engineering section. "Excuse me."

The young man was a winged fairy with dark lilac skin and green eyes. "Yes, is there something else you need?"

"Just a few questions about our destination. Do you know of Steamtop Mountain?"

The fairy seemed to stiffen, his hands clenched by his sides. "What do you want to know?"

"Well, anything you could tell me would be great."

"We do not recommend traveling to that mountaintop."

Gwen narrowed her eyes. "Why would you say that? Is it a bad place?"

"Be careful of Steamtop Mountain. The winds are dangerous there."

The blimp docked at a much smaller skyport in the quaint province of Hithertu. Due to the northern climate, snow blanketed the ground most of the year, creating a hushed environment. The picturesque province reminded Gwen of her hometown, Kalispell, which had her feeling slightly homesick. Horsedrawn sleds zipped through the snow-covered streets. Gwen and Posh donned their heavy coats, gloves and boots. Bally and LinHem had no such needs. The four of them moved down the main street and found a hotel for the night.

"Shouldn't be more than one night," Gwen said in a hopeful tone, though in truth she didn't mind it if they happened to get snowed in for an extra night or two. She had already grown to love the sundrenched beaches of Valeside, but at times she missed Kalispell's cozy nature, snow-covered hillsides and hot cocoa.

Posh, who'd never seen snow, held a look of wonder on her face. Although her skin temperature was already cool to the touch, and she disliked the colder weather, she seemed fascinated by the white blanket. She even cupped a few snowballs and threw them at Bally, which drew a warning growl.

Once they'd unpacked and changed, they met in the lobby of the wood lodge.

"What's the best path to the mountain?" Posh said.

LinHem drew out the map with his beak. "According to this, Steamtop Mountain is about half a day's travel."

"We passed a sleigh service on the way," Bally said. "It would be much more efficient than hiking there."

Posh gripped Gwen's arm. "Ooh. A sleigh ride? That sounds like fun."

"Well," Gwen said, looking down at Posh's arm hooked around hers. "How can anyone say no to that?" In truth, Gwen was just as excited.

They found the service not far from the hotel. They managed to convince the owner to rent them just the sleigh, no horses. Gwen suspected that the sight of Bally and LinHem had the owner a bit nervous when he finally agreed.

With Bally and LinHem hitched (both of them were actually larger than a horse), they thundered off toward the mountain. Soon, they were winding along snow-covered paths beneath tall pines. LinHem had memorized the directions, which allowed Gwen to sit back and enjoy the ride. Posh was giddy with excitement and explored the different compartments inside the sleigh. She found a magical oven, some mugs and cocoa powder. In short order, Gwen and Posh both had a steaming mug of hot cocoa.

With Posh cozied up next to her, Gwen almost felt like she was on vacation. For a split second, she forgot about the haunted castle, the spirits, Kershaw, Spellbinder, and all of the quests for golden sigils. Gwen just wanted to relax and unwind on the ride to Steamtop Mountain. It might be her last moment to relax, at least for the foreseeable future.

The ride took most of that remaining day. They relied on the sure footing of LinHem and Bally as they began to climb the narrow paths of Steamtop. The view was grand, though, and it was hard not to get lost in the majesty of the landscape.

Just before dusk set in, they finally made it to Steamtop Mountain.

Gwen was relieved and disappointed at the same time. Everyone spread out and explored the peak. Gwen wasn't sure what they were looking for, but in the back of her mind was what the deckhand had told her: *Be careful of Steamtop Mountain. The winds are dangerous there.*

They could see all around them in every direction for miles. But despite the warning, there was hardly any wind, which Gwen thought was a bit odd. When they neared the very center of the peak, Gwen heard a chugging noise. It was a soft chiming from above, like glitter floating on the air.

"Do you hear it?" Gwen said.

"Indeed," LinHem said.

"Look, over there." Posh nodded.

An area of the pink cloud had descended lower and was making contact with the mountaintop. The cloud swirled and pulsed like it was breathing.

Bally moved cautiously toward it with Posh right next to him, gripping his fur. Gwen followed, her wand at the ready, with LinHem bringing up the rear, his hackles raised slightly.

When they got to the undulating cloud they stopped.

"Who wants to be the first one to step into the strange cloud?" Posh joked.

Gwen swept her hand into the cloud and tiny eddies of steam flowed through her fingertips. "It's warm. This isn't a cloud. It's steam." She looked at the others, then turned and stepped into the white mass.

# CHAPTER 32

## *STEAMTOP MOUNTAIN*

GWEN STEPPED JUST inside the steam-infused cloud formation, and it took her a second to reorient.

It was hot and humid inside, the temperature much warmer than it should be atop the mountain. But this wasn't a natural cloud, she knew that now. This was a synthetic atmosphere. *But created by who and why?*

Gwen removed her overcoat and ventured deeper into the cloud. With a flick of her wand, she used a disperse spell to clear out the steam. But the foggy environment remained so thick that she could barely see a meter in front of her. Soon, she heard Posh, Bally and LinHem move next to her.

"LinHem, Bally?" she said. "Any thoughts?"

"There is strange magic here," Bally said.

"It appears to be a manmade environment," LinHem muttered. "Magic, science and machinery. Fascinating."

"It seems someone wanted this place hidden for a reason," Gwen said. "But why?"

"Maybe to keep tourists out?" Posh replied. "Let's have another look at that map."

LinHem pulled the old map out again, and Gwen used a luminance spell to light the area with her wand.

"Hmm..." LinHem hooted. "Well, this map *is* from the castle's private library. It's old and likely very unique. I see some markings on the map now." He adjusted his spectacles and pointed a talon at the corner. There was a glyph, which was glowing in a light copper tone. It was shaped like a mountain with a cloudlike halo around it.

Bally spoke up. "It would appear we've found a secret entrance. Look on the back of the map."

When LinHem flipped the parchment over, there was an intricate floor plan. Like the glyph on the front, the floor plan was etched in a copper ink. "This wasn't here before."

"It must be a map of Steamtop Mountain," Gwen said.

"Okay," Posh said. "So, we just need to figure out where we are and where we're going."

"Ah, look here." LinHem pointed at the top of a tower. Above it was something shaped like a star. "Perhaps this is where the sigil lies? It does look like quite the trek, however."

"We must be cautious," Bally said. "This place is old, and I sense sorcery."

Gwen led the way with her wand held high. LinHem walked behind her with the map to help guide them.

The lower area was thick with fog, but it lessened when they found a set of rusty stairs. The copper was patinaed from the wet environment. As they climbed higher, the fog continued to lessen until it was almost gone. Now, they could see their surroundings much better, and what they saw made them pause.

They stood inside what appeared to be a massive orb. Its framework was like a cage of steel, rusty and brown. Outside of the orb were heavy clouds, or steam, perhaps, which were pink and fluffy. It was clearly designed to deceive.

Inside the orb were thousands of catwalks that extended between gears, cogs, kettles of steam and conveyor belts. All of it huffing and chugging like an old clock. The gears were fashioned from different metals: gold, copper, bronze, brass and platinum, which flashed in the occasional daylight. It was dazzling and breathtaking. Gwen was mesmerized by the amount of skill and craftsmanship it must have taken to construct such a wonder.

"But why?" she muttered aloud. "What's it all for?"

"It's a maze," Bally said, "to hide and confuse."

LinHem nodded to an area not far away. "We might have a better vantage from there."

They moved to an area that looked to be an observation platform. On the railing was a commemorative plaque with a message. LinHem cleared his throat and read it aloud.

*Herein lies Rondu's tomb. The ancient sorcerer from Gethmeade. For the one seeking treasure within, not all is as it seems...*

Bally bent low and sniffed the tomb, then wrinkled his nose. "I know of Rondu. He was a cousin of my master and one of the Grinbers, an ancient order of sorcerers. This place is his twisted imagination."

"Was he a bit crazy?" Posh asked. "I mean, just look at the place. Sure, it's fancy, but…why?"

"I'm afraid the answer lies at rest within the tomb," Bally said.

Gwen looked upon the mechanical landscape and let out a sigh. "Regardless, we're here to find the sigil. Maybe we should split up to cover more ground?"

"Not a bad idea," LinHem said.

Posh immediately threw her arms around Bally. "We'll take the lower area."

Gwen lifted the corner of her mouth. "Okay. LinHem, you and I can take the upper area."

They split up. Gwen led the way with her wand held in front of her. LinHem fell in beside and hummed as they walked, randomly commenting on the steampunk gadgets. There were thousands of whirring contraptions. Some of the strange anomalies sent off steam, others chimed and spun. But all of them were connected to a larger system, it seemed.

That's when a thought hit Gwen. "This feels like a park of some kind."

LinHem stopped. "That never occurred to me."

Gwen pointed above her. "Could these be rides, built for entertainment?"

"Ah, yes. Interesting," LinHem said. "I see it now. I should like to ride one."

Gwen looked doubtfully at LinHem. "I don't think these are safe."

"Hmm, you're probably right, though it appears they are in remarkably good condition."

Gwen had to agree. Considering the age of the park, the rides looked as if someone had been maintaining them.

As if on cue, an object resembling a metallic robot rocketed past them. LinHem's hackles went up, and Gwen readied her wand.

The flying robot banked and flew at them but paused a few meters away.

The contraption was large, taller than LinHem, and like everything else in the park, it was made of metal. But it was also just as rusty, and a heavy patina covered much of its body. Its head sat on a thick brass rod and was shaped like an oval. It had large, almost comical eyes that blinked in a quizzical manner. Steam pumped out when it moved and made an off-gassing sound like it was passing gas. The robot's torso and arms were barrel-shaped with exposed rivets. It had no legs. Instead, it sat upon a large orb that rolled across the floor. The robot seemed to be an extension of the park.

"Ahh, you've finally come!" the robot chirped in a staccato voice and clapped its steel hands together. It bowed awkwardly. "My name is Frame. Welcome to my master's amusement park."

Gwen glanced at LinHem, who still had his hackles up. But she lowered her wand. "I'm sorry, but you've been *waiting* for us?"

"Oh, yes. Many long years. My master predicted this. I never thought this day would come," Frame said, speaking in short and brief sentences.

"Your master?" Gwen replied. "Do you mean Rondu, the sorcerer?"

"Yes. He left me in charge. I have maintained his park. Please follow me. Our time is short. I must lead you to the sigil now."

Frame turned and rolled off, bumping over the steel grate of the catwalk. It moved so fast that Gwen and LinHem had to practically sprint to keep up.

"Hold on!" Gwen huffed.

Frame stopped almost instantly and pivoted to face them. It waited and glitched slightly. If Gwen didn't know any better, she would say it seemed nervous. Yet, a robot couldn't have such emotions, could it?

"What's the rush?" Gwen said.

"Time is short, now that you've arrived. We don't have long."

Gwen glanced at LinHem again. "I don't understand."

"My master set a time limit. We must hurry."

"What's supposed to happen?"

Frame seemed to hesitate. "There is no time to waste," it said. "You must follow me now."

Gwen faced LinHem. "Do me a favor. Fly down and find Posh and Bally. Bring them back as fast as you can."

"Hmm. I don't know if that is wise, Gwenevere." Then he leaned in close. "I'm not sure I trust this robot. His system may be addled."

Gwen considered. Though she'd only just met Frame, she could sense that the robot meant no harm. "It's okay. But we might need everyone here for the sigil. Just hurry."

"Yell if you need me," he said. Then he flapped his considerable wingspan and leapt from the catwalk.

Gwen turned to Frame. "Lead on."

Frame crossed the catwalk toward a massive copper-plated orb. The orb was about one hundred meters in diameter, and the upper portion was shiny with a green patina on the bottom. There were seams and rivets around its circumference with a few vents that emitted steam, which reminded her of the great blimp they'd flown in.

"What is this place?" she asked, high-stepping to keep up with Frame.

"The master built it long ago for you."

That made Gwen almost trip, and she had to grip the railing. "Me?"

Frame rotated his body but kept moving forward. "Yes. He knew you'd come. He knew Spellbinder would find you."

"So, all of this has something to do with me?" Gwen asked, wondering how in Ambriel she was connected to this wizard named Rondu.

"It was his responsibility." Frame pivoted again and rolled on, but at a slightly slower pace, allowing her to catch up and walk beside it.

"Your master, this Rondu. What was he like?"

The robot seemed to purr—at least, that's how it sounded to Gwen—as if it was recalling a fond memory from its memory banks. "Ah, my master. How I do miss him. He created me to care for this park. It was his gift to the mountain folk who used to live here. Alas, they no longer survive. My master was a kind soul. He gave me life, and I miss him. We will soon reunite."

"These mountain folk. Who were they?"

"The Bremen Civilization of the Winter Realm. They were a hardy people of rock and stone. They mined alloys and precious metals. They saved my master. He was nearly frozen. They nurtured him back to life. To show his gratitude, he built this place for them. Yet, it also had another purpose. Only I knew of it. But tragedy struck after my master passed. The Bremen lost their way. The Chimook Winds drove them mad."

"Chimook Winds?" Gwen asked. "Are we in danger?"

"Not to worry. This place was designed to protect. It shelters those inside it from the Chimook Winds. That sound is madness. You must not go into the clouds. Avoid the clouds."

Frame rolled on, there was no emotion in his mechanical tone as he beeped, purred and released a bit of steam. Gwen followed until they hit some more stairs. The robot's large orblike wheel rolled up the steps without any problem, though. Soon, Gwen noticed they were climbing to the very top of the park's orb. They were heading to the apex. Whatever secret this place held, she assumed they'd find it there.

At the top of the stairs, Frame finally stopped and waited for her. Gwen was slightly winded as she made the top landing. Now they stood at the top of the copper orb, and she could see the clear, almost gossamer weather shield. The wind and snow bent around the shield and redirected downwind. Being surrounded by the cloud had kept Rondu's tomb hidden for all these years, thanks to the shield.

As she stood there, waiting for Frame to say something, she could hear the harsh wind howling outside. The jingling sound from inside the park—the white noise that sounded like wind chimes—drowned out the howling winds, though. She realized now that the chimes protected the inhabitants from the sound of the Chimook Winds…and madness.

"What now?" she asked.

"You must solve the riddle if you wish to retrieve the golden sigil."

"So, it's a game now, is it?"

"My master was always a trickster at heart. If someone accidentally stumbled upon this park, they might have taken the sigil. It is meant for the one Spellbinder deems worthy. You are worthy."

"Okay. When do we begin?"

"When you are ready. But do not take long. My battery life is nearing an end. You must solve the riddle before my power system fails."

Gwen heard a flapping noise. She turned to see LinHem nearing them. He landed, folded his wings, and sat on his haunches. "I have returned."

From the stairs, Bally leapt forward. Posh was seated on his back. They hurried to Gwen and stopped next to her.

"Are you okay?" Posh asked. When she saw Frame, she did a double-take. "Um, what is this thing?"

Bally padded forward and walked around the robot, sniffing it. Frame was tall, but still considerably shorter than the large cat.

"It's okay, Bally," Gwen said and placed a hand on his shoulder. "Frame is only a messenger. He is here to deliver the second sigil."

"Tis an interesting specimen," Bally said. "I sense magic and science. Might this be a creation of the sorcerer named Rondu?"

Frame turned to the ghost panther. "You are familiar with my master?"

"Through a distant connection. I never met Rondu; his sorcery was of a different kind than my master's. I had no idea he'd created such a place. Now it makes sense. He was a guardian of the sigil and a secret keeper of Spellbinder, as I was told by my master when I was a cub."

"Frame," Gwen said. "Let's begin before time expires."

"Expires?" Posh asked.

"No time to explain," Gwen said. She could already see the robot moving just a bit slower.

They all waited for Frame to speak. It seemed like it was accessing some long-lost memory. Frame made a few buzzing and ticking sounds, then straightened. "There are three riddles you must solve, Gwenevere Arris. Each one will require ingenuity and honesty. If you fail to answer the questions before my battery life runs out, the second sigil will be lost forever."

# CHAPTER 33

## *RIDDLES OF THE SECOND SIGIL*

FIRST RIDDLE," FRAME said. "What is the greatest personal attribute?"

Gwen furrowed her brow and looked at Posh, Bally and LinHem.

They were all silent as they stared back at her, just as confused.

"Can you give any further hints?" Gwen asked Frame.

The robot remained silent.

"Guess that means no," Posh said with a huff and crossed her arms.

LinHem cleared his throat. "Of course, the answer is knowledge. Without it, we would understand nothing."

Posh chuckled and shook her head. "Figures you'd say that. We get that you're smart, LinHem. But it doesn't mean that everyone thinks the same way as you do."

"Obviously, the answer is curiosity," Bally said in a low growl. "Otherwise, we would ask no questions, and therefore we would have no answers. Thus, knowledge would not exist."

Posh gave Bally a sidelong glance, then shrugged. "It appears that we all have our own theories. For me, determination is more important. Without it, we'd strive for nothing, including freedom. Isn't that the greatest attribute?"

Gwen listened to her three friends as she thought about the question. Of course, Posh would value determination and freedom. She'd been enslaved for centuries, doing others' bidding and being passed around from one master to the next. Gwen felt a special empathy for her because of this. Only determination to survive had seen Posh through. Although she now had some semblance of freedom, she would never be entirely free while working for Kershaw.

Next, she considered LinHem. He thirsted for knowledge. It was something central to his being, and he sought out the truth in everything, which made knowledge a core element in his persona.

Then there was Bally, who had a desire for curiosity. Was that because of the mysteries surrounding his upbringing and living with Speartine? Was Bally secretly searching for something more, trying to discover what had happened to his family?

But it would seem the obvious answer to the riddle would depend on *who* was being asked the question. This riddle was aimed at her in particular, not her companions. So, what did the question mean to her? What attribute did she prize the most? She thought of her dear friend Kriss. Losing her had been one of the most painful things in her life because she missed her.

When Gwen looked at her three friends, she mostly felt empathy for their struggles in life—indeed, they all had their own issues and challenges. But it was more than that. She wanted to help them, just like she had wanted to help Kriss's mother after her death. Just like she wanted to help free all those trapped spirits.

It was obvious to her now. The greatest attribute wasn't knowledge, curiosity, determination, freedom, empathy or anything else.

It was *love*.

"The answer, of course, is love," Gwen said.

Frame straightened, took a brief second as it accessed some stored files, then its eyes lit up. Fireworks shot up from the perimeter of the large, round platform. Bells and party horns blared as streamers floated down.

"That, Gwenevere Arris, is the correct answer," the robot said with a bow.

Posh breathed a sigh of relief and held a hand to her chest. LinHem hooted, and Bally flicked his plaid-patterned tail with approval.

After the fireworks and hoopla had settled down, Frame asked the next question.

"Next riddle," Frame chirped. "What is the best way to make a friend?"

At this, everyone looked around with blank expressions.

"...best way to make a friend," Gwen muttered, more to herself than anyone. She knew the question was directed at her. So, how *did* she make friends? It was something she'd never considered. She thought about Kriss and how they had met through archery. But then she thought about her more recent friends and how they'd all met in different ways. She had helped free Bally from the ghost loop, who had joined them in gratitude. With LinHem, there had been a shared interest in the tome. But when she thought about Posh and how rocky their friendship had been at first, she felt a moment of clarity. Being from different ethnicities, they had resisted each other in the beginning. But that initial resistance had been based on what others had taught them. Once Gwen had got to know Posh, and understood that she wasn't her enemy, things had changed. She knew her as a caring, thoughtful and energetic woman. Not some vile, hateful and savage genie, as many other witches would have her believe.

So, the best way to make a friend, in Posh's case, had been to understand her instead of judging her. Of all her friendships, perhaps Posh's had been the most rewarding because Gwen had been forced to see things through someone else's perspective. Again, the word empathy came to Gwen's mind.

"The answer is through empathy," Gwen said.

Once again, Frame straightened as it calculated the response, then the robot's eyes lit up. "Correct again, Miss Gwenevere."

Fireworks lit the area with booms and confetti.

Frame placed its hands behind its back. "Final riddle. Why do you deserve the golden sigil?"

Once again, Gwen was caught off guard. She blinked a few times as she stared at Frame, not sure what to say at first. *Why are these questions so hard?* she thought.

Why *did* she deserve the final sigil?

Why *did* she deserve Spellbinder's gift?

Was she being greedy?

She couldn't crack the riddle of cleansing Hidden Palm Grove on her own. In the past, she'd always done it by herself and without any help. That had made her strong, independent and confident. But she couldn't fix this one, and her ego had taken a hit. Now that she was being questioned, it brought everything to light in a way that she didn't like.

Yes. She was using the magical telescope to help her solve this one, meet Bam Jino's deadline and pay off a debt. She'd already admitted to herself and the others that she couldn't do this on her own, even with Kriss's amulet. But that also brought to light another question. Though her determination was something that drove her, and she loved challenges, the real reason she'd left Kalispell in the first place was because she wanted to help others. And cleansing homes not only fixed families, but it also helped free the trapped spirits within.

*That* was the real reward in all of this. She had declared as much to Kershaw in the beginning. She also knew that was the reason Spellbinder had sought her out.

Once again, the word empathy came to her.

The answer was because Gwen felt empathy for others, and she was driven to help them. Whether that be lost souls, tortured spirits, trapped panthers, imprisoned genies or downcast griffins.

Gwen looked at Frame. "Because I want to help others, but I need the sigils to do it."

Frame straightened, then slumped and powered down.

As Gwen, Posh, LinHem and Bally looked on, the robot literally split in half. Its metal hull began to glow. Then the robot disintegrated into dust.

The four companions stood around the pile of golden dust and stared at the sigil lying in it. The dust that had once been the robot named Frame swirled in the breeze and was swept up and over the railing. Gwen thought she heard a soft chiming in the air and felt a pang of sadness. Frame had almost felt like a living being. She'd even detected some emotions in its undertones. The sorcerer had done his job well at crafting the guardian of the second sigil.

Posh reached down and lifted the sigil from the glittering dust. The look in her eyes as she held the mythical piece of gold reminded Gwen of Posh's attraction to shiny things. But Posh quickly handed it to Gwen and shook her head as if refocusing. "What now?" she said.

"Back to base," Gwen said and tucked the sigil into her satchel. "We need that next clue from Spellbinder, assuming Bally's markings are still in place."

"The markings will remain until I remove them," Bally said.

"Well, Hidden Palm Grove has been known to do strange things," Gwen said. She looked at LinHem and Bally. "Mind if we get a lift?"

Gwen hopped on LinHem's back while Posh straddled Bally. It wasn't long before they were at ground level and heading back down the mountain in their sleigh.

It was growing dark when they left, and the moonlit sleigh ride was magical. Posh poured another round of hot cocoa from the magical thermos and cozied up next to Gwen, interlocking her arm around Gwen's.

"It's just a shame we'll be leaving all of this," Posh said. "I mean, how better to celebrate the season?"

They found a place in town to stay the night. Posh wanted to go out and explore the hamlet, but Gwen was so tired she was practically tripping over her feet. LinHem was up for it, though, and surprisingly, so was Bally. With a little cajoling, Gwen finally caved and agreed to join them for a night out.

It was snowing when they left the inn. The moon was high and lit the surrounding snow. There were locals about, having finished work for the day. The town of Hithertu appeared to be mostly tourist, and naturally, most businesses catered to them. There were more sleigh ride services, hiking ventures and even haunted ghost tours, which Gwen immediately declined. In the end, they settled for a pub near the center of town. It was part of an old town square, complete with a fountain, which seemed confusing, since it was frozen and probably stayed that way for most of the year. There was an old clock tower, a city hall and an assortment of other pubs, inns and restaurants.

"Ye Olde Yule," Posh said. "Perfect. Sounds festive to me." She pulled on Gwen and led the way inside the pub.

They were greeted at the door and seated. As they settled in, Gwen noticed the strange looks and stares of wonder from the other patrons. Seeing a ghost panther and a griffin was probably a first for many of the guests, not to mention a green witch and a genie sitting amicably together. Their table was in the back and next to a wall of windows and a balcony. There was a blazing fire in the nearby hearth, which kept them warm and toasty.

The view was amazing and once again, Gwen thought of Kalispell. They could see the tops of the mountain range, including Steamtop Mountain, and its steam halo was highlighted by the moon's light.

"May I take your order?" A waitress said. She was a rather tall gnome who gave them a wide-eyed look and tried not to stare at LinHem and Bally.

"Posh, why don't you order for us?" Gwen said.

Posh lit up. "Well, well. Let's see here…ah, we'll have a round of Burgeoning Bludgeon Bailey Blooms. Hmmm, how about some appetizers…some peppermint popcorn should do."

Posh handed the menu to the waitress, who quickly hurried off.

"Okay, crew." Posh rubbed her hands together. "We're going to play a game." She pulled out a deck of cards from her purse and shuffled them.

"Is that a Deck of Fate?" Gwen asked. "Where did you get those?"

LinHem eyed the deck through his bent spectacles. "Ah, that is a rare gift indeed."

Posh shrugged. "You pick up a thing or two when you've been around as long as I have. This is a very old set of fate cards. I get to use them only once every year. What can I say? I've been saving this for a special moment. Tonight is the night."

Bally gave Posh a stern look. "You shouldn't use such magic. It can be very dangerous, a Deck of Fate."

"Well, too bad," Posh trilled and gave him a side smile, then nudged the panther. "Come on, Bally. Loosen up. It's just a bit of fun. LinHem, you're up first."

She dealt out the cards, face down, seven total. Then slowly began to flip them over, each time making a whistling noise, as if there was some dire consequence to each card. Posh made comments like, *Ooh, that's gonna hurt,* or *Goodness, I would have never guessed…*

Each time, LinHem leaned in but then straightened as though he was indifferent to it all. But Gwen could see he was interested.

"Well?" LinHem finally asked.

Posh bent over the cards. "Yes, um…according to the cards, you have the sign of the Eagle, and you will find redemption and honor."

"Oh. Well, I guess that's fine then," LinHem said with a somewhat satisfied but confused look on his face.

"Right. Bally, you're next!" Posh said and shuffled the cards.

The panther flicked his tail as if offended. Gwen caught his expression and wondered if it was anticipation or frustration at the game. Posh caught it too and stopped shuffling.

"A steam token for your thoughts," she said.

"I'm familiar with this séance—"

"Well, it's not really a séance, Bally," Posh said. "It's your future."

"Of course," Bally said. "Please, continue then."

Posh laid out the cards. With each one, Gwen noticed the look on Posh's face though. It was one she hadn't seen from her before. There was trepidation, mixed with curiosity and concern. Posh furrowed her brow, each card coming slower and more deliberate.

Gwen also noticed Bally's expression and realized that the ghost panther understood how to read the cards as well. He'd played this game before.

"What do they say?" Gwen asked but directed the question toward Bally.

The panther faced her, his tail flicking as he blinked a few times. "It says that my desires will be fulfilled."

Posh slowly nodded. "Uh, yes. You have the Centaur, the sign of resolution. Next, we have our illustrious liege, Miss Gwenevere Arris."

"Do we have to do this?" Gwen asked, though she was somewhat curious now.

"Oh, yes. We do," Posh said with a devious smile. "Now, let's see…" She reshuffled the old cards and expertly laid them out in a different pattern this time, which Gwen assumed was for a green witch. Once again, Posh giggled and hummed as the group all leaned in with anticipation.

When Posh flipped the final card, Gwen crossed her arms. "We're waiting."

"Your sign is the Seeker."

"Meaning?"

Posh pointed to the card in the center, which happened to be a telescope. "You search for an answer to your inner being."

It took everyone by surprise.

"Well, what are the odds?" LinHem said.

"Not odds," Posh said. "Fate."

"And will we achieve these fates?" Gwen asked.

"That remains to be seen," Posh answered. "The cards reveal our desired fate. But destiny is yet to be decided. Much of it will depend on you."

Gwen sat back, then lowered her gaze at Posh. "Well. You know you're not getting out of this either."

"Unfortunately, I cannot reveal my desires. I can't deal my own wants or needs."

"Then allow me," Gwen said and snatched the deck away from Posh before she could grab it back. Gwen smiled a bit as Posh reached in and tried to pry them away a second time.

"Gentle," Gwen said in a teasing manner. "It's an old deck, right? Wouldn't want to damage them. Probably very hard to come by, these cards."

Posh sat back and crossed her arms, her golden glowing eyes darting up to the ceiling in a 'whatever' expression. "You don't know how to do it."

"That's why you're going to tell me how to 'fate a genie'," Gwen said and tucked the cards under her arm, waiting.

Posh looked at Bally and LinHem, who both appeared to want nothing of it.

"Hmm, this is between you two," LinHem said.

Bally flicked his tail. "As the griffin said. I shall stay out of it."

Posh finally sighed. "Very well." She reached out with her arm, her golden bracelets clanging together as she traced out a pattern on the table that resembled a star. "Start here, work this way, finish here," Posh said.

Gwen could tell that Posh wasn't happy about it and wondered why. Posh had been ecstatic about revealing the desired fate of her companions. Now that it was her turn, her mood had gone sour. Embarrassment perhaps? Was it the joy of revealing things to others? Some dark secret she didn't want revealed? But Gwen shuffled the cards and laid them out in the pattern Posh had indicated. First, it was a witch's hat, then an old amulet, a seashell, the sun, three golden stars, what appeared to be a genie's bottle, and lastly, a heart with an arrow through it.

Gwen looked at the cards, then glanced at Posh.

Posh remained silent as she stared at the cards. She was once again reluctant to speak, which was rare for her.

"The sign of the Cherub," Bally finally said. "She has the sign of the Lover."

Gwen felt her own skin flush as she gathered up the cards quickly and handed them back to Posh. The genie, somewhat in frustration, stuffed the deck into her magic purse.

Their waitress finally returned with the bucket of popcorn. She set it down in the center of the table, along with four jade mugs, steaming and hissing with something that smelled like coffee inside.

LinHem gripped his in a large talon and held it up. "To my new friends," he said.

Bally nudged his mug forward with his nose and tapped the table twice with one massive paw. "Here-here," he purred.

Gwen looked at Posh. She felt bashful and somewhat embarrassed now but smiled at Posh anyway and held up her mug. "To friends."

Posh took a deep breath, sighed and smiled back. "To friends." But the barely perceptible wink she gave Gwen set her heart fluttering.

# CHAPTER 34
## *A MUCH-NEEDED REPRIEVE*

THEY STAYED UP late into the night. After a few more green jaded mugs, all the awkward feelings were forgotten. Gwen and Posh led the tavern in a rousing song of snowflakes and fireplaces, an old favorite in all of Ambriel. Bally and LinHem actually joined in, and Gwen couldn't remember ever experiencing a night like it. Seeing LinHem and Bally rolling around, tipsy with joy, made her laugh. And the highlight of the night was dancing with Posh. Gwen had never been a good dancer—her footwork had always been clumsy. Posh, however, was a fantastic dancer and led them throughout the night, guiding Gwen with her arms in a way that made Gwen feel even more intoxicated. *One learns quite a bit over the centuries*, Posh had murmured in her ear as they danced.

Eventually, they stumbled off to their different rooms. Posh gave Gwen a hug. She thanked her for a fun evening and for being a good sport. That goodnight hug had turned into much more, and Gwen had been half-tempted to follow Posh to her room.

When the bellhop knocked on her door in the morning, Gwen groaned and rolled out of bed. She showered and met the others in the hotel lobby, where they boarded the small train to the skyport. Gwen noticed how Posh seemed to show no effects from their late night. In fact, Posh had been up since sunrise and had already gotten her workout in. LinHem and Bally seemed fine as well, which made Gwen feel like the lightweight of the group. But by the time they boarded the floating blimp, she was feeling better. When the airship ascended into the clouds, Gwen ate breakfast and slept the entire flight back to Valeside Beach.

Kershaw was waiting for them at the skyport. And, to Gwen's dismay, Bam Jino stood towering behind him. Kershaw held his hands behind his back and glared at Posh while Bam Jino stared at Gwen.

Passengers walked by them as Gwen waited to hear what Kershaw had to say.

"I see you've been off vacationing," Kershaw said.

Gwen set her bag down in the busy terminal and gave Kershaw a wry smile. "I wouldn't call it vacationing, exactly. By the way, mind explaining why this mountain troll is here?"

"You tell me, Gwen. He's the one claiming you owe him steam tokens. I can't have this while you and I are conducting our business."

Gwen looked at Bam Jino. "I've been sending regular payments, with interest, as agreed. The deadline is Saint Halving Day. Has something changed?"

The troll stood next to Kershaw and looked down at Gwen. She heard a low growl from Bally, and LinHem clicked his talons on the tile floor in a warning.

"I see you have some associates," Bam Jino said. "And this turncoat of a griffin isn't to be trusted."

"What do you want?" Gwen said, holding a hand to LinHem to calm him.

"Why, to check in on my investment. I'm only concerned about your well-being."

Gwen glared at the troll. She wanted to let go of LinHem and watch him shred Bam Jino. "Keep your distance. That goes for Harris as well."

Bam Jino began to chuckle. "Oh, don't you worry. I won't have to, now that I've got eyes all over the place."

Kershaw cleared his throat. He stepped away from Bam Jino and waved his hand as if trying to clear the troll's stench. "Anyway, Gwen, you have work to do, and our time is growing short. I'm getting calls from our client. She's nervous."

"This isn't the easiest task, but you're aware of that."

"Seven days until Saint Halving," Kershaw said, glancing at the four of them. "I assume you've made progress?"

"Yes, but these things take time."

Kershaw straightened his suit lapels, then grasped Posh by the arm and pulled her to a secluded area. Bally let out a low growl, but Gwen placed a hand on his shoulder as they walked off.

"Time's ticking, kitten," Bam Jino said before walking off.

But Gwen ignored him and kept her eyes on Posh, wondering what Kershaw was saying to her. It was an intense conversation, and Gwen could tell by the look on Posh's face that she was upset. Her downcast eyes and crossed arms told Gwen that Kershaw wasn't happy as he berated her for several minutes. Posh eventually returned to them, silent.

"What is it?" Gwen asked.

"It's nothing worth discussing right now. Can we go?"

Gwen put an arm around Posh and lifted her backpack. "Sure, we can talk later."

During the ride back to Java House, no one asked any questions. The merry mood around town with Saint Halving's Day approaching did little to cheer them from Kershaw's ultimatum. Gwen *was* worried, though. Despite having two of the three sigils, she was betting that attaining the last one would be the hardest. She had no idea what Spellbinder had in store for them regarding the final challenge. In the back of her mind, she sensed that things were starting to pick up. Like an approaching storm, there was a reckoning looming just ahead. Of course, she wanted to solve this riddle and free the tortured spirits. Yet, there was something else going on, and she couldn't quite put her finger on it, which made her feel anxious.

Back at Java House, everyone retreated to their quarters. LinHem flew off, (Gwen assumed to fish) while Bally vanished without a word. Posh unpacked, showered and left to walk the beach alone. Gwen let her go, knowing that she needed some space. She made a point to talk to her later when things calmed down. She felt they all needed some time to unwind, though she was anxious to get back to work. But it seemed like it wouldn't be until tomorrow at the earliest, assuming she could rally everyone.

Gwen made a cup of tea and sat on the back patio. The temperature continued to cool, though there was still plenty of sun. She wrapped herself in a blanket and watched the waves as her mind wandered. Before long, she had nodded off into a fitful sleep.

In her dreams, she could see Spellbinder. The large brass telescope was mounted atop a temple, fluted pillars supporting the massive relic. It grew in size, dwarfing everything like a god in the heavens. Behind it stood the wizard named Speartine. He was hooded in heavy robes with golden symbols and mystical stars, only his lips visible, twisted into a mysterious smirk. Beside the telescope were Posh, LinHem and Bally. Her friends were motionless, trapped by some unseen force. Before Gwen, there was a maze of walls and doors. She began to panic.

*Which way should I go? Where should I begin?*

She knew she had to free her friends. She had to save them all. Gwen rubbed her amulet and whispered Kriss's name.

*Help me save them…because I couldn't save you.*

She could hear the amulet whisper back in a low moan. It was Kriss's voice, and it gave her encouragement.

Gwen moved into the maze of wandering halls.

But she kept finding dead ends and had to continuously backtrack. After what seemed like an eternity, she stopped and dropped to her knees. She felt defeat sink into her bones, knowing she couldn't conquer this challenge. Unlike all the other challenges in her life, she had met her match. She couldn't help her friends. She couldn't free them.

The maze around her began to fade. Gwen felt herself falling through time and space. She began to panic again, reaching out for something to hold on to. She was losing her grip on reality.

Kriss's voice boomed…

*…trust yourself…*

Gwen sat up, her brimmed hat falling off her head and sunlight spilling into her hazel eyes.

Eventually, her heartbeat slowed, and she sank back into the wicker sofa. The crashing of the waves in the distance eased her nerves, and the sound of the sea breeze in the palms settled her breathing. The vestiges of the dream were already fleeting, and all she could remember was Kriss's voice whispering, *Trust yourself.*

Gwen walked back inside and sat at the large island. The afternoon sunlight spilled from the windows and across the white marble floors. But she continued to sit there as the shadows grew longer. She felt anxious, but also tired and uncertain as the day slipped away and the deadline drew ever closer.

Eventually, Gwen heard the flapping of wings, and LinHem stepped into the living room. Close behind him was Bally. They stood next to Gwen.

"You are troubled," LinHem said.

Bally nudged her with his snout. "Do not doubt yourself, Gwen."

"I…I don't know if I can do this anymore."

"You've completed the first two challenges with spectacular results," LinHem said. "Why do you doubt your resolve now?"

"Remember, you are not alone, Gwenevere," Bally said. "Spellbinder aligned our paths. We are here to help you. Let that strengthen your resolve."

"Do you have other concerns beyond Hidden Palm Grove?" LinHem asked.

Gwen thought about that. Yes, there was another concern, though she didn't speak it.

The ominous feeling. The dream.

*Was she leading them into danger?*

Gwen shook her head. "I'm just worried—"

Posh entered the room and moved over to join them. She had apparently recovered from her chat with Kershaw, and her typical smile was back. She hugged Gwen, then Bally and LinHem. "Sorry, everyone. I just needed some time to clear my head. I'm afraid I've wasted the day, Gwen. We won't be able to go to Spellbinder tonight. The witching hour is too close."

Gwen waved it away. "It's fine, you needed it. We all needed it after that last sigil. I can't tell you how much I appreciate you three. Let's get back to work first thing in the morning."

Gwen gathered her things early the next morning. LinHem, Bally and Posh were all sitting at the kitchen island, having a coffee when she entered the living room.

They walked along the beach, the sun rising above the horizon in a golden wash of rays and fireflies. It was cool that morning. With just six days until Saint Halving Day, the beachfront homes were decorated with lights and garlands. Greens, coppers and silver tones shone in the morning sun. It was a festive, though urgent reminder that their deadline was growing near.

But the Saint Halving Day deadline wasn't the only concern anymore. There was another, more ominous and unannounced threat lurking in the background that worried Gwen. She could sense it, looming on the horizon, waiting to reveal itself.

It meant harm might come to her and her friends.

The group found the hidden spiral staircase in the rock outcropping and ascended to the castle's grounds. They bumped into Tom along the way, who stopped what he was doing to chat.

"Back at it, are ya?" Tom said.

"We've still got work to do," Gwen said with a nod toward the large ogre. "Tom, I believe you've met Posh. I'd like to introduce LinHem and Bally."

"Oh, you're an ogre?" LinHem said. "Very fascinating. I met a few when I was a youngling—"

"LinHem," Posh said, clearing her throat. "Why don't you talk later. We've got business inside."

"Of course. Pardon me," he said. "I would like to visit when I have time."

"Well, y'all will be careful now, won't you?" Tom said, hooking his thumbs into his overalls and arching his back. "You know the spirits get even more restless around the holidays."

Once inside, Bally led them across the white marble tile, winding his way into the back. Like the last time, the corridors seemed to shift and bend into an unrecognizable maze. Gwen followed behind him, using her wand to light the hallways as they moved deeper into Hidden Palm Grove.

They finally arrived at the stair leading up to the lighthouse tower. Bally stood aside, offering Gwen the lead. She climbed the winding stairs to the top landing. When she stepped inside, it was dark. Strangely, the moon was already high in the night sky and shone through the colored glass, which once again seemed to magnify the stars and galaxies. In the middle was Spellbinder. Gwen walked around the rotunda, searching the floor for the outline of the vacant sigil. She found it near the twelve o'clock position and knelt, setting it in place.

The room lit up when she placed the sigil, and a musical chiming drifted through the space.

"Up you go," Bally purred, his eyelids drooping in pleasure at the sound of magic.

Gwen climbed the steps to the top of the large telescope. She felt a bit more nervous this time. What would she see? Where would Spellbinder send them for the final sigil?

When she peered into the telescope, she saw a large town nestled into green rolling hills. Beyond were tall pines and a clear lake with a mirror-like finish. The town was packed with lavish cottages built of sturdy stone and clay tile roofs. The spire-like trees lined the brick-paved roads in a copper, sepia-like tone. People moved around the town, trading in the markets for food and goods. Children ran in the streets, flying kites and laughing. The main avenue had a large, landscaped mall filled with green grass, a stream and people lying about, reading or relaxing. The sky was blue in a way she had never seen before. Gazing through Spellbinder, it felt as though the town had not a care in the world. It was probably the happiest little town she'd ever seen before, and she wanted to go visit it. No, she wanted to spend the rest of her life there—just retire and say goodbye to her worries. Seeing the little village filled her with joy and peace. It was a land of eternal happiness.

Then, the telescope dimmed, and the vision faded.

Gwen stepped back, trying to catch her breath. She leaned against the railing, her hand to her forehead.

Posh was there instantly, propping her up. "Gwen, are you alright? Talk to me. What happened?"

LinHem held out a wing and fanned her.

Bally moved over and lay down so Gwen could sit on his back. "I take it your vision was somewhat overwhelming?"

"To say the least," Gwen replied.

"What did you see?" Posh asked.

"I...I think I saw heaven," Gwen stuttered.

The four of them stared at her in disbelief.

"Heaven?" Posh said, and Gwen could see the doubt in her expression.

"I'm not sure such a place exists," LinHem said. "And even if it did, how shall we find it?"

Bally began to purr. "Ah, yes. It does exist."

LinHem looked at him, his feathers ruffled. "How could you possibly know that?"

"Because my master once spoke of it."

"And how would he know if it's real?" Posh asked, echoing LinHem's skepticism.

"Because my dear Posh, he had traveled there as a child. He told me stories of the place Gwenevere described."

But now that Gwen thought about it, her vision was starting to fade, like a fleeting dream. The nestled town, set within the greenest hills and the bluest sky with a lake so pure it looked like a mirror...the sun, the pine trees, the houses...all perfect. Maybe it *wasn't* real after all?

But Bally continued to nod, confirming what Gwen had seen. "It is real, and it does exist. The town does not age. Time stands still there. It is known as Promenade."

"Okay. I believe you," Gwen said. "Did your master say where this place was?"

"There is rumored to be a map."

Posh held out her hands. "Well? Where would that be?"

"Hidden somewhere within his castle, back where I was raised."

"Do we have time to get there?" Gwen asked.

Bally stood and began padding around Spellbinder as he considered. "Yes, I do believe so, if we leave tonight."

Posh chuckled but then shrugged. "Well. Let's pack our bags, again."

# CHAPTER 35

## *KRUBBLE*

BY THE TIME they made it back to Java House and packed up again, the night hour was deepening and the sun had dropped just over the Green Sea. They'd fortunately made it out of Hidden Palm Grove just before the witching hour. Otherwise, they'd have lost another day.

The skyport was open at all hours, though last-minute tickets were pricey. Gwen wondered how much it would cost Kershaw this time. But at least he hadn't cut their funding yet. They gathered in a private cabin of the blimp, and LinHem brought out the map of Ambriel, unrolling it gently on the table.

Bally extended a claw from one massive paw and pointed out a small hamlet on the map. "My master's keep is near the Lion's Mane Mountain Range. A dimming spell keeps it hidden from adventurers."

LinHem hummed, then checked the time on his golden pocket watch. "We will have only a few days to search for your master's keep. Time will be our greatest challenge now."

"Then let us hope Bally's intuition will guide us again," Gwen said.

Posh ruffled Bally's enormous ears. "I have faith in our guy," she said and hugged him.

Bally let loose a low growl. But it sounded less menacing now, and Gwen was beginning to wonder if Posh's charm was starting to work on him as well.

The flight took their airship a full day with a few extra stops. One layover was at another beachside resort, and Posh wanted to go shopping. But Gwen had adamantly rejected her plea, knowing they might never see Posh again if she left the skyport.

Eventually, they made it to the sprawling mountain town of Krubble. The province was practically a vertical series of roads, cottages and shoppes, at least it felt that way to Gwen after spending the last few months on the flat beaches of Valeside. It was difficult to get her bearings, and she had a brief case of vertigo due to the vertical landscape.

Krubble was carved into the mountain about halfway up, and the town's buildings dotted the main road, which was wide and cobbled with a dark stone. It snaked up the side of the mountain, switching back and forth as it steadily rose to the peak.

They stopped for a bite. Gwen wondered if they should rent a hotel room for the night but decided against it. There wasn't time to dally.

"Lead the way, Bally," Gwen urged, and they moved behind him through the busy market streets.

There was plenty of bartering. The air was light, cool and crisp. Gwen followed the ghost panther, and they actually saw several other panthers in the streets. But she also noticed that some of them were caged or being used in fights. Bally, no doubt, noticed this as well. But he ignored the cruelty in a way that told Gwen he was deliberately trying to stay focused on their task at hand.

They eventually left the town. Occasionally, they saw businesses or cottages along the mountain road, but the higher they traveled, the fewer structures they came across.

Once they neared the peak, Bally stopped and faced them. "We are here."

"We are?" Posh asked. "I see nothing."

"My master's spell is strong, even a century past." Bally moved on, nearing a darkened alcove to one side of the road. Gwen followed, wondering where they were going. But then the alcove shifted like some optical illusion. They continued deeper into the shadowy recess until Gwen could see what looked like a large wooden door.

"Well, bless me," LinHem said with a hoot. "Strong magic indeed, my good Bally."

The panther ignored LinHem and stopped in front of the door. Next to it were a few nondescript boulders. Bally placed a paw on the far one, then he pressed his snout on the middle one. The large doors swung open, and a cloud of dust rolled out to greet them.

Gwen, Posh and LinHem blinked a few times.

"In we go," the panther whispered and stepped inside, his glowing green eyes disappearing into the dark opening.

Gwen let her eyes adjust inside the dark foyer. She immediately pulled out her wand and cast a luminance spell to light the inside of the space. She could sense that this castle was old, maybe as old as the mountain it was nestled into. The vibe she got sent chills through her. Even though she was limited in her arcane knowledge, she could feel when there was magic nearby. Within the mountain keep, there was a great deal of it.

"You said your master has been dead for over a century?" she asked Bally.

"Yes. He was adept at magic and one of the Grinbers, an ancient race of sorcerers beholden to protecting Ambriel. His ability was practically unrivaled, and it was a great loss the day he passed."

Posh gave the panther a hug, which elicited another growl.

"Let's move on," Gwen said, rubbing her arms from a sudden chill. Bally's master might have been a great sorcerer, but Gwen had no desire to linger in such a place. Though she detected no spirits here, and this place required no cleansing, the magic residue didn't seem to agree with her.

"Follow me, and stay close," Bally said. "The way ahead is dim."

"Dim?" Posh asked.

"We are in a place that bridges two worlds. This is perhaps one place you would not want to be lost within."

Posh walked next to Bally, her arms wrapped around the panther, which he didn't seem to mind as much now. Gwen followed with LinHem bringing up the rear.

As Bally led the way, Gwen took in the sorcerer's palace. It was a bizarre place, to say the least. The space was vast with towering ceilings and open clerestories high above. There were rooms along the main hall, and the stone was a dark slate color. It was cool inside, and a draft hummed through the space. The sorcerer seemed to enjoy certain luxuries, though. Gwen noticed fine plates, silverware and long wooden tables for dining. The woodwork was top-notch, and even the chandeliers were fancier than some of the finest palaces she'd visited.

But it wasn't the décor that caught her attention the most. It was the bizarre oddities that were placed around the keep. Like some macabre museum, the oddities were set like statues. She noticed metallic floating balls, pulsing picture frames, large clocks that spun backwards and hourglasses with sand flowing in the opposite direction. She saw life-sized creatures, apparently frozen by some spell. There was a gorgon, a smaller wyrm, and the ever-elusive basilisk. She even saw a stream of water carved into the ceiling, which ran down the wall, out of the keep and along the mountainside.

"Bally, don't take this the wrong way," Posh whispered. "But your master was a bit strange."

The panther seemed to chuckle, which was new. "Many have said the same. A great number of his experiments were failures. But those failures led to some of the greatest inventions of our time, including Spellbinder, my dear. Once we reach the top, we will begin our search. Only at the top will we see where to go."

The group climbed more stairs, which Gwen had had enough of. But eventually, they reached the top, where she collapsed against LinHem. "What now, Bally?" she asked between gasps.

"Now, we search for the clue."

"What does this clue look like?" Gwen asked.

"I believe it to be a genie's bottle."

Posh looked as though she might be sick to her stomach.

"A what?" Posh said, raising her voice. "Is this some kind of demented joke, Bally? I don't think it's very funny."

"Please be calm," Bally said, his ears flattening back.

But Posh had her fists on her hips and leaned forward, her skin emitting a bit of steam now. "Do you know how many centuries I spent in one of those cursed things?"

"Posh," Gwen said and laid a hand on her arm, then she looked at Bally. "Please explain."

Bally settled back on his haunches. "My master felt that his secrets should be hidden away, usually within items most people were the least likely to search. The map to Promenade may be one of the most valuable documents ever created in Ambriel. Getting there is like a slice of heaven, I suppose. He knew this, and he was tasked with protecting the secrets in our land. As a Grinber, that was a burden laid upon him by the gods. When I was a cub, he used to take me into his lab, where he spent time working on his relics and inventions. He always carried a genie lamp with him—"

"Was he a slaver then?" Posh interjected.

"Quite the contrary, he freed many genies. He never indulged in the slaver's trade. The lamp was given to him by a genie he had rescued. But I always wondered why he continued to carry it with him. There was something special about it…perhaps a perfect place to hide a valuable relic. My dear Posh, you of all people would understand why."

She continued to stare at him. "If you think I'm going back into *any* bottle, you can forget it."

"Hold on," Gwen said. "What are you proposing, Bally?"

The panther didn't answer at first and waited for Posh to continue. But she looked away, still fuming with steam rising from her blue skin.

"A genie is best suited to enter a lamp and retrieve something within," Bally said. "However, no genie would willingly return to a bottle for fear of being trapped, which makes it a perfect place to hide a valuable relic."

"So, your theory is that your master hid the map to Promenade inside his personal genie lamp?" LinHem asked.

"That is precisely what I believe," Bally said. "It is our best chance to find the third and final sigil, Gwenevere. And we do not have much time. We must search this keep from top to bottom."

"This is a fairly large palace," LinHem said.

"So, we split up again?" Gwen asked, looking around the place. "I thought Bally just said it was a bad idea? Won't we get lost?"

"Or worse," Posh added and moved closer to Bally.

"I would not recommend splitting up this time," Bally said. "Many of the oddities around the keep are dangerous. If Gwen can light the way, I will use my magic to sniff out the bottle. LinHem is right. We must hurry."

"Do you still remember your way around?" Gwen asked.

Bally gave her a quick, nonchalant glance. "A ghost panther never loses their way."

"Oh, except when you stumbled into that ghost circle?" Posh said.

Bally ignored her and looked over the stone balustrade. Below them was a maze of stairs, catwalks and balconies. Above them was a high wood-raftered ceiling with some dimly filtered sunlight.

"I can feel the magic here," Bally murmured, and Gwen thought she heard a hint of joy in his deep voice. Like a child in a toy store, she sensed that Bally was happy to be home.

Bally started by circling the top level while Gwen used her wand to light the way. "My master usually kept his most prized relics at the highest level. Anyone who happened to stumble upon his keep would have to pass through the realm of oddities to get the most valuable artifacts. Touch nothing," Bally said and gave Posh a long look.

The ghost panther padded along the stone balustrade with Gwen on one side and Posh glued to his other. LinHem followed behind, his clawed talons clacking on the gray stone flooring.

There was a warm breeze from this height, Gwen noticed. It seemed to tug at her heavy robe and hair in a way that felt alluring. Like hundreds of tiny fingertips, that breeze seemed to beckon to her. *Explore, lose yourself, why not see the wonders of this place?* But that was the wizard's spell at work, she knew. It was an ethereal trap laid for unfortunate wanderers who strayed into this realm of oddities, as Bally had called it. She closed her mind to the whispers.

Gwen witnessed the same strange attractions all along the upper level. Like below, there were more paintings that seemed to move on their own, as if one could simply step into the frame and live out the scene—trapped forever. In fact, she saw just that, with real people running through a forest of colorful trees and waterfalls, likely adventurers who'd stumbled upon this castle and wandered too close.

She saw more metallic sculptures that reminded her of the ones she'd seen at Steamtop Mountain. Large gears in colorful alloys and metals. Cogs that spun and chugged under their own power. Inside the large gears were dark voids of nothingness. Coming from within were screams and shouts for help, all barely audible amidst the thrumming of the gears. There were more stone statues of creatures from different races and backgrounds, which Gwen knew now to be more wayward adventurers. They stood in different poses, kneeling, running or hands upheld and fearful looks on their faces. Some of the statues were made of gold and copper and brass, all covered in a layer of dust. Gwen moved closer to Bally and tried not to look at the oddities. She gripped her rosewood wand tighter and held it aloft to light the way forward and away from the macabre attractions.

As they moved along, Bally seemed to sniff the air occasionally, like he was following some ghostly scent. He was using his sense of smell to follow the magic, which Gwen understood now. Perhaps that was why his breed had been so desired and hunted and enslaved to near extinction. The slave traders would, of course, want to use the panthers' special scenting ability to track down hidden treasures. It made Gwen feel a pang of sadness for Bally and his kind. Their ability had been used for a more selfish purpose. That thought reinforced her desire. She couldn't care less about fixing some landmark castle for a wealthy client. She was determined more than ever to set those trapped souls free.

Bally finally slowed to a stop.

"In that room, just there," Bally said. "I sense great magic. Beware and stay focused on me. If you feel the urge to wander, grip my fur; it will help sustain you." Then the ghost panther moved through the room's stone portal with Gwen, Posh and LinHem practically riding on his back.

# CHAPTER 36

## *OF LOVE AND SACRIFICE*

WHEN GWEN ENTERED the stone portal, she felt the humidity of the breeze and its sticky fingers pulling at her. It was a sultry, heady tug that nearly took her breath away. She gripped Bally's plaid-patterned fur tighter.

Inside the room, Bally paused and sniffed. Once again, Gwen sensed a certain anticipation in the ghost panther. He had returned home. Now, they would have to rely on his guidance to get them through this particular challenge.

There was a bit more light in the room, but it was a sickly, greenish hue. Beyond, there were mountains of treasure. To Gwen, it resembled what a dragon's horde might look like. There were piles of gold coins, bullions and jewels. Gwen saw armor and swords and other magical weapons. The mounds of treasure were piled haphazardly where they nearly reached the rafters of the high ceiling above. It was dark, except for the greenish glow coming from the treasure, as if there was a substance coating it. Pathways led around the piles, like someone had portioned the treasure into allotments based on types or eras, perhaps.

When Gwen looked at Posh, she could see she was struggling to remain calm. There was a lust in her golden eyes that Gwen hadn't witnessed before. She wavered and looked to be drunk or in a trance. Bally also noticed and moved closer to her and nuzzled her face, then breathed into her eyes. Posh finally blinked and seemed to come to her senses.

"Oh my, I…I've not seen such a trove in my centuries," Posh murmured. "How did your master come to own such wealth?"

"Not all is as it seems, my dear Posh," Bally said. "Focus on me and touch nothing. There is a heavy spell upon this room."

LinHem hooted in a low whistle. "My good Bally. I am concerned now. If there is a magical lamp within, it seems it would take years to find it."

"I agree," Bally said. "There are many magical artifacts here, and my senses are muted by the sheer number. We must use logic to locate the lamp."

"Any idea what it might look like?" Gwen asked. "Can we assume there might possibly be multiple lamps within?"

"It is very possible, yes. My master would want to throw off any treasure hunters." Bally sat, considering. He closed his eyes, their green jade glow disappearing for a moment. When he opened them, he straightened. "I believe we must split up, unfortunately."

Everyone remained silent, though, looking at the massive piles of treasure.

"We shall go in groups again," Bally continued. "Posh will go with me. Gwen, fire a flare from your wand if you need help or if you do locate the lamp."

Gwen looked at LinHem, then nodded. "I suppose we'll take this area," she said and nodded down a narrow path between the mountains of treasure.

"Be on your guard and rely on one another," Bally said. Posh jumped onto Bally and nearly disappeared into his thick fur. They moved in the opposite direction.

"Hop on, Gwenevere," LinHem said. "I am sure-footed, and we must not brush against the treasure."

Gwen did so, and they moved along the narrow pathways that branched further into smaller tributaries like a river. She held her wand out, though there was plenty of light within the chamber from the glowing treasure. Gwen visually searched the piles, still not sure what she was looking for. She'd seen genie lamps in the past; such mythical bottles were rare. During the Genie Wars, only a few had ever been recovered. Once a person gained control of a genie, they kept their lamps well-hidden for fear that someone might take possession of it. Normally, a genie bottle would vaporize once the genie had been freed. But on rare occasions, the lamp remained, and they were considered very valuable artifact.

LinHem kept pace as they searched. Gwen saw more weapons and armor, likely magical. She saw chariots and tanks and flying machines. Golden statues and expensive paintings were also mixed in amongst the horde of treasure, all of them designed to lure unwary adventurers to their doom. Yet she saw no sign of the lamp and began to wonder if perhaps it was buried at the center of a mound of treasure. If that was the case, they'd never retrieve it without diving into the poisoned treasure. *What then?* she mused.

Still, they continued to search. The paths seemed to wind on forever, and she wondered if the chamber was enchanted in a similar way to the halls at Hidden Palm Grove.

Then Gwen saw the face of the mountain beyond. It was unmistakable with its dark gray slate. They'd finally reached the end of the horde. Not far away, she saw Bally and Posh. LinHem hooted, and they met in the middle.

"No luck," Posh said in a frustrated tone. She seemed to be in control now, and Gwen understood why Bally had wanted her to go with him. His magic was keeping her sane, at the moment.

'It's near," Bally said. "I am certain."

"Then we continue to look," Gwen said. "If Bally senses it, then we must look through—"

LinHem let out a hoot and dug a talon into the stone path. "Beyond," he said and pointed his beak at the side of the mountain's wall.

Barely noticeable, Gwen saw something flickering. In fact, there were several points of light.

Bally growled and moved in that direction, followed by the others. When they neared the wall, Gwen finally saw what the flickering was.

There were several alcoves carved into the dark stone, perhaps two dozen in total. Within each niche sat a genie lamp. There were all sorts of flavors: gold, platinum, silver, and bronze. There were even jade, diamond, ruby and sapphire lamps. Embedded in the lamps were all kinds of jewels as well. The lamps shone and flickered in the green pulsing light of the nearby treasure. However, the lamps themselves were not glowing, which meant they hadn't been affected by the treasure's sickness.

Gwen realized that this must be yet another test. The wizard had placed the lamps here, daring the seeker to choose the right one. And what would happen if the wrong one was chosen? Would that person become a genie perhaps, trapped forever within the lamp?

"I know this one," Posh said as she hopped down from Bally.

"What do you mean?" Gwen asked.

Posh stopped just inches from one lamp in particular. It was a dull brass lamp that appeared patinaed in the green light. It had only one small jewel in the middle, which was a sapphire so dull that it looked dirty on the inside. Amongst the other lamps, this one felt the least desirable. It certainly didn't stand out like the others around it.

"This...was my mother's lamp. It was her prison for two centuries."

The look on Posh's face was one of sadness and confusion.

"It was your mother's?" Gwen asked. She moved closer to Posh and placed a hand on her shoulder. Her skin was warm, telling Gwen that Posh was growing emotional.

"I don't understand how her lamp could possibly be here," Posh said, a slight waver in her voice.

Gwen could see that Posh was struggling to control herself. "What happened to your mother?"

"She was killed in the Genie Wars." Posh hugged her arms around herself as steam continued to rise from her shoulders.

Gwen felt suddenly ashamed. Though she hadn't participated in the wars (being an investigator only), her parents had, where they'd both been killed, landing her in a foster home. Though Posh had also avoided the wars, it appeared her mother hadn't. Gwen hated what had happened. But even worse was knowing that her race had pushed their indoctrination on younger generations of witches. Standing there as Posh gazed upon her mother's lamp, Gwen felt several emotions hit her. She wanted to wrap her arms around the genie and comfort her. She sensed Posh's pain, and the sadness seemed to extend to LinHem and Bally as well.

They waited for Posh, giving her time to work through her emotions. Gwen finally sensed Posh's temper subside. Her skin cooled, and her shoulders slumped.

"Of course, that's in the past," Posh muttered. "I miss her, but now isn't the time to rehash it. Let's get on with this." She looked at Bally. "What do we do next?"

The panther seemed to choose his words carefully. "The map is likely hidden within. One of us must go inside and retrieve it. Know that anyone who goes into the lamp may be trapped forever."

They all looked at each other before Gwen finally spoke. "It has to be me. This is my duty, and I cannot ask any of you to sacrifice for me."

LinHem shook his head. "I beg to differ, Gwenevere. Of the four of us, I am the most expendable. You must make it back to Spellbinder to set the third sigil. And we need Bally to guide us. Posh shouldn't face this; it's too much to ask for a genie to go back into that realm. I shall go—"

"No, LinHem," Bally said. "It is I who should go. It was my master's lamp, and I knew him well. Perhaps that will give me the resolve to fight my way out."

"You can't, Bally," Posh finally said. "Your magic is no good here. If anyone knows how a genie bottle works, it's me. Isn't it obvious? This task was meant for me, it's why I'm here. I mean, it was my mother's lamp. I've spent time in this very bottle. It has to be me."

"Posh," Gwen said. "There's a chance it might drive you mad. Returning to a lamp once you've been freed is a big risk."

"And it's one that I'm willing to take now. I have the best chance to return. It's my choice."

Gwen gripped Posh by her shoulders. "I won't be responsible for this. It was my people who hunted the genies in the first place. Let me make amends…let me go."

"Those days are in the past." Posh bit her lower lip. "Look at us and how much we've overcome. Holding you responsible for what others did is rubbish, so don't use that as an excuse. This is my contribution to the quest, and that's final."

Posh pulled away from Gwen's grip and crossed her arms. The others looked on, saying nothing. Gwen finally looked away. She felt tears sting her eyes and wiped her cheeks. She hated being in this position. She had grown so close to Posh in such a short time. Posh was now her closest friend. On the outside, it made no sense—this shouldn't be possible between a witch and a genie. But it worked, better than she could have hoped for. The thought of losing Posh hurt more than she could bear, and it surprised her at how emotional she felt.

Gwen turned and walked away, not wanting the others to see her tears. But she took a deep breath and faced Posh. With a quick smile, Gwen nodded. "Okay, Posh. Just promise you'll hurry back."

Posh gave her a smile and cupped one hand to Gwen's cheek. "I promise." Then she turned to the wall of the mountain. She hesitated only a second longer before reaching up and touching the lamp's patinaed surface. Posh vanished in a puff of blue smoke.

Gwen, Bally, and LinHem sat around the mountain wall, talking softly and trying to ignore their obvious concern. Gwen kept wringing her hands together and couldn't get comfortable as she sat cross-legged. She wasn't worried about what Posh would face inside the lamp, but rather, what would happen when she returned. Gwen only hoped there would be no ill effects. She tried to comfort herself by repeating what Posh had said—*This task was meant for me, it's why I'm here.*

It was Spellbinder that had intertwined Posh's path with Gwen's. It was hard to deny that fact now. Posh, a genie, had stumbled upon her own mother's lamp, which likely held the map they needed to locate the third sigil. It was no coincidence. It was just hard for Gwen to accept Posh's sacrifice on her behalf. If Posh did make it back, Gwen would never be able to repay her.

"I feel responsible for this," Gwen said.

Bally and LinHem faced her, both sitting on their haunches.

"Pardon me, Miss Gwen, but what do you mean?" LinHem said.

"When I was a child, maybe six years old, my parents joined the Genie Wars. I didn't understand what they were about at first. Only that steam was in demand at that time to run our cities. Of course, genies were a vast resource back then, before the modern inventions we have today. My race hunted them to near extinction. I feel ashamed at what my parents did, now that I understand. It's my race that's responsible for Posh's mother and countless other genies' deaths."

"Do not be hard on yourself, Gwen," Bally said in a low voice. "You were caught up in the greater scheme. 'Tis not your doing."

"What happened to your parents?" LinHem said.

"They were both killed in action, like many others. My mother and father were both red witches. Being at the top of their class, they were offered a contract by the ministry straight out of university. Once I was old enough to decide my path, I chose green, though. I believed that someday I could bring a more peaceful approach to the battlefield through observation and nature. But when I finally joined the ministry, I understood that would never happen." Gwen stood and paced around the area, shaking her hands and trying to calm herself. "I'll never forgive myself if something happens to Posh. She shouldn't even be in this position."

"We must remain hopeful," Bally said.

"Our good friend is resilient," LinHem said. "She will find her way back. I have no doubt. I'm afraid all we can do is wait for her return."

Gwen nodded and sat down again, trying to think of something else.

Since there was no daylight in the keep, Gwen didn't know what time it was. She guessed the day had turned to night, though, and she was getting nauseous from the sickly green glow. She even started to wonder if the poison was affecting her vision, since everything had a tinge of green to it now.

It felt like hours had passed when the lamp finally blew out a streamer of blue smoke. They all circled around it and waited. The lamp rattled, bobbled and sputtered. A thick blue mist flowed from the tip like a geyser, then solidified into Posh. She faltered and fell to her knees. Bally was the first to reach her and rolled on his back, allowing Posh to land on his fur-covered belly.

Gwen hurried over and knelt. Posh was out cold, her skin icy to the touch. Worse yet, her typically vibrant blue color was pale.

LinHem fanned a wing at her and tried to wake her.

Gwen tapped Posh's cheek lightly. "Posh, wake up!"

The genie finally stirred and opened her golden eyes. She blinked a few times, then sat up.

"Are you okay?" Gwen asked and climbed onto Bally's stomach and sat in front of Posh. She took Posh's hands and rubbed them, trying to warm them up.

Posh looked at her, bleary-eyed and shuddered. "I…I think so."

"What happened?" Gwen asked.

"I searched for days, through deserts and mountains…"

"How did you make it out?" LinHem asked.

Posh didn't answer right away. She looked around, avoiding their gazes.

"Posh," Gwen spoke in a calm but sturdy voice, "what have you done?"

"I made it out, that's all that matters—"

"Tell me," Gwen said, interrupting her.

"I…had to use my wish-magic to escape."

"No, Posh!"

"What would you have me do?" Posh shot back. "We needed the map, and I promised I'd return with it. There was no other way."

"You knew you'd have to do that!" Gwen barked.

"Of course, I knew. And if I'd told you that *was* the only way, you'd never have let me near the bottle."

"But..." Gwen trailed off and looked down at their interlocked fingers. "Posh. That means you've used one of your wishes on my account." Gwen noticed the new scar forming vertically across Posh's left eye. It marked the second scar now.

"I'm here, and I have the map." Posh stood and nearly tumbled over.

Gwen stood to steady her. "You don't look well. Is there a side effect to all of this?"

Posh didn't answer.

"Tell me the truth. Is there a side effect?" Gwen persisted.

"Yes, but we don't have time to talk about it right now."

"I need to hear it."

"Okay, Gwen. But please, not now." Posh pulled out the map and held it, which drew everyone's attention. "This should lead us to Promenade."

"Might I have a look?" LinHem said. Gwen realized then that LinHem would be the obvious one to decipher a map. With his extensive knowledge of the lore and history of Ambriel, the griffin was a perfect match for their team. LinHem was practically shaking with anticipation as Posh handed him the map.

The four of them unrolled the ancient map right there on the treasure room floor. Gwen held her wand aloft to provide some light.

The ancient map was ripped and torn around the edges. There were magical glyphs and words of radiance along the borders that made it feel alive. Like Spellbinder, Gwen sensed that this piece of parchment was perhaps another sentient being.

"We would do well to keep this a secret," LinHem said. "People have fought wars over the location of Promenade. If your master felt that its location should remain a secret, then let us not reveal that. Not a word gets out."

# CHAPTER 37

## *A COZY TRAIN RIDE*

GWEN FELT LIKE she was beginning to enjoy air travel. At first, she had only anxiety, as it was a new experience from the trains she was so used to. But after being aboard the blimp several times now, she could see that it was safe, not to mention somewhat relaxing. And depending on where this hidden Promenade villa was, she might even be back on board yet again. Either way, Kershaw's bank account was definitely taking a hit.

The four of them rented a private cabin again, where they could spread out their things and look over the map at their leisure. LinHem was beyond intrigued. Being a librarian, she knew this sort of document was right down his alley, so to speak. He adjusted his golden spectacles and leaned over it, moving the map gently with his talon.

"What do you make of it?" Posh said. She was wrapped in a blanket, her skin still a bit pale.

"Hmm, interesting. This map has actually shifted."

Everyone leaned in and stared.

"I believe you are correct," Bally said. "Yesterday, this port city was further north." Bally tapped a claw to one of the cities marked along the Horizontal Sea's coastline.

"Never have I seen such a thing," LinHem said. "It is likely meant to throw off pursuers of Promenade. Yet another riddle I will need to investigate. This may take time to understand—time that we have precious little of."

As Bally and LinHem continued to pore over the map, Gwen pulled Posh to the side and looped her arm around the genie. "Let's talk," Gwen said.

Posh stifled a cough but nodded. "I owe you an explanation."

Gwen waited patiently as Posh gathered her thoughts.

"A genie has very powerful wish-magic, but when used it comes at a price."

"Right," Gwen said. "But I thought it just took time to regenerate?"

"We only get three uses of our wish-magic before expiration."

"Your magic expires? I guess I never knew that."

Posh shook her head. "Not my magic, me. *I* would expire." She pointed at the second vertical scar along her left eye. "I will stay forever marked. My first wish-magic was almost a century ago. You see, the gods granted genies their wish-magic. We are punished by them, shamed for using it. Our race forbids the use of wish-magic. Our elemental-magic is fine, but the powerful wish-magic has a devastating price."

"Are you saying you will die if you use wish-magic again?"

Posh shrugged and wrapped herself tighter into her blanket.

"I forbid you to even consider using it again," Gwen said and gently shook Posh, then draped an arm around her. "And...if you do not promise me right now, I'll remove you from the team."

Posh glanced at Gwen with a defiant look on her face, one Gwen had seen so many times since they'd first met. She could see that Posh wanted to retort and snap back at her. But Posh remained silent and looked away. It seemed she had little fire at the moment.

"What would you have me do, Gwen? I will not sit by and watch harm come to you or my friends. What I did tonight was my own decision."

"I don't care. I'm serious about removing you if you don't promise me."

Posh could only shake her head. "How can I make such a promise? If you're in danger, or Bally or LinHem—"

"Then we'll have to deal with it and deal with the consequences. What I won't allow is another sacrifice from you. Going into the lamp has already taken a toll. Let that be enough, okay? Just promise me, Posh. I don't want to do this without you, but I will."

Posh finally grimaced, then nodded. "Yes, fine. Of course. I want to be here with you as well. It's what I was hired to do anyway..." She trailed off after seeing the look on Gwen's face.

"So, is that the main reason you're still here? Is this just another job?"

"No," Posh said with a cross look. "Of course not. You should know that by now."

Gwen closed her eyes, "I'm sorry. I'm...just frazzled."

Posh gripped Gwen's hand and squeezed it. "We've come a long way since we first met, yeah? I think of you a lot. You're my friend, and I won't take advantage of that."

Gwen's heart skipped a beat. She felt the same way about Posh. She loved her kind, energetic, and sassy attitude. And now, she couldn't stop thinking about her either. She was a friend. She was her—

"We've found something," LinHem said, breaking Gwen's train of thought.

Posh and Gwen stood and joined LinHem and Bally.

"This area here," LinHem said and laid a talon on a region in the far west.

All Gwen could see were rolling hills and a large lake, though. "No, I see nothing but a vast plain and this lake."

LinHem rotated the map ninety degrees, then folded three edges at an angle. Suddenly, there was a small settlement on the edge of the lake. The rolling hills surrounding the villa seemed to be trying to conceal it.

Posh's eyes lit up. "Oh, my goodness. How'd you figure that out?"

"I've spent a lifetime studying maps at the Great Library," LinHem said. "I've seen this technique once or twice, but hiding things on a map this way is very intricate magic."

"Where is Valeside?" Gwen asked, her finger tracing the area along the Green Sea's coast.

"It's here," LinHem said, pointing it out with his talon. "It's about two days' travel by train. Unfortunately, there are no skyports nearby, which would save us a day." LinHem turned the map back around and indicated a train track. "However, we're in luck. This train stops in a town close by."

"Well, what's new?" Posh said. "Looks like we're packing our bags again."

There was no break when they returned to Valeside Beach. Though Kershaw wasn't waiting at the skyport this time, Gwen needed little motivation to hurry the team back to Java House. They packed, reserved seats on the train, and they made their way directly to the depot.

It was her first extended trip aboard a train since arriving to Valeside Beach. She felt somewhat at home as it left the station. The bounce and jostle of the cabin comforted her. Unlike airflight, a train ride always settled her nerves.

They had their own private cabin, thanks again to Kershaw's account. Each of them had their own bed, restroom and a shared living space. Bally and LinHem turned in right away, as nightfall had come and it was late. Their voyage back from Krubble had drained everyone, it seemed. But Gwen was restless, her mind running in circles, and sleep wouldn't come. She sat in the living area and watched the darkened landscape zoom past, her cheek against the cool surface of the window, and her breath fogging the glass. In the corner sat a small fireplace, and a yellow flame lit the dim cabin. The soft crackle of the fire mingled with the hum of the wind outside the window, giving her cozy vibes as they sped along.

She felt someone nudge her and turned to see a bleary-eyed Posh, her blue tousled hair tied into a topknot. Her golden eyes flickered in the firelight as she yawned and leaned her head on Gwen's shoulder.

"Couldn't sleep either?" she asked, hooking her arm around Gwen's.

Gwen chuckled. "Not a wink. I should be a zombie after the last few days."

"What's on your mind?"

"Just…everything, I suppose. The Saint Halving Day deadline, what we'll find at Promenade, *if* we can even find it. Will we get the final sigil and return in time? What else is hidden inside the castle? *You…*"

"Me, huh?" Posh said in a cheeky way. "So, what about that?" she asked, propping her chin in her hands and batting her eyes playfully.

"I'm still worried about you. I don't like what's happening," Gwen replied, though Posh's skin seemed to be returning to normal.

"Our fate has been laid before us, and we can't change it. The cards tell us that much."

"Speaking of fate, what was your sign again, the Cherub? Isn't that what Bally called it?"

Posh's skin flushed, and Gwen felt a radiant burst of heat from her.

Gwen smiled. "Something I said?"

"Please," Posh said. "Can't we just let that go?"

"I've got all night," Gwen said with a wink.

Posh let out a somewhat frustrated sigh. "Yes. I have the sign of the Cherub."

"Yes. You do. And if I didn't know any better, I would think you already knew that, even before that night of cards."

Posh gave her another smirk but yawned and leaned her head on Gwen's shoulder again. "Fine, Gwen. If you want me to say it, then here you go. I've grown attached to you. Happy now? Is there something wrong with that?"

"No, not at all."

Posh smiled and closed her eyes, pulling Gwen closer. "Now that I've shared that, tell me something more about yourself."

"I suppose I owe you that. What would you like to hear?"

"What about those secrets of yours? I think now's the time."

Gwen chuckled. "It's not a pleasant tale."

"I guessed as much."

Gwen took a deep breath, then clutched her hands together, feeling suddenly anxious. "Well, I've never shared this with anyone. You were right, though. My foster parents were abusive. They didn't think I deserved any rights because I was a witch. I never knew why they felt like that, but I can only assume they'd had a run-in with a witch at some point. I became their punching bag. When it came to abuse, I experienced it all. The physical part came from my foster dad. I never wanted to be alone with a man after that. But surprisingly, it was my foster mother who was the cruelest. The physical abuse I could handle, I just tuned it out and let my mind phase. Honestly, I think that might be where my ethereal connection came from. But with my foster mother, the psychological abuse cut much deeper. She had learned a few spells from a gypsy and would practice them on me. The last spell she cast finally drove me from the house. Now, I can never bear children, and I'll never know what it feels like to have my own family or make them feel safe. I guess that's one reason I ended up doing what I do. I want to give every child a safe home. I know that being a paranormal realtor isn't the same as preventing abuse, but it's my way of helping others."

Posh held Gwen's hand tightly. "That's enough, Gwen. You don't need to say anything else. Thank you."

They didn't speak any more that night. Posh seemed to know that it had taken everything for Gwen to share her past. Gwen knew she'd never have to speak about it again. She knew that Posh would never ask again, either.

The train ride lasted through the night and into the next day, not stopping along the way. Gwen finally managed to catch some sleep. Having Posh near helped soothe her mind. The genie's comforting vibe was something that Gwen had recently come to like more and more. Posh seemed to fill a missing piece of her soul, at least, that's how it felt. But it was something foreign, something she had never known before, after being independent for so long. She had purposely distanced herself from men, at least the ones looking for a romantic connection. She had never felt the need to fill that physical void. But recently, that had all changed. She'd been so caught up with sigils and telescopes that her relationship with Posh had snuck up on her.

*Posh…*

Gwen liked thinking about her, and the cool, effortless synergy surrounding the genie. Her cheeky comments, her unapologetic approach…her confident moves that night they had danced.

And yet, Posh also felt vulnerable in a way that made Gwen want to protect her. It was an intoxicating mystery wrapped up in a rather short, toned and confident lady that had Gwen feeling somewhat tipsy. And, of course, Posh seemed to feel the same way about her, too. She'd said as much just the night before and hadn't necessarily been shy about it either.

But Gwen was still struggling with those feelings. Or maybe it was how she planned to deal with it amidst all the other things happening right now. She had so many plates spinning that sooner or later one of them was bound to fall. Worrying about which plate would break was one reason she felt so anxious. She didn't know what she would do if any harm came to Posh, and that's what concerned her the most.

Their train finally arrived at a small hamlet in the far west named Everfield. It was early morning, the sun peeking over some of the rolling hills in that region. Even in the early light, Gwen could see the lush green fields that spread out before her. It looked like a green quilt that disappeared along the horizon, some never-ending perspective that carried into the sun.

Posh bumped into her, a groggy stumble that nearly tumbled them both onto the boarding platform. Gwen caught her and held her close as LinHem and Bally followed behind. Gwen let go of Posh amidst the turmoil of other passengers exiting the train. They were soon pressing their way through the thicket of travelers amidst the steam and commotion. Gwen noticed how the crowd was a mix of different races of people and creatures. She saw red, green and yellow witches, smaller firedrakes, striped centaurs, and a slew of other winged creatures like fairies and pixies. It was the first time that Bally and LinHem didn't stick out like sore thumbs.

Once they exited the platform, Gwen led them to the nearby hamlet. The streets were cobbled with brown stones and thatched buildings lined the alleyways. There were all sorts of businesses just opening up for the day. They passed bakeries and restaurants with fresh bread wafting through the crowded streets. There were cobblers and blacksmiths propping open their doors. They meandered through the busy markets, past parks and tranquil ponds and pastures. It was the most picturesque little town she'd ever seen. She was well-traveled throughout Ambriel, thanks to her days in the ministry, and yet she'd never heard of this hamlet called Everfield.

Eventually, the cobbled street dead-ended into a small sign that read: *The End of the Road*. Beyond that was a green pasture with trees sprinkled along the rolling hills. Purple shadow lines were growing lighter as the morning sun lifted into the perfectly blue sky. Small puffy clouds wafted over the fields, casting pastel shadows onto the landscape.

"Well," Posh said, looking at LinHem. "What now?"

LinHem pulled out the map and held it up to the sky. The sun shone onto it in a strange way. "Hmm. This map seems to lead us to this point, though I must admit, I'm at a loss as to why that is."

Bally stepped closer to LinHem and bent the three corners of the map back to their original position with his snout. Then he let out a soft growl. "Posh, my dear, I believe your question has been answered."

As LinHem held the map, Gwen and Posh stepped closer and looked. The sun revealed a phrase scrawled across the parchment, which was glowing in a golden ink.

Gwen read the phrase out loud. "The Beginning of the Road starts here."

# CHAPTER 38

## *THE BEGINNING OF THE ROAD*

"WONDER WHAT THAT means?" Posh asked.

"My dear," Bally said. "Is it not obvious?" The ghost panther laid his massive paw on the road sign.

"Are you saying…" Posh stepped off the cobbled road and walked behind the sign that read: *The End of the Road*. She abruptly vanished.

Gwen and LinHem looked at each other and then back to the area where Posh had just been standing. Suddenly, Posh's blue-haired head reappeared, though the rest of her body was missing. "The road begins here, apparently," Posh said.

The others did the same and walked behind the street sign.

When Gwen stepped around it, she let out a gasp.

The cobbled road continued, but it was no longer the smooth brown stones. Instead, it was a golden-hued brick. The hamlet continued on, and the town expanded out around them.

"The sign, it must be a hidden marker," Gwen said.

"Aye," LinHem said. "One only revealed to those who have the map with them, configured in the proper way, I might add. Intriguing."

"Precisely," Bally said, his tail flicking with satisfaction. "Ah, my master was indeed a genius." Bally led the way, using his nose to sniff the air. He seemed to be following some invisible scent again.

As they followed the panther, Gwen took in the town known as Promenade. It was as she had seen in her vision from Spellbinder. There were unbelievably green fields and pastures and hills. A blue sky with what looked like golden glitter floating on the breeze. There was a barely audible chiming in the air, and the wind seemed to tug at her, trying to pull her into a dream. The feeling she got was like nothing she'd experienced before. Gwen knew one thing. She never wanted to leave this place.

Like on the other side of the street sign, this one too was filled with all manner of creatures. It was as if some unspoken declaration stated that *all are welcome here*, and it brought a smile to her face. In this utopia, there was no discrimination or judgment or segregation. Everyone was accepted.

But strangely, as they continued walking through the hamlet, the citizens seemed to ignore them. Could they not see them? Were they invisible? Did they even exist in this world?

Eventually, she stopped and tapped a yellow male witch on the shoulder. He turned to face Gwen but didn't smile or show any emotion.

"Excuse me. What is happening here?" Gwen asked.

"It would seem you are here through discovery," the male witch said in a monotone voice. "You have not been invited. You must speak to the master."

Gwen looked at her friends, confused. "Okay. Can you please tell me where that is?"

But the witch didn't answer and turned and walked off.

"I know the way, Gwenevere," Bally said.

They followed Bally, no one speaking now. Posh hooked her arm around Gwen's and pulled her close as they strolled through the picturesque hamlet.

But to Gwen, it was such a strange feeling. Though she felt happiness here, there was also a lingering 'imposter' feeling. She *was* an uninvited guest in this town, apparently. Though no one told them to leave, she understood that she needed an invitation from this 'master', whoever that might be. They had accidentally stumbled upon a great secret, and the other inhabitants here knew it as well.

The small cottages grew less dense, and at the top of a knoll stood an old hut with the golden street dead-ending into it. It was something that didn't fit into the rest of the perfect little cottages, like a black duck in a group of swans. It was round and built of rotting wooden planks. A rusty stove pipe poked through the thatched roof, with a greenish colored steam spewing from it.

Bally walked up to the front door and tapped one large paw against it and waited. Seconds later, the door cracked open, and an old man with a crooked purple hat stepped through and looked at them. Bally let out a roar, then nuzzled the old man.

The old man chuckled. "It's nice to see you, too, Bally."

"Come inside, all of you," the old man said. "We have much to discuss."

The man led them into the small hut. Gwen noticed how dilapidated the hovel appeared from the outside. There was only one window, and the walls were made of vertical wood planks, faded and checked from age. The small hut was round, perhaps three meters in diameter. She wondered how it was large enough for even one person to live in, let alone four guests, including a rather large griffin and ghost panther.

But when she stepped through the door, her mouth fell open.

As if by magic, there was somehow plenty of room inside. It was also much nicer than it appeared on the exterior. It had high ceilings, with clerestory windows that emitted plenty of daylight. There was a main gathering space with a round fireplace in the center made of stone. The ceiling was pitched upward and surrounded the rotunda-shaped room. Alcoves and hallways extended from the main rotunda to other antechambers, which she assumed were sleeping quarters. A large countertop surrounded the perimeter, littered with old books and maps, drafting tools and pencils. Some of the maps were pinned up on the walls. But the one thing that caught her attention the most was the shiny robot that scooted about the space. It zipped from one room to the next with the sound of mechanical clicking. If she didn't know any better, she could have sworn that it was Frame.

"Welcome to my humble laboratory," the old man said and tipped his tattered wizard's hat.

Gwen did the same and tipped her hat as Bally moved to stand next to the old man. The wizard smiled and ruffled his ears affectionately. Then, Bally tackled the old man and began licking his face. He chuckled as they rolled around on the floor. Gwen had never seen Bally act in such a manner, and it reminded her of a baby cub the way he pawed at the man.

When they finally stopped, the man stood. "Ah, as you have likely guessed, I am Speartine, the wizard, and the creator of Spellbinder. You have finally made your way to me, as was designed long ago."

"Long ago?" Posh said. "Are you saying that we're supposed to be here?"

"Precisely. Bally was meant to help guide you here, though he didn't know it at the time. I apologize for the ghost loop, young Bally. But had I told you, fate might not have taken its true course."

The four companions looked at each other, dumbfounded.

Gwen cleared her throat. "Excuse me, Speartine. Can you give us a little more background? Why the four of us? Why is…well, this quest so important?"

"Your three companions are here to help you along, Gwenevere, and you are meant to help them in return. Your friends have their own desires to fulfill as well, and all of them are noble. But I think you may have surmised that already."

Gwen fidgeted with her wand, not sure what to say. Everyone stared at her, waiting. But she was so flummoxed that she could only stare back at the old wizard. She felt uncertain that she could finish her own quest, let alone help her friends achieve their desires.

Speartine continued. "Well, you have a special ability, do you not? It is one that not even I possess. You are in a place and time where you can set some wrongs to right. I have always championed equality and fairness. I have tried to create things through my inventions to help maintain balance. But some things are beyond my ability, and I was limited in my life in Ambriel."

"Limited in your life?" Gwen asked. "I don't understand."

"I am no longer in the land of the living."

"Does that mean we're also no longer alive?" Posh asked.

"It means that you are not yet invited to Promenade," Speartine said. "You are only here as guests."

"So, that's why we got the dirty looks," Posh muttered.

"Yes, you have not earned your place here yet. I am afraid you cannot stay."

"What is this place?" Posh asked.

"Is it not obvious," Bally said. "This must be heaven."

The wizard leaned against his wooden staff and rubbed his brow. "Well, it isn't that simple. This is just one reality that we know from the time we are born. It has been called many things, though, it is what you make it. Promenade is known as an *after* reality, and there are many of those."

"An after reality?" LinHem hummed. "Fascinating. I have not heard it described in such a way. However, I am curious to know more about your telescope. It is a very curious relic."

Speartine's eyes wandered to the heavens, and a slow smile creased his weathered face. "Ah, Spellbinder. Yes, after I built the telescope, it took on a life of its own. You might even call it a sentient being. Its essence resides mostly in another realm, and even I do not understand how it exists here. I only know that as a Grinber, I was ordained to construct the telescope by the god of desire himself. You four are now called upon, and you must answer. Beware, Spellbinder gives nothing for free. In the laws of its kind, the sigils must be earned. You four must work as a team to attain the final sigil, if you hope to return and free the spirits."

"The four of us, master?" Bally said. "Yet, after nearly a century, I have finally returned to you. I wish to remain by your side."

The wizard looked at Bally, a sad smile on his face. "No, Bally. I'm afraid you are not invited…not yet. You still have much to do in your current reality, and there you shall remain for now." The wizard gave the large cat a hug, then stepped away. "You four are on a noble quest. As each of you builds your resume for your own after reality, you have this opportunity to help thousands of souls. Listen well. This final challenge will be a greater test than the previous two. Do not forget that you are a team. Are you prepared?"

Gwen gathered her friends. "Thank you. I owe the three of you more than I can say. It sounds like this might be dangerous. If any of you want out, I'll understand."

Posh snorted. "Really, Gwen? After coming this far, you seriously think any of us would turn back now? Besides, you heard the wizard. This is *our* responsibility."

LinHem laid a feathered wing on Gwen's shoulder. "We are with you, Gwenevere."

Bally did the same, laying a large paw on her other shoulder. "Shall we begin?"

Gwen took a deep breath, then gripped her wand. "Okay, Speartine. We're ready."

# CHAPTER 39

## *A TEST OF GOLD*

POSH, LINHEM AND Bally stood next to Gwen, waiting for the wizard's response.

The old man leaned on his staff and spoke slowly. It was in a language that Gwen didn't recognize. It sounded ancient, guttural almost. But she understood by the tone that the words were filled with power, some long-forgotten dialect known only to the Grinbers in Ambriel, perhaps. His staff began to glow white hot, then fire erupted from the tip.

Speartine's form began to shift.

He elongated, then morphed and stretched. In a matter of seconds, he sprouted horns and web-like wings from his back. Golden scales shone in the light as his form grew, slowly at first, then faster and faster. The roof of the old hut flew apart, and the walls pulsed from the energy radiating from his being.

Gwen, Posh, LinHem and Bally moved away and stepped outside of the hut just as it splintered into pieces. They watched in awe as a golden dragon finally emerged and reached its full height. It roared and shot a jet of fire at the ground, scorching it.

"Spread out, one to each corner!" Gwen yelled. She pulled the brim of her hat lower and held her wand out in front of her defensively.

Bally leapt to the right side of the dragon, then vanished. Posh turned to mist and shot under the dragon's belly and behind it as LinHem took to the air and held his position on the far left.

The dragon, momentarily confused as they split up, turned and swung its tail at where Bally had been. Posh took the opportunity to shoot an icy bolt at it, which hit the dragon on the back. Its golden scales changed to a blue and purple color. But the dragon shook off the effects and whipped around, shooting a jet of fire at Posh. Gwen had never seen the genie move so quickly before. She transmuted into a cloud of mist and zipped out of the rain of fire and to the opposite side.

The dragon reoriented on Bally, or at least where Gwen thought Bally was. It seemed that the beast could see into the veiled world of the ghost panther. It lunged at thin air, and suddenly, Bally was visible again, now that he'd been spied. But the plaid-patterned panther was quick, and Bally used his strength and leapt to the dragon's horned head, striking with his massive paws. At the same time, LinHem swooped in and lashed out with his talons and beak. The attack seemed to disorient the dragon as Gwen moved closer and pointed her wand at some nearby wheat stalks. She muttered a sentinel spell, and the stalks came to life, forming a dozen straw foot soldiers. They circled one of the dragon's clawed feet and began attacking it, which didn't do much but annoy the beast. It shook its head, and Bally flew from it. LinHem took flight again, his beak and claws having little effect on the golden scales.

The dragon looked down at the straw soldiers and let loose a massive jet of flame, causing the straw soldiers to erupt in fire.

Gwen was already moving toward a stand of trees and used a green-thumb spell to wake one. This was a large oak, ancient and old. Its gnarled tree bark was thick, and its branches long and strong. It uprooted and marched toward the dragon. Gwen climbed one of its branches and wedged herself there, directing the giant oak to engage the dragon. Soon, the two massive figures were intertwined. The dragon's strength was immense, though, and it finally managed to rend one of the oak giant's limbs from its main trunk. But the tree held firm and pressed in closer so the dragon couldn't use its fiery breath.

LinHem and Bally engaged the dragon again, hammering at the beast's horned head. Gwen noticed a thick frost form near the dragon's face where Posh had shot a stream of ice into the dragon's eyes, clouding its vision. Gwen continued to urge the massive oak in closer and soon every limb of the golden dragon was tied up in branches. They had finally managed to immobilize the dragon. Still, Bally and LinHem's attacks had little effect on the dragon's thick armor. Even though it couldn't see and was immobilized, they struggled to slow it. Gwen's thoughts raced as she sat amidst the tree branches.

*How are we going to defeat this dragon?*

She watched LinHem wrench on the dragon's horns. Bally swatted at the beast with his sharp claws. Posh flew around the dragon, using her icy mists and heated steam to slow it. The oak giant still had the dragon's arms, legs, wings and barbed tail immobilized.

And yet, they were losing the battle.

They had to find another way.

Then the dragon let out a loud roar and flexed its serpentine body. With a loud crack, the block of ice Posh had created to slow the dragon shattered into a thousand little ice cubes. LinHem was thrown forward, along with Bally, where they plunged into the wheat field. The massive oak tree splintered in half, causing Gwen to tumble from her perch.

The four companions stood their ground while the dragon spread its wings and blotted out the sun. The ominous shadow engulfed them, and Gwen felt her hope fade into the darkness. The dragon would bathe them in flame, and that would be it. They had come so far, only to fail the final test. She would never finish her task. She would never free those unfortunate souls from the castle.

The dragon arched its back and prepared to douse them in fire.

Gwen braced for the dragon's breath.

But it never came.

She looked up to see Posh floating in front of the dragon. The genie hovered in place with her legs crossed like she was riding a flying carpet. She held her thumbs and forefingers together, a pulsing golden light bathing the entire area. Gwen could see that Posh was about to use her final essence of genie wish-magic.

"No!" Gwen yelled.

She broke free of LinHem and Bally and raced toward Posh. When she got there, the dragon's head was racing downward, the red-hot magma about to spew forth. The golden beast's chest was bright, lit all the way up its long neck.

Gwen grasped at Posh, but the genie shifted higher and out of her reach.

Just as the flame left the dragon's mouth, the light surrounding Posh turned a bright blue. Then it leapt from her and struck the dragon's fire. The impact created an explosion that leveled the entire area. It blew Gwen into Bally and LinHem, and she bowled them over in a cloud of dust. The shockwave flattened the wheat field like a hurricane's wind.

Gwen watched as the dragon's flame dissipated in a cloud of steam. Then the dragon began to float. Its golden scales glowed bright as the dragon fragmented into small pieces, and it eventually lost its form. But Posh didn't let up. She winced as she concentrated, her brow creased in effort and pain. Finally, when there was nothing left of the dragon but dust particles, Posh relaxed and dropped to the ground.

Gold glitter from the dragon swirled in the air. The warm breeze held it aloft in the midmorning sun. Around Gwen's feet was a pile of golden shavings. It shifted, like sand in the desert. Sitting on top of it was the third sigil.

But the only thing Gwen could think about was Posh.

She sprinted over to the genie and slid on her knees. Posh's skin was ice cold, the color almost white. "Posh, what have you done!" Gwen hugged Posh close to her.

Posh looked up to Gwen and brushed some of her hair away from her brow.

"Why, Posh?"

"Do you have the sigil?" Posh whispered, her voice no more than a whisper.

Gwen felt a tear trickle down her cheek as she held Posh in her lap. Across Posh's left eye, Gwen saw a third and final scar begin to develop. "You promised not to do this!"

Posh wrapped her arms around herself to fight off an involuntary shiver. "Seems…like fate strikes again."

Gwen watched as Posh continued to fade. Her vibrant blue changed to a pale white, reminding Gwen of a ghost. "I won't accept this."

"You don't get to choose my fate. I do."

"Take it back, please." Gwen felt hysterical, like she was losing grip of reality. It was that same morning in Kriss's room all over again. Losing Kriss had hurt. Losing Posh felt devastating. It hurt her soul to see the beautiful genie withering away before her eyes.

But Posh continued to fade, becoming a transparent, gossamer sheet…like all those lost souls Gwen had tried to help.

And there was nothing she could do to save Posh.

"Tell me how to fix this," Gwen begged, her voice raw with emotion. "Please…tell me! Where can I find you?"

"I don't know," Posh said. Her eyelids finally closed, and her voice was barely a whisper. "The gods will punish me for using their forbidden wish-magic. No power in the universe can save me now. I am forever cursed. My after reality is the Friar's Inferno."

"Why did you do this…why? I asked you not—"

"For you, and I'd do it again." Posh took Gwen's hand and held it to her chest.

Gwen felt her body go still.

Then, Posh's form disintegrated, and the genie was no more.

Gwen continued to kneel in the wheat field with LinHem and Bally standing next to her. A warm breeze swept through, bending the stalks flat as it swirled around them. Posh's remains were lifted, then scattered to the wind.

# PART THREE

## THE DEVIL'S PADDOCK

# CHAPTER 40

## *INTO THE UNIVERSAL LENS*

GWEN CONTINUED TO sit in the wheat field for the rest of the afternoon. Bally and LinHem stood beside her the entire time as a deep feeling of loss consumed her. She gripped the sigil so tightly that it cut into her hand—the regret she felt was more than she could bear this time. Posh was gone forever, and it was her fault. The genie had sacrificed herself yet a second time to save her life.

Was she destined to always be alone? The loss of her parents, then being forced from her foster home, followed by Kriss's death, and now Posh was gone. Gwen had thought she'd finally found someone to hold on to. For a short time, she'd dared to hope things could change for her.

But right now, things felt pointless. Gwen had the third sigil, but the one she cared about the most wasn't there to celebrate with her.

Eventually, Bally nuzzled Gwen's green hair and began to purr. He sat down in front of her.

Gwen leaned into Bally and wrapped her arms around him, and she finally broke down and cried. LinHem knelt and wrapped his wings around them, trying to give what comfort he could.

"Gaining the third sigil has been costly for us all," Bally said.

Gwen nodded. Not only had they lost Posh, but Bally had lost his master as well. The sacrifice given to attain the third sigil would not soon be forgotten.

They moved past the road sign and back to the other side. Gwen walked dejectedly down the cobbled road, passing by all the shoppes that were closing down for the day. Most of the citizens were heading home and largely ignored them. Luckily, they were able to catch the last train out of Everfield.

When Gwen got to her private cabin, she literally collapsed onto the living room sofa and curled up.

LinHem lit a fire, but left her alone and went to his room, along with Bally. She pulled a blanket around her and stared into the fire, eventually dozing off.

Her dreams that night were filled with self-doubt and regret. Had her decision to let Posh continue with their group been the right thing? A familiar sense of claustrophobia hit her, like when Kriss had passed.

Throughout the train ride home, LinHem and Bally continued to check on her. But eventually, they left her alone. She needed time to herself, and it took the entire train ride back before she could face either of them. There wasn't much time to grieve, and she knew it would take longer to fully recover, but she needed to focus. Afterwards, she could spend time grieving. But mission one was Hidden Palm Grove. She owed it to Posh. Failure now would be an insult to the sacrifice she'd made.

But now that Gwen had the final sigil, she wondered what there was left to face. Obviously, they needed to return the sigil, which shouldn't be a problem. Then, according to legend, Spellbinder would grant her deepest desire. Only...there was more to it, and somehow, she knew this. Nothing had been easy so far.

In the morning, Gwen showered and left her private cabin.

On the boarding platform, Bally and LinHem waited for her. Near them stood Kershaw and his group of ogre bodyguards.

He seemed impatient, his arms crossed and one index finger tapping his sleeve. Kershaw was dressed in his typical pinstriped suit, pressed and impeccably tailored. He held her gaze as she approached. "Where, may I ask, is Posh? I have a bone to pick with her."

Gwen stopped in front of him, her arms hanging at her sides and her fists clenched. But the look on Kershaw's face told Gwen that he already knew what had happened to Posh. Somehow, he knew she was dead, and Gwen wondered if he'd been notified by the golden chain around Posh's waist. Either way, if he was shocked or even saddened by it, he showed no emotion.

"You know what happened," Gwen said coolly. "Do you have anything to say? No condolences…nothing?"

Kershaw held his hands calmly behind his back. "Posh knew the danger in this assignment. She served her purpose. It still doesn't relieve you from our contract."

Gwen wanted to reach out and strangle Kershaw with her bare hands. "How can you say that? Posh was loyal. She worked in your service for nearly a decade, and all you can say is—"

"The only thing that matters right now is fulfilling the contract. Posh knew that. It's on you, Gwen. I will hold you accountable if you fail. Your time is almost up."

Kershaw stepped close to her and hissed in her ear. "You're used to working alone anyway, so what does it matter? Figure it out." He turned and walked off, leaving her in stunned silence.

Bally crouched low, as if waiting for her command to shred him to bits. Even LinHem, who was typically softhearted and docile, had a glare in his eye. He clicked his front claws on the stone in anger. Gwen knew he'd be right behind Bally, if she gave the word.

Instead, she took a deep breath and turned to face them. "Enough of that. I'm not working for him anymore. We're doing this for Posh."

"Indeed, we are," LinHem said.

"Yes," Bally growled.

"Let's get back to Hidden Palm Grove and place this sigil," Gwen said.

As they hurried through the busy train depot, Gwen walked close to Bally. "Any idea what will happen once we set the final sigil?"

"I cannot say. I've never heard of anyone completing one of Spellbinder's quests. Only that the answer will become clear to the bearer of the sigils."

*The answer will become clear,* Gwen muttered to herself. That phrase rang oddly within her thoughts, though she had no idea why.

They made a quick stop at Java House, then set out immediately along the beach and toward Hidden Palm Grove. They walked rapidly, practically running when they neared the hidden spiral staircase in the rock outcropping. With less than a day until Saint Halving Day, the air had finally turned cold in Valeside Beach. To Gwen, there seemed to be an ominous pall hanging over the tropical paradise. That heaviness sent a chill up her spine, even with the festive atmosphere around the bars and coffee shoppes.

When they finally reached the castle, the evening air was gray and gloomy. Clouds were rolling in from the Green Sea like black mountain tops. In the distance, Gwen saw Tom working around the grounds, his hounds nearby. Odd, considering the late hour and the colder temperature.

Tom eyed her the entire way into the castle. He tipped his feathered hat and mouthed something to her, which she didn't understand. Before she could stop to think about it, they were pushing into the foyer and across the polished marble floors of Hidden Palm Grove.

"We must hurry," Bally said. "The witching hour is near."

The three of them followed closely behind Bally as he wove his way into the back corridors of the castle. The keep felt different now. To Gwen, the same ominous feeling had crept into the corridors. Like tiny fingers that worked their way out of the stone walls, she felt a tingle on her skin. Everything seemed to be accelerating to a boiling point, and at the center of it was Spellbinder.

Soon, the corridors grew dark and heavy, and Gwen knew they'd missed their window. The witching hour was upon them. When she turned to look for LinHem, the griffin was gone.

"Bally!" Gwen hollered and stopped. She turned back and hurried down a long corridor, looking for LinHem. She called out, her voice echoing down the corridor and off the walls.

When she turned to look for Bally, the ghost panther was also gone.

"Oh no," Gwen whispered. She was alone.

All her friends were gone now, and Gwen was lost in Hidden Palm Grove. If she could somehow manage to find her way to the lighthouse, how long would it take?

A moment of paralysis hit her, and she slumped to the floor and leaned against the wall. She removed her wide-brimmed hat and ran her fingers through her tangled hair. A cold chill gripped her, and the hair stood up on her arms. For the first time, fear settled in, and she wrapped her arms around herself.

It didn't take long for the spirits to find her.

She was in danger of getting caught in another ghost loop, like the first time she'd ventured here alone. She had barely managed to break free of that cycle, and it had taken the entire night. She couldn't afford that right now. Time was short.

*Guide me, Kriss*, she whispered. *Tell me what to do.*

Her ruby amulet lit up.

It was no more than a flicker at first, like a fire struggling to ignite. But then it pulsed and grew stronger until it was glowing a bright red. Gwen stood and steadied herself. She clutched the amulet in one hand and held her rosewood wand forward. Gwen took a steady breath and began to walk through the darkened hallways.

Occasionally, she heard a voice. Whether it was Kriss or Posh or some entity, she didn't know. But when she did hear it, something caught her eye. On the wall next to her was a massive paw print. It was Bally's markings.

The amulet was allowing her to see his ghost marks.

Encouraged, Gwen hurried on, moving with a bit of urgency now while hoping her amulet's energy would hold. Soon, she heard another whisper and found another ghost mark. Buoyed by hope, Gwen blocked out the spirits that threatened to pull her into their ghost circle. Gwen practically sprinted down the corridors. She thought about Bally and LinHem. Maybe Bally had tracked LinHem and ferried him safely out? She only hoped they wouldn't follow after her.

It felt like hours had passed when Gwen found the final marking.

She stood at the foot of the lighthouse, looking up the long winding staircase. She'd made it, and there wasn't much time left.

She gripped the handrail and moved up the staircase like a wraith in the night, shivering all the way. At the top landing, Gwen paused. She reached into her leather satchel for the golden sigil and felt the cool golden trinket in her palm. The group had sacrificed so much for her to be here for this moment. With a deep breath, she pushed through the doorway and into Spellbinder's inner sanctum.

Once inside, Gwen closed the door and leaned against the wall to catch her breath.

It was hauntingly dim, the constellations casting their ethereal light onto the floor. Gwen pulled the sigil from her satchel. She held it up to the stars and galaxies, memorializing its outline in her mind's eye. The golden dragon, and the final piece of the puzzle, would finally be laid to rest.

Spellbinder will give you the answer you desire…

*The answer I desire*, she whispered to herself.

Gwen began walking around the lighthouse floor. In the center was the hulking form of Spellbinder. The wizard had stated the telescope was a sentient being and imbued with the essence of the god of desire. It appeared that this god was a benevolent being, seeing that it had appointed her to rescue thousands of trapped souls. And yet, the only soul on her mind was Posh.

Gwen moved quickly around the lighthouse rotunda, stooping in the dark and searching for the outline of the dragon's sigil. She was aware of a higher presence within the chamber. The air seemed alive, like the room was taking in breath and steadily letting it out. She wasn't alone. Spellbinder, the god of desire, was with her.

But despite that, she was also acutely aware of the ticking clock. The time was near, and in the back of her mind was Harris's deadline, too.

Her hands continued to shake as she searched. "Come on, come on," she whispered, dropping the sigil in her haste. *It's got to be here somewhere!* All this effort—searching for the sigils, traveling across Ambriel, dealing with setbacks and the sacrifices. Her nerves were on edge.

Gwen dropped to her hands and knees, feeling for the sigil's void.

That was when a realization finally hit her.

The sigil's placeholder was no longer on the floor.

*Because it's within the telescope*, a voice whispered.

Gwen grabbed her wand and leapt up the wide stairs and to the top of the telescope.

The tube's surface was warm, vibrating almost. *Breathing…*

Something shone at the top of the telescope. It flashed golden in the light of the stars.

"That's it," she muttered.

Gwen scaled up the telescope and straddled the enormous tube of Spellbinder. She began to shimmy her way toward the end.

When she placed her hands on the metallic surface, a buzzing sensation radiated through her palms and up her arms. It flowed through her entire body, giving her a lightheaded and weightless feeling of euphoria.

There, in the observatory, she clung to the barrel until she finally made it to the end. In the sky, she witnessed the planets beyond starting to align, and the stars morphed into a strange pattern.

Something grand was about to happen.

Gwen looked down into the end of the telescope and saw the gigantic lens within. Just in front of it was the void for the third sigil. It matched the outline of the golden dragon.

She slid inside the opening, splaying her legs out to prevent herself from sliding into the massive lens. When she gazed into it, she saw things of wonder, things that mere mortals were not meant to see. If she had to guess, she was witnessing the beginning of creation: swirling masses of dust and matter and time. Things that her mind could not comprehend. Her body stretched and elongated as she suddenly realized something. Spellbinder's lens wasn't an object to see through…

*…it was a portal.*

Gwen pulled her gaze from the disturbing vision.

She held the golden sigil in her shaking hands and finally placed it within the void. As she did, her body began to tingle. Then she fell limp and slid into Spellbinder's lens and disappeared into the inky void beyond.

# CHAPTER 41

## *INTO PURGATORY*

GWEN SLID INTO the giant lens of Spellbinder, her body in a state of paralysis. It felt like slipping into a dark void of blackness where nothing existed, save a vacuum of empty space. She let out a yelp in fear as she sank further into the void.

She could see all of Ambriel below her. Between the continent and the heavens was a soft haze, and beyond that she could see starlight and other heavenly bodies. The paralysis that had taken her body persisted, though. All she could do was wait and see where Spellbinder was transporting her.

She floated at a tremendous speed, zipping past galaxies and stars. She sensed that she was being projected through Spellbinder's lens in the direction it had been aimed. She tried not to panic, telling herself this was all part of the process, at least she hoped.

Eventually, she slowed, and her body felt somewhat normal again. She didn't feel elongated, and the numbing sensation was gone. She flexed her hands and felt the tingling ease, and the circulation returned.

Gwen floated above a landscape of steam and starlight. To her, it appeared as a comet's surface might, and a long tail trailed behind it. The surface was faceted, shiny and mirror-like. Each facet seemed to represent a different event or timeline. Inside each one was something like a moving picture playing out in real time. She wondered if perhaps these images were aligned to a specific person or creature and represented their own existence. But there were so many facets that she couldn't count them all.

Her body started to descend, and soon she was standing on the comet's surface.

She stepped around the faceted craters while avoiding jets of steam. She didn't know what she was searching for; she only assumed that Spellbinder had brought her here for a reason. Beyond was a large mountain, and at its base was a large gate made of crystal. When she approached, the gates swung open, beckoning for her to come inside.

Gwen felt unsettled and confused as she stood before the gates. She wondered if this was all a dream. How could she be here, on the surface of a comet? None of it made any sense. She was trusting in Spellbinder now and that the telescope had a plan for her.

Gwen stepped through the gates.

On the other side was a vast amphitheater of cosmic proportions. It was carved into the side of the mountain with the stage set far below. Behind the stage, like some grand backdrop, was the universe and all of creation. The view stole her breath, and she felt like she was sitting on the edge of time.

Seated in the amphitheater was a multitude of people and creatures of all kinds, like witches, ogres, fairies, gnomes and giants. Near the bottom of the amphitheater was a line of people who seemed to be waiting to step onto the stage. Upon the stage were a dozen people sitting in chairs.

Gwen found a red witch seated near the top of the amphitheater. "Excuse me," Gwen said.

The red witch faced her. She had war marks on her forearms and palms and wore a red cloak with glyphs. "Yes, what is it, dear?"

"I…I'm new here. I was just wondering what this place is?"

"Why, you are in purgatory. These people wait for their judgment."

"Purgatory?" Gwen said and arched her brows. "As in…limbo? But that would mean these people are dead."

"Yes, I suppose it does."

"But I'm not dead."

The red witch looked closer at Gwen for the first time. She stood and walked around her, poking her with her wand. "Why, you're right! You are not dead, and you should not be here. How did you come to this place?"

"I was brought here, and I don't know why."

The witch stood back, glancing over Gwen while shaking her head. "This just won't do," she said. "Come along. We'll get to the bottom of this."

The red witch took Gwen by the arm and led her down the steps of the amphitheater, which seemed to take an eternity. When they finally reached the bottom, the witch led her to the base of the stage and waited.

The dozen people sitting around the stage were busy conversing with each other, and they didn't notice Gwen and the red witch at first. One lady, whom Gwen assumed was in charge, called out a name from a podium made of crystal. The next person in line, who happened to be a small pixie, glided up to the stage and stopped in front of the council. After a brief testimony from the pixie, the council members seemed to write something on a tablet made of crystal.

"What are they doing?" Gwen whispered.

"This is the Elder Council. They are judging this creature and how it will live out its after reality. These signs will determine which realm the pixie must go to.

Gwen recognized that word again—*after reality*. It was the same phrase Speartine had used when he explained Promenade. This caught Gwen by surprise, though. She'd always assumed the afterlife—or after reality—was less personal than what she was seeing right now. People standing in line, being judged by a mystical council, seemed a bit cliché and somewhat silly. Nonetheless, here she was, standing in purgatory and watching it in real time.

"That's Gaia," the red witch whispered.

The lady at the podium was a human, though she was much taller than any human Gwen had met. Her skin had a golden hue to it, and her hair glowed white. She wore white robes that appeared like clouds, and when Gwen looked closer, she could see them shifting and churning as the lady glided elegantly across the stage.

"You've been mischievous during your time on Ambriel," Gaia said to the pixie, who was shaking uncontrollably. "But where shall we place you in your after reality?"

The other council members cupped their hands around their mouths again as they conversed quietly. Then they grew silent.

Gaia held up her crystal tablet. One by one, the other members did the same. All the tablet's symbols matched. They glowed in kind as the pixie phased to a transparent state, then vanished to some far corner of the universe, Gwen assumed.

"When do we ask about me?" Gwen said in a low voice. She felt anxious all of a sudden.

"Only when they call for you, my dear," the red witch said.

"But how will they know?" Gwen said. "I'm not even supposed to be here—"

"Gwenevere Arris," someone called out and it boomed from the stage.

Gwen turned to see the same lady wave her to the front of the line.

Gwen marched over, leaving the red witch behind, and nervously climbed the steps of the stage, hands behind her back.

"You are not supposed to be here, I see," Gaia said.

"I…I'm not sure why I am here, to be perfectly honest."

The council murmured behind Gaia, then went silent as she held up a hand. "I am Gaia, and I lead this mystic council. What can you tell us?"

"Spellbinder sent me. I was following the sigils and—"

"Spellbinder?" Gaia interjected. Her flowing robes swirled a bit faster, like thunderheads building on the horizon. "You were sent by Spellbinder, the god of desire?"

Gwen furrowed her brow, confused by her sudden change in attitude. "It's a telescope, actually. And yes, I was sent here on a quest."

That caused another stir amongst the council.

Gaia raised her hand again for silence. "Please, continue."

"I had a task in Ambriel, that's where I'm from. It was a quest to free some trapped spirits."

Gaia turned to the council, and they talked softly for a few minutes. Finally, Gaia returned to the podium. "We have reviewed your case. What you do is noble, Gwenevere Arris. The universe chose you, and your friend Kriss has blessed you. Thank you, I know your life has been difficult."

Gwen stood there in shocked silence. She didn't know what to expect, but it certainly hadn't been sympathy from a mystic court.

"Do you wish to see the history of the spirits you seek to free?" Gaia continued.

Her tone caught Gwen off guard. It seemed that she knew more than she was letting on. "I…I don't know," Gwen said, her voice a bit unsteady now.

"It is not a pleasant tale, but you deserve the right to know, if you choose."

Gwen hesitated again. In all honesty, she much preferred to free the spirits and just move on. Completing the quest didn't require her to know the details, and she wasn't sure if she wanted to witness the cause behind the spirits' entrapment. She felt ashamed of her attitude. After all, if she was going to help save these souls, the least she could do was to understand their grief. Though it might be difficult to see, she owed it to them.

Gwen finally nodded. "Please. It's the least I can do for them."

Gaia moved to the side, allowing Gwen to see the towering mountain beyond. Once again, she noticed the thousands of facets shining like glittering mirrors. Within each facet, a motion picture began to play, each one telling its own unique story. Gwen witnessed every single spirit's former life. It was too much to take in, so she focused on a few instead. The motion picture sped through each spirit's life, only slowing when it got to their final moments. Gwen saw centaurs rounded up and caged, stripped from their families and worked to death. Ogres, gnomes, witches and fairies, each story the same. Rounded up, caged and forced to work until their death. The ones that didn't die during construction had been auctioned off by the slavers. The connection in all of their storylines was Hidden Palm Grove.

The common thread was the castle itself.

But what *was* it about the castle that pulled them together?

If she could resolve that, then she could free them all in one fell swoop.

"The spirits you seek to free were imprisoned, forced into slave labor, and then worked to death or murdered," Gaia said. "The one you work for was responsible for covering up these atrocities, along with their entire family. When that one's time comes for judgment, it will not be pleasant. But I digress."

All along, Gwen had believed that Kershaw was representing some high-profile client. However, if what Gaia said was true, then his family had been slavers. Was that the real reason he was so anxious to sell Hidden Palm Grove? Was Kershaw ashamed of his past, or was he covering up the atrocities of his family instead?

Still, it felt like there was more to the story. She wasn't convinced of anything just yet.

"Why would Spellbinder bring me to this place?" Gwen asked. "Why wouldn't it just grant my desire when I returned the third sigil?"

"We do not interpret Spellbinder's intentions. That god is veiled from us. Our council exists only to pass judgment on those who were once living." Gaia paused momentarily, leaned forward and lowered her voice. "I may remind you, however, that the right to choose a desire belongs to you alone."

Gwen looked back at Gaia, confused. Was the lady giving her a hint?

Someone yelled from the top of the amphitheater, making Gwen and the other council members turn and look.

From the middle of the amphitheater, which was too far for Gwen to see, someone came rushing down the steps toward them. As the person drew closer, Gwen caught her breath in surprise. She could hardly believe it.

It was Posh.

# CHAPTER 42

## *A PENULTIMATE DECISION*

POSH RUSHED TOWARD Gwen at a full sprint. She was out of breath when she reached the stage but threw herself at Gwen and wrapped her arms around her.

"Posh!" Gwen said and held her tight.

The genie clung to Gwen, her body heaving with exhaustion and joy. Gwen breathed in the ocean aroma of Posh's vibrant blue hair. She felt the heat coming from Posh's skin, which had regained its radiant color. It was a somewhat awkward moment as they stood on the stage, in the middle of the Elder Council, with the multitude of people staring at them. But Gwen didn't care and hugged Posh until she calmed down and her cries subsided.

Gwen finally let go and held Posh at arm's length. "I didn't think I'd see you again, but I guess it all makes sense why you're here."

"It feels so strange and confusing. I guess I'm going to my after reality now."

But Gwen could see the worry on Posh's face, and why shouldn't there be? She was sure this new reality was unexpected and sudden. She continued to hold Posh by the shoulders and look down into her golden-flecked eyes. She felt a moment of guilt again at seeing the three vertical scars over her left eye. Posh was only here because she'd sacrificed for Gwen.

"I…I don't know what to do, Posh. Why did Spellbinder bring me here?"

"Sure, you do," Posh said. "Just do what you've always done. Figure it out."

Gwen held Posh's hands, not caring what the others around them thought. She gave Posh a squeeze. "Walk beside me for a moment, won't you?"

Gwen didn't ask for leave from the council as she pulled Posh with her. The council members went back to their work as she stepped off the stage. The soft murmur returned as people continued to file into long lines.

Gwen held Posh's hand as they walked behind the stage and into the strange landscape beyond. It was nothing like Gwen had ever seen. There were some crystal-like trees, faceted and ghostlike. There was a lake with boulders and trails, all in the same crystallized look. She thought maybe this purgatory place was caught between planes, and the physical things around them were stuck in both worlds. But the backdrop was still incredible, with the heavens before them and the stars and galaxies creating a kaleidoscope of colors beyond. It was like standing on the largest mountain Gwen had ever witnessed and looking upon creation in a way that maybe only the gods had ever seen.

Gwen and Posh continued to walk a good distance from the amphitheater until the noise quieted. She found a large boulder near the lake and settled down, half expecting to fall right through the ghostly rock.

"Talk to me," Posh said and sat next to her.

Gwen chuckled. "Where should I begin? My friend just sacrificed herself for me, I have no idea why I'm here, and I just found out the real reason behind what's happening back at the castle. Did you know that Kershaw was really the one behind all of this?"

Posh gave Gwen a confused look. "Are you certain? Kershaw's devious, but that doesn't sound like him."

"Honestly, it's not Kershaw I'm worried about. There's something else going on, something much bigger."

"I wish I was there to help you figure it out." Posh looked away, her skin growing cold.

"I'm sorry," Gwen said gently. "Here I am, talking about my problems, and you're here in this place."

Posh stood and stepped away from Gwen, hiding her face.

Gwen stood and placed her hands on the genie's shoulders. "Posh…look at me."

Posh straightened and faced Gwen. She wiped her hand across her cheek. "It's alright. Don't worry about me, okay? You've got to finish this."

Gwen fought for words while struggling with her guilt again. "It's my fault, Posh. You shouldn't even be here. It should be me."

"I don't regret what I did for you," Posh said, and touched Gwen's cheek. "I'd do it again."

"I know you would. Any idea how much time you have until—" Gwen broke off, unable to say it.

"Until I'm sent to the Friar's Inferno?" Posh finished with a sigh, then a chuckle. "Who knows? I don't think time exists here. Never thought I'd be on the brink like this. I don't know what to expect there, only that it won't be pleasant. I'll deal with it, no matter what happens."

Gwen couldn't face Posh, not sure of her emotions again. It was just in Posh's nature to stay positive, which was another reason she felt so drawn to her.

She sat on the boulder and looked at the ethereal lake beyond, watching the waves ripple across it. The stars twinkled in the vastness like tiny fireflies on a black canvas as Gwen thought about what she could say or do to help Posh. After all, she owed the genie her life.

A muffled voice boomed from beyond, and it was difficult for Gwen to understand.

"They're calling for me," Posh said. She stood and pulled Gwen with her.

"Hold on. We need to talk—"

"I have to go…I think this is it."

Gwen stared into Posh's golden eyes and wrapped her arms around Posh's petite frame. She buried her face in her hair, breathing in the ocean breeze one last time. Posh's skin grew warm, and Gwen felt like she could stay that way forever. She didn't want to let go, not like she had with Kriss. She still recalled that day and what would've happened if she'd only delayed her friend for a few minutes longer. The stray bolt would have never pierced her chest, and Kriss would still be alive.

Here she was again, and that same feeling hit hard.

Gwen felt a sudden urgency. She needed to prevent this from happening again.

*But how?*

Her heart was breaking at that moment, like a thousand tiny shards scattering to the wind. She couldn't bear the thought of losing Posh a second time.

The voice boomed again, calling for Posh, and Gwen began to wonder why Spellbinder had really brought her here. No doubt, it was for a specific reason.

And that's when an epiphany hit her.

Posh pushed back, wiping her eyes. "What is it?"

Gwen wandered toward the lake, scratching her brow and trying to focus her thoughts.

"Gwen. What's wrong?"

"I think I know what to do."

Gwen grabbed Posh by the hand and pulled her. They ran along the trails and past the tall ghostly pine trees, eventually slowing in front of the stage. The twelve council members stood and motioned to Posh. But Gwen held on to her hand and stepped up to the stage. She walked into the center of the council and waited.

Gaia stepped forward. "I am sorry, Gwenevere Arris. You are not allowed on this voyage. It is not yet your time."

But Gwen stayed next to Posh and didn't let go of her hand. "I know why I'm here, Gaia. I know now why Spellbinder has sent me."

"Are you ready to declare your desire?" Gaia said.

Gwen understood that she had to make her announcement in front of the council. They were meant to bear witness. "Yes. I am ready."

"Gwen, what are you doing?" Posh asked.

"What I was meant to do all along."

Posh seemed to understand then and reached for her left cheek, tracing the three scars. "I am forever marked with the curse of the gods. My after reality has been determined, and nothing can change that. Not even the gods, Gwen. You can't save me."

Gaia nodded in agreement. "This is true, I am afraid. Fate determines our after reality. Once set, it cannot be changed. This genie has used forbidden wish-magic, and she is destined for the Friar's Inferno. That is her after reality."

"I won't accept that," Gwen said, feeling her anger boil over. After all she'd done for others, and after all she'd been through, why couldn't she get a break for once?

Posh began to shake her head. "Don't do this, not for me. Think about the spirits. You have to free them. That was the deal."

"And I can't do that without you." Gwen turned back to Gaia. "I don't care what you think, or what the gods say. My desire is to bring Patricia Oshner back to Ambriel with me."

Gaia faced the council, and they gathered close and began to murmur.

While they were talking, Posh pulled Gwen to the side. "Stop this! I did what I did for a reason."

"And I'm also doing this for a reason."

Gaia returned and faced Gwen and Posh. "Never before has something like this happened. You test fate, and risk breaking the rules of our universe and beyond."

Gwen took Posh's hand. "It changes nothing. This is my desire, and I feel it in my soul. Who am I to say otherwise or deny that truth?"

Gaia gazed down upon the two of them, a barely perceptible smile lined her face, and Gwen thought no one else noticed it. It was a smile meant only for her.

"So be it," Gaia said.

The other council members quieted. Each of them etched a symbol on their crystal tablets, then held them up. Gaia finally did the same. Written on it was a round symbol with the image of a telescope sitting upon a pyramid-shaped fulcrum. The sigil of the god of desire, Spellbinder.

Then, the air around them began to thrum. Gwen thought she could hear a strange chanting. The space between them glowed a bright white until she couldn't see anything. Gwen felt Posh grip her hand, then her arm. Gwen hugged Posh tightly to her as the light engulfed them, and she lost consciousness.

# CHAPTER 43

## *BACK TO REALITY*

When Gwen opened her eyes and looked around, all she could see were blue skies. The sound of crashing waves and seagulls filled her ears. Warm sand cradled her body and sifted through her fingers. She craned her neck and saw Posh lying beside her, who was just waking up. The genie blinked her eyes a few times, their golden light glowing a bit brighter.

Gwen rolled over and sat cross-legged on the beach. She witnessed the smile on Posh's face as she sat up and breathed in the salty air. Then Posh sat forward and hugged Gwen.

It was early morning, the sun just cresting the Green Sea. A soft, balmy breeze ruffled Gwen's hair as she held her friend tight. A few passersby looked on but said nothing. Eventually, Gwen pulled back and held Posh by her shoulders.

"It feels good to be home," Posh said, the corners of her lips turning up.

Gwen could only nod, not trusting her voice.

"I guess we need to figure out what to do next," Posh said.

"So, you're…not upset with me?" Gwen asked, tentatively.

Posh shrugged with the hint of a smile. "Well, I suppose I'll just have to live with it. The Friar's Inferno can wait."

Gwen hugged her again. "It's good to have you back."

"What did you have in mind now? Saint Halving Day has passed."

"Has it?" Gwen said. She stood and looked around. The Saint Halving Day lights along the beach were still up and the trees lit with festive colors. "I don't know, maybe it hasn't passed."

Gwen stopped a couple of ogres passing by. They held their sandals in their hands, and the girl leaned on the broad male ogre. "Excuse me. Do you know what day it is?" Gwen asked.

The couple looked at each other, brows furrowed. "It's…Saint Halving Eve," the girl said.

"Thank you." Gwen pulled Posh with her as the couple continued down the beach.

"What in Ambriel is going on?" Posh said.

"Spellbinder," Gwen said. "It sent us one day into the past."

"Why would it do that?"

"I think it's because I made the right decision. I saved you because of your sacrifice for me."

Posh placed her hands under her chin, then batted her eyes playfully. "Thank you, but now we don't have the third sigil. How is our situation any better?"

"I'm not sure yet. Let's find Bally and LinHem."

"I'd really like to stop by Sephora Bean." Posh glanced down the beach to see beachgoers already lining up for their morning coffee. "I really miss it, though."

"Posh, seriously?" Gwen chided. "You can have all the lattes your little heart desires after we figure this out. Come on." She grabbed Posh by the crook of her arm and dragged her toward Java House.

When they stepped through the doors, Bally was sitting on his haunches, eyes closed. LinHem was busy around the kitchen, frying up his morning's catch. Bally's eyes snapped open, and LinHem turned to look at them.

"Ah! How is this possible?" LinHem squawked and removed his apron. He literally flew over to greet them.

Bally stood and began purring when he met Posh's gaze. She flung herself at him and threw her arms around his neck. She buried her face in his plaid-patterned fur coat and didn't let go.

"What, may I ask, is happening?" LinHem said. "First, Gwenevere vanishes into thin air. And now, Miss Posh is back as well?"

Gwen held up her hands. "I know it's all very confusing. Everyone, just have a seat and let me explain."

Bally sat back on his haunches, Posh still dangling around his neck, while LinHem tried to get comfortable on the couch.

Gwen launched into the events, telling them about the third sigil, her trip to the mystic elder court, and how they'd made it home.

"Gaia, you don't say?" LinHem said thoughtfully. "A legend, apparently a true legend at that. She has been around since the beginning of time and helped the gods form Ambriel."

"She was very gracious," Posh added.

"Well, it suddenly hit me," Gwen continued. "All along, it had been destined for me to return with Posh. I think it was a test from Spellbinder. Should I solve the mystery of Hidden Palm Grove and make the deadline to satisfy my own drive? Or should I do the right thing and save my friend, who sacrificed herself for me? The choice was simple, once I understood the question."

"It really wouldn't have been selfish," Posh said. "After all, you're trying to free those trapped souls, as well as your friend Harris."

"Well, yes, I suppose that's true," Gwen admitted. "But Spellbinder gave me the choice, and I couldn't stomach leaving you, especially after all you did for me. I knew I'd figure it all out afterwards."

"What do you propose we do?" Bally said in a low voice.

Gwen shrugged her shoulders. "I don't really know. But we've been granted another day, courtesy of Spellbinder. It would seem this entity is rooting for us, and that gives me some hope."

"Fine, challenge accepted," Posh said and clapped her hands.

"Perhaps we should visit the castle," LinHem said, adjusting his spectacles. "I know just the place."

"Which would be where exactly?" Posh asked.

"Where we can find all the information we need," LinHem replied. "The library, of course."

The group of companions had a quick meal, and by midmorning, they were walking along the beach, hurrying back to Hidden Palm Grove. Gwen and Bally had to literally drag Posh in the opposite direction of Sephora Bean.

"Just one latte," Posh had begged.

But soon they were ascending the hidden spiral staircase behind the tall rock formation. The skies had grown cloudy, and tall thunderheads stood along the horizon.

"There's a storm brewing," Bally said. "The wind has shifted."

"Come on, let's get inside," Gwen said.

When they made the front lawn of the estate, Gwen saw an expensive coach lined with horses. Kershaw stood at the front door, arms crossed and a scowl on his face.

Gwen stopped in front of him. Behind Kershaw was the same group of ogres as the day before.

"His personal bodyguards," Posh whispered.

At first, Kershaw didn't show any emotion as he looked at Posh. Gwen wondered if the loophole in time had reset his memory. Since Spellbinder had brought them back a day, was it possible that Kershaw didn't remember their last meeting? If so, he didn't know about Posh's passing into purgatory. Regardless, Gwen knew his true feelings about Posh. Despite his early cordial nature toward Gwen, it appeared he was nothing more than a business-minded, cold and uncaring realtor, even though Posh might argue otherwise.

"Step aside, Kershaw," Gwen said. "We're going in."

"Oh, I have no intention of stopping you. I'm only here to warn you that this will be your last chance. If you do not cleanse the castle by the end of the night, I plan to take back everything, and more. By force, if necessary."

The six ogres moved closer, each of them towering over Gwen. Bally and LinHem stepped forward, and Posh brought her index fingers and thumbs together, ready to dispel some of her powerful wish-magic.

"They're not laying a hand on anyone," Posh said, giving Kershaw a glowering look, her golden eyes glowing a bit brighter.

"I assume you know that you're no longer employed by Aloe Realtors," Kershaw said, glancing at the golden chain around her waist. "Therefore, I will collect on your indentured servitude and what is owed me. I could have you reimprisoned at any time. In fact, if you fail in your contract, Gwenevere, I promise to do just that."

"And if I succeed, Posh goes free," Gwen said.

Kershaw chuckled and considered for a few seconds. "If you succeed, the genie is yours. But I recommend that you don't fail me." He moved to stand directly in front of Posh and was about to hurl another insult when Bally breathed into his face. Kershaw blinked, as if he'd lost his train of thought, then hurriedly stepped off the veranda and walked back to his coach. The ogres brushed past them, careful to steer clear of LinHem and especially Bally.

"Come on," Gwen said. "We have until midnight. I don't want to get caught in the witching hour again."

They made their way to the library. As soon as they walked in, LinHem began directing them. "There has to be some information here. Look high and low. Leave no niche unsearched."

The four of them split up and scoured the large library. Gwen had never really ventured into the corners and nooks, and in fact had only visited the library a few times since being at the castle. Perhaps she should have spent more time researching the place. LinHem had a point. They'd found Speartine's codex here; maybe there were more secrets to uncover.

She looked around every corner, noticing for the first time how unique the library layout was. But she wasn't surprised, based on what she'd learned about the rest of the castle. Everything here was a mystery. There seemed to be an endless maze of intricately carved wood niches and reading rooms tucked away from view. The craftsmanship was immaculate, the artistry a long-lost trade of Ambriel. She got caught up in the details, tracing the scrollwork with her fingertips. She delved deeper, lighting the way with her wand. As she continued to venture down dusty niches covered in cobwebs, Gwen noticed more elaborate patterns, which were unlike the others she'd first seen. It was then she realized how closely the patterns resembled Spellbinder's sigil, which she'd just seen in purgatory at the elder court: a circular symbol with a telescope atop a pyramid-shaped fulcrum.

Gwen whistled loud enough to break the silence. "Posh, Bally, LinHem. Over here."

Soon, the others were gathered around her.

"Look, the patterns in the woodwork, here…" she said.

LinHem leaned in closer. "Ah, Miss Gwenevere, I do believe you may have found something indeed. I recognize this work. Alfred the Woodford. He was one of the greatest carpenters during the Vione Era, which would have been about the time this castle was built. He was legendary for what he achieved. It was said that he wove spellwork into his carvings and etchings. Alas, this is a long-lost craft. This is the sigil of the god of desire, Spellbinder himself." LinHem tapped the wood carvings with his talon.

"Yes, I recognize it from the elder court," Gwen said.

"I do sense magic," Bally said, sniffing the air. "We are close to something. This nook is special."

The four of them searched the wood-clad nook. Posh knelt to the floor, checking the baseboards while LinHem flapped his wings and examined the ceiling and crown moldings above. Bally climbed up a large wall, and Gwen explored the stone fireplace, which was set in an ornate bookshelf of rosewood. When she stepped inside the soot-covered fireplace, she noticed a repetitive carving of thorny rose nettle, her favorite plant. Gwen wondered if this was somehow in reference to herself.

But there was also a section of the carving that didn't match.

"I think I found something," she called out.

Posh was there, then LinHem and Bally. They gathered inside the fireplace.

Gwen pointed out the pattern. "That's thorny rose nettle."

"Your favorite," Posh said. "Coincidence?"

"That's what I'm wondering. But look at this area." Gwen pointed at the variation in the carving. "It's out of sequence with the pattern."

"What's this?" LinHem hummed and adjusted his spectacles. He reached out with a talon and pressed the area.

There was a loud groan as the fireplace shifted in a flurry of flipping stones that eventually rearranged into a staircase. Beyond, there was a dark opening that led downward.

Posh gave the others a wide-eyed glance.

Gwen shrugged. "Follow the breadcrumbs, right?"

She led the way with her wand held before her. Framing the narrow staircase was a stone balustrade. She gripped it nervously as the others filed in behind her. Together, the four of them glided silently down the stairs like a group of wraiths.

Gwen noticed that the deeper they went, the carved stone began to change to a rougher, more unfinished state. Soon, there were rock striations in the walls, and a pungent smell rose from below. The air felt stagnant, heavy and humid.

When they reached the bottom landing, Gwen paused to listen. In her wand's light, she could see strange outlines beyond.

"Bookshelves?" LinHem whispered. "Odd, indeed. He moved closer and looked through the racks."

They were old stone shelves, cut from the bedrock. It was a black granite with gold flecks that shone like stars. When the light from Gwen's wand hit the rocks, the flecks seemed to magically absorb the green light. As the shelves of stone gathered light, the chamber lit up in a haunting way. No longer needing her wand, Gwen stowed it in her satchel.

"This place is ancient," Bally said. He padded softly around the shelves. "I sense old magic here. Be cautious."

"Wonder what we should be looking for?" Posh whispered.

Gwen shook her head. "There must be something down here. Let's spread out."

Gwen felt the sides of the shelves as she searched. They were warm and seemed to pulse with the light, reminding her of a furnace. The steamy air had her sweating, and she rolled up the sleeves of her robe.

"Gwen," Posh called out.

Posh stood above a large steel hatch, which was set into the floor's bedrock. There was a massive steel rung on it, like it had been designed for some giant mountain troll.

Posh handed Gwen a scroll. On it was a pattern of thorny rose nettle. Scrawled in a spidery font was Gwen's name.

# CHAPTER 44
## *DOWN THE HATCH*

GWEN TOOK THE scroll, somewhat hesitantly, and held it up to the golden light of the stone shelving. Embossed on the scroll was a wax seal with the sigil of the wizard, Speartine, which was a golden dragon in the shape of the letter "S". Below the sigil was her name. It was dated 127 D.B., over a century ago.

Posh patted Gwen's shoulder in excitement. "Go on, open it!"

LinHem and Bally gathered near as Gwen broke the seal. When she did, the golden light of the granite flickered and surged. A low howl drifted down from the staircase. Gwen paused a few seconds longer before reading the scroll aloud.

*To the one chosen by Spellbinder, I write to you.*
*Seek within to travel with one you knew.*
*May your mind be steadfast and hand be true.*
*Trust in your heart for what you must do.*
*Fear not the Devil's Paddock. –S.*

Gwen flipped the scroll over, but it was blank on the back.

"In true style, my master," Bally said. "This quest has personal touch upon it."

"What do you mean?" Gwen asked as she rolled it up and slipped it into her leather satchel.

"I knew him to speak in riddles, as was his character in life. It appears his writing is the same. He is asking you to find something below, and only one of us may assist you." Bally moved to the hatch leading down. He placed a claw through the iron rung and, with his massive paw, lifted the trap door. The heavy hatch clanged open, and dust spilled out. "Who shall it be?"

Gwen considered as she looked at her three companions. But it was already clear who she would take. After all, why else had Spellbinder guided her to Posh? It only reinforced her decision to use her wish and revive the genie. The scroll, in fact, was telling her as much: *Seek within to travel with one you knew.* She'd known her before her death, and the genie had practically been resurrected.

"It has to be Posh," Gwen said.

Posh moved close to Gwen and took her hand. LinHem bowed low along with Bally.

"Please, go with our blessing, and we shall await your return," Bally said.

LinHem gently laid a talon on her shoulder. "Of course, Posh seems destined for this, given the recent events. Be careful, the both of you."

Gwen turned to Posh. "Are you ready?"

Posh took a deep breath and let it out slowly. Then nodded.

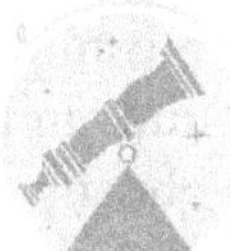

The two of them dropped down the hatch, and Gwen held her wand aloft to light the way. The square hatch turned into a circular tube that widened as it sloped downward. The sides were a smooth, rock surface, like some blackened and charred onyx, Gwen thought. In several places, it was so slippery that they found themselves on their hands and backsides. But eventually, the tunnel morphed into a roughhewn staircase, rudimentary and ancient. It continued to grow hotter as they descended. Eventually, the tubelike cavern grew so wide that Gwen could no longer see the walls.

As they made their way down into the dark and steamy environment, Gwen wondered what lay at the bottom, though. Was it the answer to this never-ending quest or simply another breadcrumb? That thought circled her mind as they crawled deeper into the Devil's Paddock.

It felt like hours had passed when Posh asked to take a break.

"Wonder how deep this tunnel goes?" Posh said, trying to catch her breath from the humidity. She leaned back on her elbows, sweat glistening off her blue skin. "Even the floor is getting warmer."

"We must be getting close," Gwen said. She pulled on Posh. "We need to keep moving."

Five minutes later, they broke free from the massive tunnel, which opened to a breathtaking view. Gwen and Posh paused to take it in.

They stood at the upper portion of a cavernous space. Far above was a dark sky with clouds and stars. There didn't seem to be a ceiling to the cavern, which was bizarre, since they were standing below the castle. To Gwen, it seemed as if the sky was an extension of this ghostly world, maybe even a portal bridging the two planes. But it was no ordinary sky. It felt dim, like when she phased into the ethereal plane. Even though she wasn't currently phased, both of these realms felt eerily similar. It was like looking through a dirty lens and seeing everything in that same russet color.

The ground level was perhaps a few hundred feet below, and the stairs continued down along the cliff face. There was a field beyond, at least, that was the best description she could think of. The rocky terrain and craggy boulders were backlit in a reddish light as if the ground beneath had been fractured. Steam poured from the cracks with a loud hissing sound. Gliding around and in between the boulders were thousands of spirits. Like ghostly whisps of smoke, the gossamer apparitions wandered lazily in random patterns, phasing through the rock formations.

Posh drew close to Gwen and grasped the crook of her arm. "What in Ambriel have we found?"

Gwen remembered the scroll and reached into her satchel. She knelt on the stair landing and smoothed it out. Posh knelt beside her.

"Well…what do you know?" Posh said.

The writing on the scroll had disappeared. In its place was some sort of crude map that fluctuated and flickered in the supernatural light.

"Oh, I've heard of these," Posh said. "It's a dungeon guide."

"I think you're right," Gwen said. "It must change as we make our way through each chamber." She read the text below the map. "Beyond the Cracked Realm, find the Realm of Copper Fields. Take the Green Path through the Realm of Shadows and into the Realm of Eternal Flame."

Posh gave Gwen a concerned look. "The Realm of Shadows? I don't like the sound of that."

Gwen could only shake her head. "Let's just keep moving."

They descended the remaining steps and set foot on the ground level, which, according to the dungeon guide, was known as the Cracked Realm. When they stepped away from the stairs, the ghostly spirits grew clearer.

"Are these the same spirits inside Hidden Palm Grove?" Posh said.

Gwen nodded. "This must be an extension of the castle."

"I bet this place, the Devil's Paddock, has bled over into Hidden Palm Grove."

"It would seem so," Gwen replied. "The map says we go this way."

They hurried past the spirits, who seemed oblivious to them. Gwen got her first good look at the spirits and saw gnomes, ogres, and pixies. She even noticed a few centaurs and trolls. There were winged creatures flying above in every race imaginable. These trapped souls should be heading to purgatory and Gaia's court. But instead, they were trapped and tortured and would find no rest until they were freed.

Gwen and Posh followed the dungeon guide, crawling across the Cracked Realm and past numerous ravines filled with fire. The lava flowed around the rock like some volcanic river, and the heat and steam increased as they traveled onward. But eventually they approached a large stone portal with a pair of black iron gates. A sign hanging over the gates read: *The Realm of Copper Fields*. Gwen and Posh both pushed on the large gates, and they swung open with an ominous groan.

Beyond, there was a thick mist, or maybe it was steam. When they stepped through the portal, the mist cleared, and they could see deeper into the realm. At their feet, the path was filled with a green, luscious grass. To either side of the green path were thick fields of copper wheat stalks. The stalks whipped and shimmered in the gentle breeze, creating a soft whispering sound. It reminded Gwen of a choir, though the voices belied a more sinister message, despite their whimsical tone. What she heard was a warning not to stray from the path.

Referring to the dungeon guide again, they found the right trail amongst the dozens that forked out, which was named the Green Trail. When they reached the next intersection, they paused. Stuck on several deformed iron poles were dozens of trail signs with strange names. Gwen looked at the confusing jumble of directions. She counted at least a dozen paths meandering off through the wheat fields. It appeared that there were quite a few realms within the Devil's Paddock, and she had no desire to get lost in any of them.

Posh pointed at a new phrase that appeared on the dungeon guide. "Be hasty, lest you become stagnant." She shrugged. "You're the sleuth. Any clue what that means?"

Gwen could only shake her head.

She led the way through the wheat fields, making sure to stay on the green trail. When they entered, the wheat stalks changed color to a copperish tone. Even the sky and clouds transmuted to a coppery hue, like everything was slowly being coated in a metallic substance. When she looked down at her robes, the dark green fabric was now coppery and shiny. Her skin was no longer green either. Gwen glanced at Posh to see her blue skin also changing to the same metallic color.

Then she began to taste something funny, like she'd swallowed a coin. The metallic sensation was followed by stiffness in her right foot.

"Something's wrong," Posh said. "My legs feel stiff."

Gwen reached down with her wand and tapped on the lower portion of her robe. A hollow sound, like someone knocking on a metal statue, answered in a resounding thud.

"I think we're changing into copper," Posh said. "I can even taste it." She held up her hand and gave it a tap.

"Run!" Gwen said and bolted down the trail.

Ahead, she could see a massive cave opening with darkness beyond. It looked like the gaping mouth of a giant, ominous and grim. But to her, she saw a safe zone from being transformed into a copper statue.

Gwen's legs continued to stiffen, and her lungs struggled to take in air. With Posh right behind her, Gwen could feel herself slowing, her body growing heavier.

With the cave just ahead, Gwen made a final lunge forward. She fell face first into the green grass, and Posh landed on her legs. But Gwen managed to reach her hand into the shadow of the cave, then her other hand. She watched as the copper color instantly faded, and she could feel her fingers again.

"Grab my waist," Gwen said, her voice sounding hollow.

Posh wrapped her arms around her, and Gwen pulled with all her strength. It was enough to get her torso into the shadows. Gwen turned immediately and pulled Posh up by her arms and slid her body into the cave. Posh's blue color returned, and she bent and pulled Gwen into the cave. The copper hue faded, and Gwen's skin and robes returned to their normal green color.

Both lay at the mouth of the cave, letting the shadows soothe them. Gwen finally caught her breath and rolled to face Posh.

"That was close," Posh said. "Thanks."

Gwen gave her a quick smile. "Let's try not to get turned into statues on the first challenge." She pulled the dungeon guide from her satchel. "Says here we're passing into the Realm of Shadows next." She stood and helped Posh to her feet.

"This place is so odd, more than Speartine's palace even," Posh whispered. "I feel like I'm inside someone's nightmare."

Gwen led with her wand as they moved into the cave. The walls were etched with runes that glowed blue, and the ceiling arched up and over them for miles, it seemed. The strange runes filled almost every niche of the glasslike cavern, casting shadows in every direction. On closer inspection, the runes were shaped like creatures. Gwen thought she recognized a few: fairies, trolls and gnomes, amongst others.

Posh stuck close as they walked cautiously across the smooth cave floor. Gwen heard noises echoing in the background, and the shadows leapt in odd directions like they had a mind of their own. Was it some trick of her eyes, or were the shadows moving toward them?

"We're being surrounded," Posh whispered.

"I noticed," Gwen whispered back.

The shadows multiplied and moved closer. Within a few more steps, Gwen and Posh were surrounded. The shadowy figures thickened and blotted out the light from the runes. It was like a black cloud covering the sun, only it was denser, like an eclipse. Gwen felt suffocated, as if a heavy weight was grinding her body into the obsidian rock floor.

In the diminishing light, she held the scroll above her head, trying to read the new phrase written on it. "In the Realm of Shadows, take your passage *literally*."

Posh tried to stand but seemed to be feeling the same heavy weight upon her. "Let…me see." She gasped in short breaths, as if breathing was also difficult. Posh pointed to the last word in the sentence. "I think…it means for us to pass *through*…the shadows, literally. See? It's…italicized."

Posh took Gwen's hand and led them directly toward one of the shadows. It was large, maybe from an ogre, based on its shape and size. When they stepped into it, the lighting of the runes glowed a bit brighter. The shadow vanished and let them pass. Gwen felt lighter, and it seemed the oppressive weight had lessened slightly.

Posh found another shadow, then another. It was like playing hopscotch, skipping from one shadow to the next. They worked their way closer to the end of the cave's mouth, feeling lighter with each step. After passing through a dozen or so shadows, they were past the cave and into the light.

Gwen placed her hands on her knees to catch her breath. "Good job, Posh. Who's the sleuth now?"

Posh pointed with her chin at the sign beyond. "The Realm of Eternal Flame ahead. Sounds like fun."

The sign was on fire, as well as the smoking hamlet beyond. It looked like the once quaint town had been burning for ages. Sleeping in the center of the town was a massive golden dragon.

# CHAPTER 45

## *SLEEPING DRAGON*

GWEN AND POSH stood next to the trail sign and stared at the sleeping dragon beyond.

The sky was covered in black ash, and the strange, unearthly sun cast a muted red stain across the burnt landscape. The entire area was a smoking ruin, the small town charred, and there was no other living creature to be seen. Even the spirits were missing here, perhaps fearful to wake the dragon.

But when Gwen looked closer, she noticed that the flames seemed to be flickering backwards. The smoke and ash floated down into the homes and buildings, not upward towards the sky. It was a strange sight, and she wondered if it was an optical illusion.

Posh turned to Gwen. "I don't know about this. Remember what happened the last time we faced a dragon? Didn't go well for me." She rubbed at the three vertical scars across her eye and cheek. "I'd rather avoid using any of my magic."

"But it's pretty obvious that we'll have to face the dragon." Gwen mused, tapping a finger to her lip in consideration.

"Okay. But how? If I use my wish-magic again, I don't think Spellbinder will send you back to purgatory to retrieve me this time."

"Well, there were hints for the first two realms. Maybe there's another one on this dungeon guide."

Posh sat across from Gwen as she plopped down and crossed her legs. She unfurled the scroll. A spidery script soon appeared below the dungeon guide, labeled, *The Realm of Eternal Flame*. Below the phrase was the outline of a strange pattern or symbol, perhaps. Gwen read the passage aloud.

"In the Realm of Eternal Flame, be wary of sleep. Do not let your thoughts wander far, but rather, breathe fire into life. *Join* your forces within the *talisman* to *break* free."

Posh rubbed her chin. "So…the dragon is sleeping. Don't wake it. Sounds easy enough."

"Or maybe it means the opposite. Everything in this realm seems to be backwards. Look at the flames and the smoke. Even the ash is floating downward."

"You think it's that simple? All we have to do is *wake* the dragon!" Posh said, raising her voice.

Gwen shrugged. "Well? Do you have a better idea?"

"Umm...okay," Posh trilled. "Who wants to test that theory first?" Posh crossed her arms and gave Gwen a sidelong glare.

Gwen tucked the scroll back into her satchel and walked around the charred buildings and closer to the dragon. It was a large golden dragon, just like the one they'd battled in the town of Promenade.

"Gwen," Posh hissed. "I was kidding. I mean...maybe we should think about this." Posh tugged at Gwen and tried to slow her. "Look around you. Even the spirits aren't here. That's telling, isn't it?"

"If we want to solve this, we have to go through that dragon."

"I understand, but are you sure the right thing to do is wake it? There's no going back if you do."

"You're usually the one jumping in headfirst," Gwen said.

"Purposely waking a sleeping dragon is where I draw the line."

Gwen sighed. "I'm trusting my instinct. It's served me well so far." Gwen tried to sound confident but heard the slip in her voice.

Posh finally nodded. "Alright, Gwen. I trust you. But do you have a backup plan if that thing wakes up angry?"

"I'll figure something out," Gwen said and began trudging toward the dragon again. She pushed her way through burning wreckage and blacked tree stumps. She had to cover her mouth with her robe from all the soot in the air.

When they neared the dragon, Gwen slowed and stopped just outside of the clearing where the dragon slept. The golden beast was curled up with its tail wrapped tight around its legs and partially covering its face. It had an enormous snout that ruffled the dirt when it exhaled. Otherwise, it was completely still.

"This thing's bigger than the last one," Posh whispered.

"Yes, I can see," Gwen said. She tiptoed into the clearing with Posh right behind her. Then Gwen walked close enough to touch its snout...

...and she began to yell.

It was loud enough to echo around the town's square and surrounding cottages.

Posh immediately ran to Gwen and tried to cover her mouth. "Gwen! I changed my mind," she hissed.

But Gwen pulled Posh's hand away and continued to yell.

Eventually, Posh gave up trying to quiet Gwen and joined in.

Together, the two of them ran circles around the dragon and screamed and stomped and clapped. But after several minutes, the dragon hadn't moved and continued to slumber. To Gwen, it almost seemed that the beast was under some enchantment.

Gwen finally stopped and sat down, breathing hard. Posh collapsed next to her.

"Any more ideas?" Posh said and leaned back on her elbows.

Gwen pulled out the dungeon guide and flattened it on the gravel path. She reread the phrase again. Just like the other realms, she was betting there was a hidden riddle tucked somewhere within the passage.

Posh stood and leaned against the dragon's neck. "Okay, there's talk of joining, talismans, and breaking. Thoughts? Ideas?" She held up her hands.

Gwen could only shake her head and hunched forward. She was tired, sweaty and had dirt caked around her neck. There was still an urgency in the back of her mind, though. The Saint Halving Day deadline was nearing, and she wasn't leaving till they figured this out.

But the phrasing on this riddle had her stumped.

As Gwen leaned forward and rubbed the kinks from her neck, her hand brushed across her amulet.

She paused, her thumb and forefinger tracing the ruby. She looked down at it, noticing the strange pattern again and how similar it was to the amulet's shape.

Why couldn't the amulet be considered a talisman? It had certainly protected her over the years.

The sketch in the dungeon guide matched the amulet's six-sided shape. She quickly removed the amulet and held it up.

Posh's eyes went wide. "What are you doing?"

"This amulet isn't mine. I stole it. Maybe it's time to return it."

"You mean to destroy it? But it's your most valuable keepsake."

"And perhaps it's a key destined for this moment. Maybe that's why I took it in the first place?" Gwen held the amulet over the ancient dungeon guide, then laid it inside the sketch's outline. "Posh. Sit in front of me and take my hands."

Posh did so, sitting cross-legged with the scroll and amulet between them.

"I believe we need to join our forces. Between us, it should be strong."

"I'd say so. Genies have some of the strongest enchantment energy, second only to witches."

"To do what I'm thinking, it'll take our combined energy," Gwen said. "Now it makes sense why Spellbinder wanted you on this journey."

"You sure destroying the amulet is the answer?" Posh said, a bit of hesitation in her voice.

"The dungeon guide seems to be leading us that way." Gwen read the entire phrase again. "In the Realm of Eternal Flame, be wary of sleep. Do not let your thoughts wander far, but rather, breathe fire into life. *Join* your forces within the *talisman* to *break* free."

Posh rubbed her brow, still uncertain. "What if we need your amulet later?"

"There won't be a later if we can't get past this stage. If we do this right, we can breathe life into fire."

"In other words, wake the dragon," Posh said.

Gwen nodded. "This ruby amulet was forged from fire. It's the talisman we're meant to break by joining our life forces. Just…follow my lead, okay?"

"Right," Posh muttered, still a bit nervous. "Sounds…easy."

With hands joined and the guide and the amulet between them, Gwen and Posh closed their eyes.

"Repeat after me," Gwen said. "Once we start chanting, open your mind. I'll take it from there." Gwen took a deep breath and began to chant the phrase from the dungeon guide. As she did, her amulet glowed a bright red.

# CHAPTER 46
## *WAKING THE BEAST*

GWEN JOINED POSH, chanting and pulling her energy force closer. To Gwen, it was like some strange séance. She felt at one with Posh in a way she'd not known with anyone before. She could see into Posh's past, and her entire life was laid bare, going back hundreds of years. Gwen felt her pain over the loss of her mother. Gwen witnessed the scars and abuse from former masters Posh had served. She experienced Posh's decades of isolation and physical and mental exploitation. Posh's life was heartbreaking, with very few instances of joy, at least until recently. How she managed to be so upbeat and confident was telling of her character and determination. This, however, was something Gwen sensed she'd been a part of, and that thought made her feel warm inside.

Together, they floated in some cosmic void of time and space. Stardust swirled around them as Gwen held onto Posh's hands tightly. She felt unnerved by the infinite void of space around them. But Posh's effortless energy calmed her.

*...speak the phrase...*

Gwen did so, and Posh joined in, their voices echoing across the empty void. They kept repeating it, and soon, Gwen could feel the ground shaking. It made her open her eyes, and she snapped back to reality. The ruby amulet glowed brighter, and fire shot from the jewel. It grew so hot that the amulet finally ruptured into a thousand tiny shards. Posh let go of her hands, and they stood and raced from the clearing.

They hid behind a burnt pine tree. Gwen felt a moment of grief at the destruction of Kriss's amulet but soon forgot about it as they watched the dragon begin to wake.

The golden beast snorted and sent out a huge plume of smoke. The nearby fires extinguished as the dragon stood and stretched from its long slumber. It let out a roar, arched its back, and shook its body like a wet dog coming in from the rain.

Finally, it looked around the clearing, searching the shadows with its glowing eyes. "Come forth," it said in a deep voice.

Gwen felt compelled to do so, though, apparently, Posh wasn't affected by the dragon's command.

Just as she was about to move into the clearing, Posh gripped her and shook her.

"Stay silent," Posh whispered.

Gwen's head cleared, and she knelt, her wand at the ready. She had no spells that could defend her or harm the beast. But Posh could, and she appeared ready, her forefingers and thumbs held together, prepared to dispel wish-magic. But Gwen didn't want to risk that again.

"It's okay, Posh. This dragon means no harm."

Posh stared at her in disbelief. "Dragons kill, that's what they do."

"Because most of them have been trapped or hunted to extinction. Just like you and the rest of the genies. But I think this dragon is different."

Posh still held her fingers together, uncertain.

"Think about it," Gwen pressed. "Why would Spellbinder send us down here? It purposely guided us to this place. It wanted us to wake this dragon for a reason. It's time to find out why."

Gwen stood, turned and marched into the clearing before Posh could stop her.

The dragon rose above the burnt trees as it watched her with its glowing eyes. Gwen stopped directly in front of it and held her hands calmly at her sides, though she could barely control her shaking knees.

Like the other dragon, this golden dragon (which Gwen knew to be the eldest and wisest of their race) was large and had magical abilities other dragons didn't possess.

It stood on all four legs and craned its long neck. "I do not recommend sleeping for such a long period," it said, then brought its snout within a meter of Gwen's face. Its breath blew her wide-brimmed hat off her head.

Gwen stood paralyzed with fear, not daring to pick up her hat.

A few seconds later, Posh stopped beside her, knelt and dusted off Gwen's hat. Then she calmly set it back on Gwen's head with a pat.

The dragon eyed the two of them, then spoke in a low rumble that sounded like thunder. "I am Thiden from the Isle of Moraile. Might I ask who the two of you are?"

"I…I am Gwenevere Arris. This is Patricia Oshner."

"Hmm. A green witch and a genie. Such an unlikely pairing. Are you friends?"

"Oh, yes," Posh said. "We're good friends, in fact."

"I know of genies and their plight," Thiden said. "Finding a friend in a perceived enemy brings me hope. I have been trapped here for over a century; an enchantment has been placed upon me. Thank you for breaking the spell."

Posh finally relaxed, and so did Gwen.

"I'm confused," Posh said. "Aren't we supposed to fight you or something?"

The dragon began to laugh, which was the strangest thing Gwen had ever heard. The ground rumbled like a miniature earthquake, and Posh steadied herself by grabbing Gwen's arm.

When the dragon calmed, it brought its snout closer to them. Its large teeth were like spears that gleamed in the ruddy firelight. "Let me first explain how I came to be trapped within the Devil's Paddock, and it may answer some of your questions. I was enslaved by a powerful spell that bound me here. The spell enchanted me into a century-long slumber. I am mostly a peaceful dragon, unlike some other races. The Green Goslithe of the south and the Blackened Scales of the north, for example, are fierce breeds and prefer destruction. We golden dragons of Moraile hold life as sacred and avoid taking it when we can. Patricia, as a genie, you would know all about enslavement, I imagine."

Posh nodded. "Yes, but I have been freed from my lamp, and I will never go back."

"My plight is similar to the genies'," Thiden said. "I have been caged here in this paddock until the enslaver is ready for me. A great conflict is coming. The enslaver's plan was to use me to build an army."

"Are you still under the slaver's control?" Gwen asked.

"Not anymore, thanks to you."

"Thanks to Spellbinder," Posh said, "and with impeccable timing it would seem."

"Ah, Spellbinder. Yes. My husband's creation, of sorts—"

Gwen held up her hands and paused the dragon. "Hold on. Did you say *your* husband? You're a female dragon?"

"Speartine was a dragon in human form, which is one of the golden dragon's powers. And yes, I am the last female golden dragon in Ambriel."

Posh and Gwen looked at each other in shock.

"So, your husband *was* the great wizard, Speartine?" Gwen continued, recalling the wizard's words now. "That would mean he built Spellbinder for more than a single purpose. He not only wanted to save these lost souls, but to free his wife as well."

"And, to help prevent a war, it seems," Posh added. "Pretty obvious now that there's more to this quest."

"We were meant to rescue you, Thiden," Gwen said. "We just weren't aware of it."

Thiden let out a jet of steam. "Ambriel has been at peace for over a century. I fear that might not be the case for much longer."

"But that changes, now that we've freed you, right?" Gwen said.

"I cannot prevent a war that has been in the making for a century."

"But you can sway it, no doubt," Posh said, a hopeful tone in her voice.

The dragon considered. "There are powerful forces on both sides. Other dragons: the greens, blacks and reds are also enslaved."

"This war, can it be stopped?" Gwen asked.

"The first step is to release the trapped souls. They are meant to be used in the war. Spellbinder knew this."

"So, the Devil's Paddock was designed to hold these enslaved souls?" Gwen said.

The dragon nodded. "This is not the only paddock. There are others sprinkled around Ambriel. Dragons are like magnets and tend to gather lost souls to them. This is why other dragons have been enchanted into slumber. Where there are other haunted castles, you will find a slumbering dragon beneath. Think of them as a disguise, haunted to steer others clear until the enslaver is ready."

Posh looked at Gwen, raising her brow. "Then why in Ambriel would Kershaw want us to cleanse this one so quickly…unless—"

"Kershaw knew," Gwen said, finishing Posh's thought. "He knew about the coming war."

# CHAPTER 47

## *A NEW ENEMY*

THIDEN SAT ON her haunches and folded her wings as Gwen and Posh worked out the details of the revelation.

"Okay," Gwen said. "So, Kershaw knew about this whole thing, obviously. But who is this client, and why would he assist them if he knew it would lead to war?"

"Kershaw never told me the name of the client," Posh said. "He kept that under lock and key. Typical for him. He rarely shares that information with even his closest associates."

Gwen thought for a few seconds. "This just throws everything into chaos. I can't believe Kershaw would do such a thing."

"He always has an ulterior motive," Posh said. "I've learned that much over the years."

"I think it's time we return to the castle," Gwen said.

"What's on your mind?"

"Not sure yet, I just feel like we need to get back."

"What about Thiden?"

The dragon curled up and lay across the steaming rock. "Attend to your matters. I am free now, and I will make my way back to my homeland across the Green Sea soon. I do have a few things to attend to before I leave."

"Your husband, Speartine," Gwen said. "He was the final sigil, which allowed us to free you. He sacrificed himself."

"I would have done the same. It was wise to hide the sigil in that way. But a dragon's rebirth only occurs every century, and that reincarnation will take place in our homeland. I will wait for him there."

Posh looked to the spirits beyond. "You say that we have not finished our quest. How do we finally free the spirits?"

Gwen and Posh watched as the dragon closed its eyes and fell to sleep again.

"Guess a century of sleep wasn't enough?" Posh muttered.

"Maybe it wasn't a restful sleep," Gwen replied. "And our quest continues, it seems. We should move; the day is running out."

They hurried from the Realm of Eternal Flame and along the Green Trail toward the lower realms. Across the Shadow Realm, the Realm of Copper Fields, and finally the Cracked Realm. Now that they knew how to cross them, it was easier to make their way back. They helped each other ascend the wide tunnel that snaked up and through the iron hatch. Gwen and Posh raced past the stone shelves and onto the large spiral staircase, where they sprinted up, stopping only to catch their breath. After what felt like an eternity, they breached the top portal and spilled into the basement level of Hidden Palm Grove.

Posh lay on Gwen's back, panting and gasping. When Gwen eventually caught her breath, she sat up and called out for Bally and LinHem.

"Wonder where they could be?" Posh said. "They said they'd wait right here."

"Well, we were gone for quite a while."

"Yet the day isn't even half over," Posh said.

"They must be here somewhere," Gwen said and pulled on Posh. "We still have till midnight to meet the contract."

They made their way up to the castle's ground level. It was past midday, the sun high in the clerestory windows, spilling daylight across the polished marble floors. But the castle was silent.

"Maybe they went back to Java House?" Posh said, though Gwen could tell she wasn't convinced of that.

"No…I don't think they did," Gwen said.

She felt the presence of something within the castle. It was a foreboding presence, something she'd not felt before. Gwen turned slowly to see the silhouette of a creature she'd only heard tales of.

Outlined in the light of the foyer was a creature with a lion's body, large, black, fleshy-type wings, and the head of a human. But it was the tail that drew her attention with its long, spiked end.

It was a mythical beast known as a manticore.

Of all the creatures in Ambriel, the manticore was probably the oddest thing to Gwen, especially since she'd never seen one in real life. The sketches and tales didn't do the creature justice. It was large and very rare in Ambriel, almost as rare as dragons. They were known for their prowess on the battlefield.

The female manticore moved into the living area, its sharp claws clicking on the marble tile. The tall creature stopped directly in front of them.

Gwen held out her wand, running through all her defensive spells. Posh brought her thumbs and forefingers together as steam began to rise from her warming skin.

"What did you do with our friends?" Gwen asked.

"Why, shouldn't we have introductions first?" the manticore said.

"It seems that you already know us," Posh replied.

"Well, it is my job to know who I hire to sell my castles." The manticore lowered her front torso in a mocking bow.

"So, you're the client?" Gwen said.

"Indeed. I am Lucinda."

Lucinda's facial features were youthful, though Gwen knew she was much older. She had long, flowing black hair and iridescent eyes that shifted in the light like a raven's feathers. When she smiled, Gwen noticed her fangs. Lucinda wore a silver corset of armor over a long surcoat made of swords, which looked more like trophies from her conquered foes, if Gwen had to guess. She smiled in a way that felt malicious and deceitful. Her smile alone told Gwen that she was dealing with a creature who had no remorse. Lucinda would kill anyone who got in her way.

"I believe your mission was to cleanse my castle by midnight on Saint Halving Day. Was it not?" Lucinda said.

"It isn't Saint Halving Day yet," Posh said coolly.

Lucinda scoffed. "The day is almost up; you have no way of ridding these spirits. Only one creature can do that. Yes…I know what else lies below Hidden Palm Grove."

"And what might that be?" Posh said, her hands on her hips.

Lucinda twitched her tail and looked like she might slam it into Posh. "That dragon is to be slain!" she said, raising her voice. "Tell me that you did not wake the beast."

Gwen wasn't as well-versed in mythical creatures as LinHem. Still, she knew that manticores and dragons were fierce adversaries, and they'd been pitted against each other in many wars throughout Ambriel's history, much like genies and witches. Now it was starting to make sense. Lucinda had placed the enchantment on Thiden only to attract the spirits. A war was coming to Ambriel, Thiden had warned. Lucinda was building her army in castles across Ambriel. Her intent was to slay the dragon as it slept, but only after she'd gathered enough spirits, which she'd been doing for a century. But Gwen also knew something else about manticores.

They were afraid of spirits, and the spirits had not yet been cleansed from Hidden Palm Grove.

"Why don't you do it yourself?" Gwen said. "What's preventing you, a manticore, from marching down there right now and destroying the dragon as it sleeps?"

Lucinda looked down at the two of them. Gwen could see her lion's mane shaking with rage. "You promised to cleanse my castle, and I expect you to finish the job. Slay the dragon! If you rid the beast from the Devil's Paddock, I will return your friends. I give you till sundown." Lucinda leaned in close enough to show her fangs. Then she marched off, having to compress her massive body through the oversized doors of Hidden Palm Grove's foyer.

Posh waited till Lucinda had left, then turned to Gwen. "Why would she want us to kill the dragon? Couldn't she have done it herself while Thiden was asleep?"

"I think it's because manticores are afraid of the spirit realm," Gwen said.

"Okay, but killing the dragon would free the spirits, wouldn't it?"

"That's what I don't understand," Gwen said, rubbing her brow. "If Lucinda is building an army, that's the last thing she'd want to do. I think we're missing something, and I know just who to ask—"

"Thiden," Posh said, "if she'll talk."

"Let's hurry before she leaves."

Gwen and Posh rushed down the hatch again. Gwen felt an urgency to find her friends, and Lucinda had only given them till sundown. With Posh glued to her side, they reached the bottom of the long spiral stair in record time. Using the dungeon guide, they followed the Green Trail across the lower realms. Gwen finally breathed a sigh of relief when she saw that Thiden was still sleeping on the burnt hill surrounded by flames.

The dragon raised its head as the two of them approached. Gwen had to take a knee to catch her breath, and Posh did the same.

"Well, I didn't expect to see you two back so soon. This must be important."

"We...we need your help, Thiden," Gwen panted.

The dragon stood tall and expanded its wings. "What seems to be the problem?"

"The manticore…Lucinda," Posh said, trying to catch her breath.

"Lucinda," Thiden said. A tiny lick of flame escaped the dragon's nostril when she spoke. "I've not heard that foul creature's name in centuries. We last faced off on the battlefield long ago. I thought her dead. It would seem that I was wrong." The dragon spouted a jet of flame into the air, and her roar shook the ground. "Where is she now?"

Posh pointed upward.

"Climb aboard," Thiden said and lowered to the ground.

Gwen and Posh quickly climbed onto Thiden's back and grasped its golden scales.

"Hold tight." Thiden leapt and flapped its great wings. The flames beneath extinguished as it rose upward.

Gwen began to wonder how the dragon would escape the Devil's Paddock, though. She'd seen no openings large enough for a dragon. But Thiden seemed to know where to go. Gwen held tight and trusted the dragon.

Thiden ascended through the levels via a different route than Gwen had taken, though. As if by magic, a series of portals appeared, seemingly woven into the strange sky. Like the shifting walls of Hidden Palm Grove's corridors, the portals disappeared and reappeared each time they achieved a new level. Then, they were free of the castle and soaring into the clouds.

The sun was lowering closer to the Green Sea. Splashes of pink and purple painted the ocean waves as Gwen and Posh watched from Thiden's back. She felt Posh wrap her arms tighter around her waist and laid her head on Gwen's shoulder. They were moving faster than anything Gwen had ridden before, and soon they were clear of Valeside's downtown district. The citizens who saw the dragon screamed and fled for cover, which made Posh cackle. Gwen knew that a dragon probably hadn't been seen in Valeside Beach for at least a century, and a sighting would definitely cause a stir.

They flew low over the mountain range, and Gwen wondered where Thiden was taking them. Thirty minutes later, they circled a high rim top that looked to be a dormant volcano. Though there were many in the Lion's Mane Mountain Range, this one was filled with activity amongst the lush green and pink rose nettle, which seemed to be everywhere. Green sprites and fairies labored over cauldrons. Gnomes and dwarves worked around the rim of the volcano, building vehicles and other strange contraptions.

"What is this place?" Posh said from behind Gwen.

Gwen shook her head. "No idea, but there's something going on down there, and it looks like we're about to find out."

# CHAPTER 48

## *SHOWDOWN AT SUNDOWN*

THIDEN SETTLED ONTO the volcano's rim amidst the lush vegetation and thorny rose nettle, causing dust to plume up. The creatures below scurried away, cowering in the shadows. Thiden let out a long roar that shook the ground, and the nearby birds took flight. There was a commotion from one of the caves, and Lucinda stepped from the tunnel as Thiden flew down into the crater. In shackles behind her were LinHem and Bally. They were both tethered with glowing ropes and held by dozens of mountain trolls. Leading the procession was none other than Bam Jino. Gwen almost tumbled off Thiden's back at seeing the mountain troll. *What in Ambriel was he doing here?*

Lucinda and Thiden faced each other. Though Lucinda was smaller in stature, her barbed tail dripped with venom. Gwen had heard tales that a manticore's spiked tail could penetrate even a dragon's scales. But Thiden didn't seem concerned as she settled to the ground and caused a tremor.

"We're not leaving without our friends," Gwen said and hopped off Thiden's back, her rosewood wand at her side. She eyed the group of trolls from below the brim of her hat, her gaze settling on Bam Jino.

"You said you would cleanse my castle, green witch," Lucinda said. "And you've broken the contract, a magically binding contract."

"No, I never guaranteed that," Gwen stated. "Maybe Kershaw did. I made no such promise. And may I ask why this particular troll is here?"

Lucinda gave Gwen a wicked smile. "Is it really a surprise? I had to get you here, Gwenevere. Bam Jino was simply another channel to force you into this. As a reward, I've promoted him to be my new general. He will lead my army."

Gwen glared at the mountain troll, then back at Lucinda. She took a step forward, her wand at the ready. "I should skewer you, Bam Jino," she said.

The troll grinned at her, showing his fanged teeth. "We'll soon see if your tone changes."

"Meaning what?" Gwen asked.

"Wait and see, little kitten."

Thiden took a step forward, which caused Bam Jino to shuffle backward behind Lucinda. The manticore looked from Gwen to Thiden to Posh. Gwen could see growing hesitation in her expression now. But even facing the dragon, she didn't seem to want to release LinHem and Bally.

Thiden finally spread her wings, causing several trolls to tumble over. "Ah, Lucinda. Stubborn as ever. I see that you were the one who placed the enchantment over me."

"Does that surprise you, Thiden? You always were so naïve."

"You mean to gather an army, and it would appear you have already begun."

"Are you here to stop me?"

"I have no intention of involving myself in Ambriel's disputes, so long as you release these two captives."

"And what assurance do I have that you will leave this land?" Lucinda said, her barbed tail twitching anxiously.

"I go where I choose. But, if you must know, I will head back to my homeland beyond the Green Sea, and there I will wait for Speartine to reemerge."

Lucinda seemed to consider again. As she did, Gwen felt something begin to rattle around inside her satchel. She opened the flap to look inside and saw something glowing green from within. There was a low wailing noise that morphed into a deep growl. Gwen reached in and pulled the glowing object out.

It was Matilda's butter knife.

The bejeweled pommel felt warm in Gwen's palm, and the emeralds shone bright in the shadow of the crater. As she held it, she felt herself phase into the ethereal realm. This had never happened to her before. She'd been pulled involuntarily from the living realm by the knife, by this *spirit blade*. She was a shade now, seeing things through the familiar russet-colored lens. What she witnessed was a moving picture that played out before her. Gwen saw a short female gnome dressed as a chef who had to be Matilda. In front of her was a large manticore, which had to be Lucinda. Lucinda was wearing the same armor she had on now and berated the gnome, and their argument escalated. Soon, Matilda was backed into the corner, which happened to be the main kitchen of Hidden Palm Grove. Matilda held the knife up defensively as Lucinda pressed in. The hulking manticore forced the smaller gnome into one of the storage coolers. Lights flashed, and the door flew from its hinges. All Gwen could see were shadows strobing in the light as a fight ensued. Then, Matilda's lifeless hand hit the tiled floor with the emerald knife still clutched loosely. As Lucinda stood over the gnome, the hilt of the butter knife glowed brightly, and a strange mist gathered around it, causing Lucinda to hurry off. Then, Gwen's vision faded, and she was pulled harshly back into the living realm.

Gwen stumbled back as the vision faded, and her form solidified.

She looked up to see Lucinda standing before her, a confused look on her face. Then, the butter knife roared to life at the sight of the manticore.

A few things clicked in Gwen's mind at that instant.

The butter knife was more than it seemed. It was Matilda's legacy, and her spirit had taken possession of it to avenge her death. The fact that it had been triggered by Lucinda's presence reinforced what Gwen had just witnessed. The manticore had, without a doubt, been a part of the slavers who'd entrapped the spirits in Hidden Palm Grove all those years ago. And over time, she had taken possession of the castle.

"That blade!" Lucinda shrieked. "'Tis not meant to be used this way." She reared back on her hind legs and slashed her spiked tail toward Gwen. Her batlike wings fanned dust around them. But the butter knife had placed an orb of protection surrounding Gwen as the manticore's tail hammered down. Green sparks shot from the impact. Gwen moved her wand to cross the knife, and it glowed brighter. The manticore backed away, along with her legion of followers. Gwen could sense that Lucinda had no desire to tangle with the spirit blade, a golden dragon and a genie.

Lucinda finally stepped aside with her hands held out in a mocking gesture of submission. "You win this round, green witch. We shall see about the next meeting, when Thiden is no longer present."

The trolls released the glowing ropes at Lucinda's command, and the griffin and ghost panther seemed to wake from a trance. Lucinda watched with contempt, her batlike wings fluttering with rage. Next to her, Bam Jino leered at Gwen, as if memorializing the whole thing for later retribution.

Lucinda and her entourage of creatures began filing back into the volcano's caves.

"Hold on, Bam," Gwen said.

The large troll stopped and faced her, along with the rest of Lucinda's horde.

"We have unfinished business," Gwen continued.

"Ah, the deed," Bam Jino growled and pulled a piece of parchment from his kilt. "I assume you'll be wantin' this?"

"That, and your promise to leave Harris alone."

The troll grinned, showing his fangs. He used the deed to tap his lower fang, considering. "And why would I do such a thing? You still owe me a considerable amount of loot."

"You don't care about the tokens, Bam. You never did. So, how about this? If I win, you return the deed and leave Harris in peace."

"And if you lose?"

"I'll come work for you, as part of your mob, free of charge."

There was a split second of shock on Bam Jino's long face. But it quickly faded.

"What'll it be?" Gwen asked. "Surely you're not frightened by a little ole' green witch."

Posh stepped up beside Gwen and whispered in her ear. "Gwen, look at the size of this guy. What are you doing?"

"Something that needs to be done. And I'm going to end this right here, right now."

"Maybe it's not such a good idea. We need to get back anyway—"

"Fine," Bam Jino said. "You want this piece of parchment that badly, then come get it." The troll set the deed on a large boulder behind him. "If you can get past me, it's yours."

Gwen gently maneuvered Posh behind her, then pulled the brim of her hat a bit lower. She held her wand in one hand and Matilda's spirit blade in her other. Behind her, she heard Bally growl and LinHem scrape his talons through the gravel. The glint in Posh's eyes told Gwen that she was also ready for a fight. On Bam's side, the creatures hollered, and Lucinda whipped her spiked tail in the air. But everyone went silent when Thiden let loose a roar that shook the nearby rose nettle and vegetation. That was everyone's warning—this battle was between Gwen and Bam Jino, and no one was to interfere.

Gwen's eyes didn't leave Bam Jino as they circled each other. The troll was more than twice her size, and his muscled arms and shoulders twitched in the volcano's ruddy light. As the sun lowered behind the canyon's rim, she knew a physical confrontation was a bad idea; she needed to keep her distance and use ingenuity to outsmart Bam Jino.

The big troll was quick and launched at her.

He brought his fists down toward her head. Gwen parried with the spirit blade and her wand, creating an orb of green energy. Embers burst outward from the impact when his fists hammered down. But the energy orb held, and Gwen rolled in the gravel and moved to a nearby cave. Her smaller frame fit inside, but Bam Jino was too large to follow.

Gwen melted into the shadows.

Bam Jino roared in anger. "Come out, kitten. What are you hiding from?" He reached into the cave, his clawed fingers grasping at her robes. Gwen brought her spirit blade down, and green fire erupted from the tip as it struck his thick skin.

Bam Jino howled in pain and pulled his gray-skinned hand back. There was a large burn mark on his palm, and he punched the ground with both fists, causing small tremors to shake the area.

But Gwen was trapped now with the troll standing just feet from the cave's mouth. She pressed deeper into the recess, her hands feeling the rock until she noticed a void.

*This must be a network of caves.*

She lowered to her knees and pushed through the thick rose nettle, finally popping into a larger chamber. She used her wand to light the way. In front of her, the cave forked several times. She followed it until she found another opening. She peered out from beneath the vegetation to see Bam Jino still trying to get into the far cave's opening.

Gwen took a deep breath, then leapt forward, using the spirit blade to strike the troll. She landed a blow on his back, which seared his skin and cut through several of his leather belts. She tried to roll beneath him, but Bam Jino was quicker than she had anticipated. He whirled and caught her by the waist, pinching her arms tight to her sides, and she dropped the spirit blade. The troll's strength was tremendous, and Gwen screamed in pain. From the corner of her eye, she could see Bally, LinHem and Posh start to charge across the volcano's floor. But Thiden held them back by cupping a large wing around them.

Bam Jino brought Gwen close to his long face. She could smell his stench, and his fangs gleamed in the waning sunlight. His narrowed black eyes were bottomless and lustful as he leered at her. She knew then that she was doomed. His strength was overpowering—she wouldn't be able to break free. She'd made the cardinal mistake of getting too close, allowing him to use his one advantage. His strength.

Bam Jino raised his other hand and gripped her waist. With both hands, he began to squeeze.

Gwen nearly passed out.

Stars erupted in her vision. In the background, she could hear Posh screaming. Bally and LinHem roared. She felt like she was phasing into the ethereal realm. If she'd only kept her amulet, she might have been able to slip through Bam Jino's grip. But she'd destroyed Kriss's amulet to free Thiden. There was the spirit blade, which she could've used if she hadn't dropped it.

In her thoughts, she sensed Kriss's presence nearby. She felt a sudden longing to be with her friend. Perhaps now was the time to let go and join her. She hated to go like this, in front of her friends, especially Posh. She worried about how they might blame themselves. Then again, Gaia might invite her into her court, then send her along to one of the after realities. Maybe even Promenade.

*…not yet…*

The whispered voice brought Gwen back to the present and away from the precipice. It felt like time slowed, and her wand grew warm in her hand. An epiphany came to her. *Maybe from Kriss.*

The thorny rose nettle!

It was everywhere. How had she missed it?

The stems were strong, the thorns coated with a duress toxin. Their constricting strength could choke even the largest creature unconscious.

And thankfully, she hadn't dropped her wand.

With a subtle flick, she commanded the vines to move. The pink roses rippled like a breeze descending around the volcano. The green thorns glistened in the setting sunlight. Then, the surrounding rose nettle shot toward them.

Bam Jino's legs were quickly covered. Then his arms, his hands, and his face, and he dropped Gwen in shock. The sinewy stems latched onto his neck with their thorns and constricted so tightly that his eyes bulged. Bam Jino was forced to his knees as he pried at the rose nettle. He managed to tear several from his arms and neck. But soon, he was covered in the pink and green mound of roses and thorns.

Gwen rolled to her feet, bringing the spirit blade and her wand up defensively. But there was no need, now that Bam Jino could barely move. Gwen heard his muffled cries from beneath the tangle of rose nettle.

It was too much for her.

Though she disliked the mountain troll, she couldn't stand there and watch him slowly suffocate to death. With a flick of her wand, the thorny rose nettle instantly relaxed, then wilted until there was nothing left but dust.

# CHAPTER 49

## *UP IN FLAMES*

POSH RUSHED TOWARD Gwen, along with LinHem and Bally. But Gwen didn't take her eyes off Bam Jino and held out a hand to stop them. She waited to see what the mountain troll would do.

Thanks to the toxin, he wavered unsteadily. He was out of breath, and large red whelps crisscrossed his bare chest from where the rose nettle had constricted. Behind him, the horde of creatures looked on, seemingly at a loss. At first, Gwen thought the horde might rush them. But whether it was Thiden or perhaps respect for the victor, Lucinda held her army in check.

Towering amidst the horde, the manticore stared at Gwen, seeming to reevaluate her now. Gwen placed the spirit blade back into her satchel, along with her wand. She calmly walked over to the boulder, took the deed and stuffed it into her satchel.

When she turned to face the mountain troll, he had a look of rage on his face. Gwen knew he wasn't used to losing, and his pride would likely take a hit. News of being defeated by a witch would spread quickly. His reputation was more important to him than anything. She wondered if others who were in his debt might purposely default on their payments now.

When Gwen walked past him, Bam Jino lowered his shoulder and rushed at her. Before she could get her wand or spirit blade out, the troll was practically on top of her. Just as he leapt at Gwen with fangs bared, a large shape shot down and lifted the mountain troll into the air.

Thiden caught Bam Jino in one clawed foot, then flung him even higher into the evening sky. He cartwheeled through the air, arms and legs flailing helplessly. As he descended, Thiden opened her massive jaws. The screaming troll tumbled inside, and Thiden clamped her teeth shut. A smug look of satisfaction eased across the golden dragon's face as a streamer of smoke trailed from her nostrils. It had all happened so quickly that no one else moved or spoke a word.

Thiden let out a long roar that sent Lucinda's army scrambling for the caves. Within seconds, Gwen, LinHem, Bally, Posh and Thiden were the only ones standing inside the crater.

"What?" Thiden said with a devious grin on her fangled snout. The look on her face, in spite of the situation, made Gwen want to laugh.

"I thought you said you weren't getting involved in Ambriel's disputes?" Posh chuckled. "Not that I mind. Please, participate all you want."

"The rules of engagement must be upheld," Thiden rumbled. "Gwenevere won a fair fight. I see no issues here."

"Then neither do I," Gwen said. "Thank you."

LinHem turned to Gwen. "Thank you. I am once again in your debt."

"As am I," Bally purred.

"Thiden is the one you should thank," Gwen said with a nod toward the dragon.

The ghost panther and griffin glanced at Thiden, both with uncertain expressions. Gwen understood their hesitation. After all, the last golden dragon they'd faced had tried to kill them.

"Fascinating," LinHem said. "There are not many golden dragons left in Ambriel."

"I am the last of my kind in this land, now that Speartine, my husband, is no longer here."

Bally walked up to the dragon and bowed. "Your husband was my master. He rescued me and was a father to me. But unfortunately, he has gone on to the after realms."

"Part of him, yes. But golden dragons reincarnate every century. I will wait for him in my homeland. This is where I bid you all farewell. The least I can do now is ferry you back to Valeside Beach."

"Great," Posh said. "After all of this, I'm ready to go home and relax. I think I'll spend a week at Sephora Bean. A mint latte should hit the spot." Then she faced Gwen. "I'd hold on to that butter knife."

Thiden flew Gwen, Posh and Bally on her back while LinHem followed, struggling to keep up. The golden dragon told them more about her history in Ambriel and the ongoing war between manticores and dragons. "You've not seen the last of Lucinda, I'm afraid," Thiden said. "Don't be fooled. She backed down because she was not ready to show her hand. She is a fierce and cunning adversary. Be wary."

But Gwen would cross that bridge when the time came. She was just happy to have her friends back and be at the end of this quest, or mission, or whatever it had morphed into. She had no idea what the future held for them. All she wanted right now was a little down time, and perhaps, as Posh had so eloquently stated, a latte at Sephora Bean with her friends.

They landed on the campus grounds of Hidden Palm Grove. Thiden lowered as they climbed off and waited.

"This is where I say goodbye," Thiden said.

"Before you leave, I have a few questions," Gwen said. "Why would Lucinda want you dead? Wouldn't that free all the trapped spirits and defeat her quest to create an army?"

"If I were to die, the spirits would by default transfer to the castle's owner. It's referred to as a Blood Escrow. The manticore is preparing an army of spirits, which is why she's placed an enchantment on many dragons held within castles around Ambriel. She is searching for people to slay those dragons and build her army. She cannot use dragons; they would never fight for her. By eliminating them, she is also diminishing potential foes as well."

"Why didn't Lucinda have Kershaw tell me that?" Gwen asked. "What if I never found out that I was supposed to slay a sleeping dragon?"

"Would you have done so if they had asked?"

"No, I don't think I could."

"Even if it meant freeing thousands of trapped spirits?" Thiden said, lowering her snout at Gwen.

Gwen considered that. Would she willingly murder to save others? Fight, perhaps, yes. But murdering an innocent being as it slept? "I... just don't know if I could do that."

"Lucinda and Kershaw wanted you to figure it out on your own for that very reason. Had they directed you to do so, there's a chance you might have balked. However, with your sleuthing skills, they were betting that once you found Spellbinder and understood the mission, you would've followed through with it."

"They knew I would find Spellbinder…" Gwen muttered. Now it was starting to make sense. "But it sounds so wrong, killing an innocent creature. Doesn't sound like a quest Spellbinder would support."

"One dragon, whom many consider a threat to life, in return for thousands of innocent souls?" Thiden mused. "Sounds worthy to me. No one else could have found their way to the telescope but you. It calls to you. Pair that with your special abilities, and that makes you a perfect candidate. Not just for this castle, but *all* the castles where Lucinda has gathered her spirit army. They've likely been targeting you for a long time, perhaps even waiting for you, while applying pressure from others, like the mountain troll."

Gwen felt her temperature rise, knowing now that she *had* been taken advantage of—Harris had been right. She disliked being fooled, and it made her feel a bit embarrassed as she stood there with her friends.

Thiden seemed to sense her guilt and let out a puff of steam from her nostrils. "Do not fret, Gwen. Be steadfast in knowing that your noble character prevailed. Once again, this is why Spellbinder speaks to you. One thing Kershaw and Lucinda didn't count on was your kind and caring spirit. You discovered the truth behind the Blood Escrow. You also chose Posh over duty. Remember, love is more powerful than greed. Kershaw and Lucinda could not fathom someone choosing love over money, which was their downfall."

Gwen blushed green at the compliment and waved it away. "I still don't understand how I was supposed to slay a dragon. Even a sleeping dragon would be difficult to defeat."

"Through the spirit blade."

Gwen pulled out Matilda's butter knife. She looked at it with confusion and some new respect. "This thing?" She thumbed at the short, bent blade, which was dull and probably couldn't slice through a loaf of warm bread.

"Do not underestimate a spirit blade. It can pull you into the ethereal realm, Gwen. It is a very formidable weapon, especially in your hands, once you understand how to use it."

"How would I even know that this could slay a dragon, though?"

"Spellbinder, of course," Thiden said. "It would have given you the exact instructions on how to use it to slay me, and Lucinda knew that."

"Okay, got it. There are two ways to free the spirits," Posh said. "It appears we've avoided the wrong one. But we still haven't accomplished our mission. Are these spirits doomed to always haunt Hidden Palm Grove?"

Thiden stood to her full height, blotting out the stars and moon. "To free the spirits, their bond with the castle, or the property they haunt, must be broken. That is their common thread in this case. These are the souls that built and constructed this castle. Therefore, the castle itself is their bane."

It was as Gwen had already guessed. Thiden was telling them to destroy the castle, and, unfortunately, Gwen had no means of achieving such a feat, unless the 'almighty' spirit blade could do it, and she doubted that. After all she'd been through, she still wouldn't be able to free the trapped spirits on her own.

"It is time," Thiden said, ready to take flight.

"Wait," Gwen said. "Are you sure you won't stay?"

"I will not stay in Ambriel. I will return to my homeland with Spellbinder, where it will be safe under my protection."

Gwen didn't know what else to say. She was sad to see the dragon go but understood Thiden's desire to return home. "Thank you, and good luck on your journey."

The dragon bowed, then spread its wings and took flight. They watched as Thiden circled up into the night sky.

Then, the dragon did something unexpected.

It dove into Hidden Palm Grove.

The dragon crashed into the middle of the castle, scattering huge blocks of limestone across the campus grounds. The loud crash brought Tom and Nat from their cottages, dismay on their faces. They all stood around and watched as Thiden ransacked Hidden Palm Grove.

Thiden pounded on the ramparts with its massive tail. It gripped turrets with its talons and ripped chunks of stone from the walls. Soon, everything was on fire, and smoke billowed from the turrets and large windows. The dragon took flight and circled the castle. It let loose a final jet of flame that engulfed everything in fire. At last, Thiden landed atop the lighthouse and ripped the roof off. She lifted the massive telescope out with her claws. With Spellbinder clutched tight, Thiden soared into the sky.

Then, Gwen heard the sound of wailing, like the ground was screaming in agony. It was low at first, then it grew to a fevered pitch. As she watched in awe, a light shot from the rubble near the castle's center. It beamed into the heavens, a green light so intense that she could barely look at it. Like lightning, thousands of ghostly shapes shot up from the flames in an endless stream. With each freed spirit, the wailing noise receded until the last one had left the castle. With a thunderclap, the light disappeared, and the sound died away.

Gwen and company stepped back from the heat as the castle finally collapsed in a burst of embers.

"Wow," Posh muttered. "I guess that solves our problem of destroying the castle, a parting gift from Thiden."

"She also took the telescope," Gwen said.

"The dragon has done what we cannot," LinHem said. "Dragon fire has the ability to break the bond that entrapped the spirits."

A stagecoach drew their attention as it raced up the gravel drive. The horses slid to a stop, and Kershaw hopped out. He looked at the burning castle in dismay. "What have you done?"

"What needed to be done," Gwen said.

"You understand that you'll have to pay for this!" Kershaw roared.

"I don't think so," Gwen answered calmly. "But I am curious about your role in this whole ordeal."

Kershaw lowered his gaze at Gwen, then Posh. "You have no idea what you're talking about."

"At first, I thought you were creating a diversion for us," Gwen continued. "That you were trying to help free the spirits. But now I realize you were only after the castle for profit. I'm guessing that you promised to help Lucinda build her army. In return, she would deed you the castle once the dragon was dead. Isn't that true? Part of your deal with her was finding and hiring me. I was one of the few in Ambriel who could get to the dragon. Thankfully, we woke it instead of killing it."

"And you broke our contract in doing so."

"Did I?" Gwen said. "I was asked to cleanse the castle by Saint Halving Day, and there was no stipulation as to how it was done. The spirits have been freed, and the clock hasn't struck midnight."

"And you destroyed a very lucrative property in the process!"

"Wrong. It was the dragon that did that. I have Tom and Nat here to vouch as eyewitnesses."

Kershaw faced the two groundskeepers. "Well? Is that true? May I remind you who I am before you speak."

Nat looked at Tom, then looked up at Kershaw. "I was employed by the castle's owner, not you, Mister Kershaw. I don't think I'm interested in joining Aloe Realtors, now that I know you work there."

Tom grumbled, then tipped his feathered cap. "Aye, I'm with Natalie on this one, Mister Kershaw."

"So, you two are vouching for the witch?" Kershaw said, and his ogre bodyguards stepped forward.

Nat crossed her arms. "That's right. Gwenevere had nothing to do with the castle's destruction."

"Looks like you'll have to track down the dragon and sue it. Good luck with that," Posh said.

"I could still have you imprisoned, Posh," Kershaw said.

"Are you sure you want to fight that battle?" Gwen chuckled. "I know you withheld information from Aloe Realtors. That's a breach in ethics. You could be fired from the company, and your license barred if they find out."

"I practically own the company!" Kershaw said, gritting his teeth. He straightened his suit lapels, though Gwen could see he was flustered now.

"If it goes public, that you were in on this, it could sink Aloe Realtors," Gwen replied. "And I have all the evidence I need. So, what's it going to be? Let Posh go free, walk away from this, or I go public."

Kershaw seemed to consider as he glanced at his bodyguards. For a split second, Gwen thought he would actually give the command for his bodyguards to assault her. Kershaw stood defiantly looking at the smoking castle, an uncertain look on his face, though.

Gwen gripped her wand as Bally and LinHem tensed, ready to fight. Posh held her fingertips together, magic pulsing. Even Tom and Nat appeared ready for a scuffle.

"Well, Kershaw?" Gwen asked.

Kershaw finally slouched, his shoulders rolling forward in defeat. "Fine," he said and pulled a golden pen from his vest pocket. He muttered something and then performed a quick spell. The pen glowed, then vanished. Suddenly, the golden chain around Posh's waist disintegrated into a scattering of shimmering dust.

Posh let out a yelp, then threw her arms around Gwen and kissed her cheek.

Kershaw leveled his eyes at them. Gwen could see that he wanted to hurl another threat at her, but instead, he kept his mouth shut. He returned to the stagecoach with his bodyguards and left. Gwen knew she'd just made another enemy, but at the moment, she couldn't care less. Feeling Posh wrapped around her was the only thing that mattered.

Just knowing that Posh was free forever was worth all the sweat and effort over the last few months.

"Thank you, Gwen," Posh said when she finally pulled back. She gave her a grateful kiss and wiped tears of joy from her cheeks. "Now…if you don't mind, can we finally get to Sephora Bean and have that latte?"

# CHAPTER 50

## *A WELL-DESERVED LATTE*

GWEN, POSH, LINHEM and Bally spent most of the next day at Sephora Bean. It was Saint Halving Day, and Gwen couldn't think of a better way to spend it than with her friends at their favorite place in Valeside. When she couldn't keep her hands steady from all the caffeine, they finally strolled leisurely down the beach and back to Java House.

Java House was officially Gwen's now. She'd fulfilled her promise and cleansed Hidden Palm Grove, and the deed had been magically transferred into her name. The binding of the deed didn't care that the castle had been destroyed and now lay in a smoking ruin. And Kershaw, as shrewd as he was, hadn't thought to place that particular restriction in the contract. And the best part—there was no escrow to pay for Java House. It was tax-exempt, and there were no additional fees. Gwen owed nothing for the beach house. Furthermore, there was plenty of room for all of them, assuming everyone wanted to stay. Gwen had even offered Tom and Nat a room, but both had declined, likely from their ongoing dispute with each other, though Gwen had seen them talking quietly after the castle had been destroyed. There was hope yet.

LinHem had received a letter from his parents, offering him a place in their home again. Apparently, word had already spread about the freeing of the thousands of spirits. Since LinHem had been a part of that act of bravery, he'd regained their respect and was anxious to fly home.

Bally, too, had other business, tracking down more of Speartine's artifacts. But he also promised to visit when he could. Posh, of course, was bursting to relocate from her tiny uptown apartment. And, since that lease had been held by Kershaw, she was now homeless anyway.

The next day, Gwen contacted Harris on her globe and gave him the good news. "I promise, Bam Jino is gone."

But Harris sat in the tavern, a look of doubt on his ruddy face. "You tellin' me that a dragon actually *ate* Bam Jino? Well, that must've been one hell of a dragon. I mean, he was a mountain troll!"

Gwen held up her hands. "I swear it, by my wand, Harris. Anyway, you shouldn't have any more issues from him or his crew. And, as promised, I'll be sending you the deed to our agency by raven tomorrow. It's yours now."

Harris wiped his eyes with the back of his thick hands. "Thanks, Gwen. I don't have the words. You sure you won't come back? I sure miss you."

Gwen shook her head without hesitation. "Sorry, Harris. This is where I belong now. You will come visit me, though, won't you?"

"Yeah, course I will. Found my swimmin' trunks. Maybe next summer I'll make the trip."

"I'm holding you to that," Gwen said and smiled at him.

"You said something was callin' to you down there in Valeside Beach. I take it you found what you were lookin' for?"

"Yes, I'd say so."

Harris drummed his hands on the table. "Then I'm happy for you. And if you need me, you know where I'm at. Goodbye, Gwen."

After Gwen closed the connection, Posh joined her on the deck. She sat next to Gwen and stretched out, soaking up the last rays of the late December sun.

Despite the slightly cooler temperatures, there was still plenty of sun, and the warmth had Gwen in a dreamlike state. She still couldn't believe her fortune. She'd met new friends, helped free thousands of trapped spirits, owned an incredible beach home on the coast of Valeside, and she'd helped Harris out of the mess he'd created. But in retrospect, if it hadn't been for Harris and his mess, she might never have come to Valeside and met Posh. Now, she'd finally found her soulmate in someone she would have rejected only a few months back. It was almost magical how quickly things could change in a person's life, if only they allowed fate to work.

She glanced over at Posh. The genie had on her favorite blue polka dot bikini and was stretched out on the lounge sofa. She had her eyes closed, dozing with a smile on her face, some steam gently rising from her skin.

"Wait here," Gwen said and went back inside. She returned with a small, gift-wrapped box in blue polka dot paper and handed it to Posh. "Merry Saint Halving," she said.

Posh sat up and draped her sundress over one shoulder. She blinked at Gwen in surprise. "What is this? Saint Halving Day is over."

"Just a little gift I picked up for you during our shopping spree."

"Gwen…no. I can't—"

"Oh, yes, you can. You're going to take it because I said so."

"But I have nothing for you."

"I don't care, Posh. I never did."

Posh reluctantly took the gift. Flustered, her skin color turned a deeper shade of blue, and steam rose from her cheeks as she unwrapped it.

Inside was the golden sapphire amulet.

"It reminded me of you," Gwen said. "The sapphire matches your skin, and I know you like jewelry. It's from the Holland Empire. I had it engraved."

Posh turned it over and read the inscription.

*Freedom.*
*Your friend,*
*Gwenevere*

Gwen reached over to help her put it on.

Posh wiped her eyes. "Damn you, Gwen. Stop it." She reached out and gave Gwen a hug.

Gwen inhaled the ocean scent from Posh's hair, felt the heat begin to rise from her skin…felt lost in her golden eyes. "What was your first wish?" Gwen murmured.

The question caught Posh off guard and seemed to pull her from the moment. "What?" she whispered.

"Your first wish-magic," Gwen said. "I want to know what it was."

Posh looked to the ocean and propped her chin on Gwen's shoulder. "I'd never known love, and it was something I desired more than anything. So, I wished to find the one who could heal me from the abuse, the nightmares." She walked around behind Gwen and wrapped her arms around her waist, then leaned her head against Gwen's back. "That night, when you used my deck of fate cards, I got the sign of the

Cherub. But in truth, I didn't need the cards to tell me that. I knew when we first met that you were the one. It was worth the wish-magic."

Gwen felt her breath catch in her chest as she turned and traced the three scars over Posh's left eye. She felt the heat from Posh's skin warm her, and she placed her hands on Posh's arms.

"I said I didn't have a gift for you," Posh whispered. "But that's not entirely true. I've been thinking."

Gwen pulled back. "I'm intrigued. I'm frightened. What is it?"

"Well…I thought…since we make such a good team, why not start a company together? Valeside could use a few honest realtors. As a bonus, I think we could put Kershaw out of business."

Gwen let out a long chuckle. She hadn't had such a good laugh since she'd first arrived in Valeside Beach. It was something long overdue. "I'd like that very much," Gwen said and squeezed Posh's hands. "But we have no office, no capital…I mean, I guess we could set up here at Java House, and I do have a little left over from Kershaw's signing bonus—"

"Gwen," Posh said and stopped her. "I'm a genie."

Gwen shrugged. "Okay. And?"

"Contrary to popular belief, genies *do* have a treasure trove. They just can't spend it on themselves. You knew that, right?"

Gwen blinked a few times, shocked. "No, I had no idea."

"Well. I bought office space a long time ago in Lower Valeside. At the time, it was a gift for Kershaw, which I never gave to him. But I can gift it to you. It's not too far from here, in fact. We could go see it—"

Gwen reached out and shook Posh. "Of course. What are we waiting for!"

Posh and Gwen practically sprinted across the beach, then along the main boulevard. A few blocks later, Posh pulled Gwen to a stop. They stood in an older part of town, the buildings around them slightly outdated. But otherwise, it was a clean area. The colors of the surrounding businesses were bright pastels mixed in with some steam: pink and purple and yellow. The area had a cozy charm to it, and there was plenty of foot traffic walking along the sidewalks and window shopping. Restaurants, retailers, and coffee shoppes dotted the block. In the middle was a two-story cottage with pink siding and mint green trim around the pitched slate roof. There was a tall, round turret on the corner, which Gwen thought might be a set of stairs.

"Well, this is it," Posh said. "What do you think?"

"My favorite colors…it's perfect, Posh. I mean, it'll need some updating, a coat of paint, maybe some work on the roof, but…I love it. How long have you been thinking about this?"

Posh looked bashfully at Gwen. "Umm, I guess just after we met."

Gwen shook her head. "Oh, really," she said, giving her a good-natured shove.

"I even took the liberty of placing the company name. Hope that's okay. We can change it, of course."

Gwen read the plaque on the door: **Arris & Oshner Realtors.**

Posh stepped forward and playfully polished the brass sign with her elbow. "I have one more thing to show you."

Posh opened the ornamental door and pulled Gwen inside.

The interior was old and had an antique, almost timeless feel about it. There were two large offices along the street side and plenty of space for additional offices in the back, in case they ever needed to expand. To the left, there was a kitchen and more storage space. Further down the hallway was a copy room. The large windows gave a view of the street and all the people walking by. The bakery next door filled the room with the aroma of fresh-baked bread and pastries.

"I don't know what to say, Posh," Gwen said, her voice catching in her throat.

"Come on, there's one more thing I want to show you upstairs." Posh took Gwen by the hand, then guided her by the waist up the stone staircase. It wound upward a few flights and ended at a wide top landing.

When Gwen stepped through the door, her jaw nearly hit the floor.

Sitting in the middle of the large space was the telescope, Spellbinder, which occupied the entire second floor.

"How…how'd you do this?" Gwen stuttered. "Thiden just flew off with it. And, how the hell did you get this thing inside here?"

"I got in touch with Thiden last night and talked her into it. Dragons and genies have a way of making things happen, magic portals and all. Well, we managed to get Spellbinder inside. Wasn't easy, the floor'll need some work, but we did it. She was okay giving her husband's telescope to a good home. I guess she felt we'd take care of it and keep it a secret."

"Well, you said you didn't have a gift, but I'd call this a big one, Posh. I don't know what to say."

"Just say yes. I'd love to call you my partner."

Gwen took Posh's hands and smiled at her. "Of course. But I think we're officially beyond partners now."

# EPILOGUE

## *ARRIS & OSHNER*

SIX MONTHS LATER

BUSINESS AT ARRIS & Oshner went off swimmingly. Gwen and Posh brought in several of Aloe Realtor's clientele rather quickly, after someone leaked the news about Kershaw's involvement in the Hidden Palm Grove incident. Gwen suspected Nat, though she had no proof of that. Either way, they had their hands full with real estate opportunities and were quickly forced to hire several new employees. Gwen insisted on hiring locals from all backgrounds and races. Soon, the office was filled with pixies, fairies, witches and even a couple of ogres. Within six months, Arris & Oshner was one of the top real estate firms in Valeside Beach. Gwen began to worry that they'd already outgrown their new office and might be forced to open branches across Ambriel.

Gwen and Posh still made time for low-income clientele—Arris & Oshner wasn't in need of steam tokens. Since Gwen came from an underprivileged background, she sought out those families in need. It felt good to be helping them again, and it brought her full circle to her roots. She even threw in the occasional haunted cottage for old times' sake.

But in truth, Gwen missed her days dealing in the ethereal realm. And she missed her ruby amulet, though she thought that Matilda's spirit blade might fill that gap, once she learned to use it. In the back of her mind was also the threat from Lucinda and what she was planning to do in other areas of Ambriel. Though Valeside Beach might be safe now, what was Lucinda doing in other regions? Might they suffer a similar fate if no one stepped up to cleanse the castles she owned? Did anyone even know that Lucinda was trying to raise an army of spirits? Gwen felt compelled to at least send out a warning, possibly even seek out those other castles, now that she understood the plight and how to free the trapped spirits. But that would take effort, and right now she was enjoying her time with Posh as they built their new business together.

It was nearing the end of summer in their first year of business when Posh pulled Gwen onto the deck of Java House. It was close to dusk, and several beachgoers strolled along the shoreline. The sun was slowly drowning amidst the Green Sea, reflecting pastel colors into the pink sky. Fireflies buzzed across the bay like tiny dancing sprites. It was a perfect evening for sitting out with a glass of wine, and Gwen stretched her legs across Posh's lap and kicked off her sandals. Posh tickled the soles of her bare feet with a devious smile.

Gwen set her wineglass on the coffee table, sank into the sofa, and closed her eyes, letting the crooning of the waves soak into her soul. In the corner hearth, a fire popped and hissed as gulls cawed in the background. The afternoon sun on her skin and the heat from Posh's skin had her head spinning in a good way. She moaned as Posh gently massaged her feet.

Not long after Gwen had dozed off, she heard a flapping sound and opened her eyes to see a raven. It settled onto the railing and squawked at them. Tethered around one of its talons was an old piece of parchment.

Posh gave Gwen a curious look, then untied the message and shooed the raven off. She unrolled the yellowed piece of parchment and read it under her breath.

"What does it say?" Gwen asked and sat forward. She watched as Posh's eyes grew wide.

"I don't believe it," Posh whispered. She handed the note to Gwen.

*Dear Miss Gwenevere,*

*I am writing to you in a plea for help. I am the mayor of the City of Cross Knot, and I beseech you to travel here at your earliest opportunity. I have come to understand your special ability within the ethereal realm. The castle named Vain Court, in the center of our town, has exhibited signs of paranormal behavior. One of our residents, a ghost panther named Bally, has recommended you. I hope you will consider helping us, as strange things are occurring within our province. I fear the castle may be overwhelmed soon with spirits. Please hurry.*

*Sincerely,*
*Pascal Quillint*

Gwen set the note down and stared at Posh. "Well?"

"Oh no, no, no," Posh said and stood. "Not this again."

"Posh, surely you knew it would only be a matter of time until this happened. Thiden said as much."

"We did our part, Gwen. Let someone else step up and do the next one."

"And who would that be?" Gwen said. "We have the knowledge, experience and ability."

Posh sat down and put her chin in her hands. "I was really hoping to just sell normal cottages, you know?"

"Yeah, I know," Gwen said and placed an arm around Posh's waist and pulled her close. "I feel like we have a responsibility, though. Spellbinder called to me first, maybe now it's calling to both of us? Valeside might be safe, but if Lucinda builds an army of spirits, no place in Ambriel will be safe."

Posh leaned her head on Gwen's shoulder. "If we do this, we bring LinHem and Bally along."

"Of course. We'll have to track LinHem down, but it sounds like Bally's already there."

"Just promise me that once we're finished, we'll come straight back to Valeside and continue our lives together."

Gwen gave Posh a long look. "You know I'd have it no other way."

Posh finally nodded, then stood again. "Alright. Let's pack our bags."

Gwen stood and held Posh. She didn't know what to expect and almost regretted having to go through the whole ordeal again. But she also felt that ache in her bones for a good challenge, which was something that no amount of cozy beachside lounging, living or selling of cottages could ever fill. Even though she didn't say it to Posh, Gwen was anxious to get back on the road. If anyone was going to stop Lucinda, it would have to be Gwen and her friends.

THE END